Ode to

Joyous Cooking

Ode to Joyous Cooking was designed by The DePlano Group of New York City. The Cookbook
Committee is deeply indebted to Marco and Roberta DePlano and Loreena Persaud-Gomez for their
gifts of time, support, and artistry in creating a stunning book that is without peer in the realm of
community cookbooks.

ISBN: 0-9754995-1-3

1st Printing   September 2004   110,000 copies

WIMMER
COOKBOOKS

A CONSOLIDATED GRAPHICS COMPANY

800.548.2537   wimmerco.com

Sovereign Bank

Thank you for being a loyal Sovereign Bank customer. We appreciate the confidence you have placed in us to provide solutions for your banking needs.

Please accept the enclosed cookbook, *Ode to Joyous Cooking*, as a gesture of our sincere gratitude. We hope you'll enjoy it in the years to come.

Bon Appetit!

Jay Sidhu

Jay Sidhu
Chairman and CEO
Sovereign Bank

Legends, Love, and Culinary Traditions

of

Pennsylvania, New Jersey, Connecticut,
Rhode Island, Massachusetts, New Hampshire, and Maryland

The role of Pennsylvania and its historic place in the founding of our country is well-known to every American school child. Almost as well-known are the legendary peoples who, in the early 17th century, fled religious persecution in their homeland to settle in the southeastern part of the state. Known as the Pennsylvania Dutch (a corruption of *"Deutsch,"* their true Germanic origin), Amish or Plain People, they are fascinating to the modern world because of their simple ways, quaint clothing and horse and buggy transportation. Many of their traditions speak of restraint and discipline, however, their colorful quilts and hearty foods allow us to glimpse into an entirely different aspect of their lives.

Although they brought taste preferences from Germany and Switzerland, the geography and climate of the region where they settled shaped the recipes and variety of foods, which appeared on their Amish tables. A totally agrarian society, their large and prosperous farms are located on some of the most fertile land in America and can easily sustain their large, extended families. In fact, the land is often so productive that Amish cooks undertake massive "pickling" and "setting food by" operations. Cookbooks rarely existed, and special dishes are passed on from mother to daughter, often with imprecise instructions and measurements, such as "a handful", "a pinch", "a very hot oven", or "cook until done."

For a people reluctant to express their feelings, food has become the way for the Pennsylvania Germans to show affection, sympathy, and gratitude. Whether a wedding, funeral, barn raising or Sunday lunch after worship, community gatherings are held in the home and follow an almost standard menu. This simplifies preparation for the host household and discourages the temptation to be competitive in the kitchen, thus committing the sin of pride.

Not more than an hour to the east of this bucolic scene is the bustling city of Philadelphia, fourth largest in the country, and site of many important events in our nation's history. Philadelphia also can lay claim to several food firsts—Philadelphia Pepper Pot Soup and the Philadelphia Cheesesteak sandwich.

Legend has it that Pepper Pot Soup was created by a desperate chef, who was given the challenge of feeding the starving Continental troops at Valley Forge. General George Washington begged him to transform the meager rations into a rib-sticking, nourishing meal. The result was mixture of tripe and potatoes liberally dosed with black pepper. In the 19th century, this soup was sold from milk cans on the streets of Philadelphia. Pepper Pot Soup (see page 67 for the recipe) continues today in the local food repertoire, appearing on the menus of such venerable institutions as the Union League, an exclusive Philadelphia men's club.

The Philadelphia Cheesesteak was created in the 1930's in the Italian neighborhood known as "South Philly." Since that time, there has been an ongoing rivalry and debate continues about which shop serves the best and most authentic version. Hot contenders for the title are Jim's, Pat's, or Geno's, with the latter two squaring off on opposite corners in the heart of South Philly—24 hours a day—and both doing a thriving business for more than 60 years.

The main ingredients of a "real" Cheesesteak are good quality, thinly sliced beef, cooked on a grill until well-browned, but not crispy or burned, and gently shredded during the cooking process. Added to the beef are one's own choice of sautéed onions, peppers and mushrooms, all topped with cheese and piled onto a fresh 8 to 10 inch long, crusty "Italian" roll. The cheese selection may be American or provolone slices, placed on just before serving, so they can melt into the meat, or even Cheez Whiz slathered directly on the bread.

Eating the Cheesesteak requires a special, acquired technique called the "Philadelphia Lean." To be authentic, the sandwich must be dripping with juices when it is served. To avoid ruining their clothes, Philadelphians have learned to bend forward over the sandwich, rather than bringing the sandwich up to their mouths.

PHILADELPHIA CHEESE STEAK

1½ pounds sirloin steak or sirloin tip roast, sliced paper thin and then cut again into ½-inch ribbons (To make this part easier, partially freeze the meat before slicing.)

2 tablespoons light vegetable oil

American or provolone cheese slices, or a jar of Cheez-Whiz

4 crusty 8-inch long Italian rolls sliced lengthwise; they can be warmed or grilled, just before serving

ADDITIONAL CONDIMENTS:

Sautéed sweet bell peppers, green, red, or mixed
Sautéed sliced onions
Sautéed sliced mushrooms

Worcestershire sauce
Salt and pepper

1. Prepare the onions, peppers, and mushrooms ahead of time and keep warm in separate bowls.

2. Heat the oil on a grill or in a skillet over medium heat. Working quickly, place about half the meat in the pan, turning and shredding it until it is brown throughout.

3. Transfer to a plate; repeat with the rest of the meat; return the first batch to the skillet to reheat, tossing well, adding a dash of Worcestershire sauce, salt and pepper to taste.

4. Assemble the sandwiches. Divide the meat onto the four sliced loaves, using the pan juices as well. Add sautéed vegetables as desired, and finally, the cheese selection.

5. Some people prefer to mix the peppers, onions and mushrooms into the meat, just before assembling the sandwiches, and then top with the cheese. It is a question of choice (and great debate) as to which combination is best. You decide—and meanwhile, enjoy your authentic Philly Cheesesteak!

Yield: 4 servings

When told that a soloist would need six fingers on each hand to perform his concerto, Arnold Schoenberg replied, "I can wait."

The first colonists to arrive in present day New Jersey were the Dutch in the early 1600's. They found the land already inhabited by the Lenni Lenape, a peaceful tribe whose name aptly translates as "original people." The Lenni Lenape lived in wigwam villages scattered along the rivers and got along remarkably well with their new European neighbors, showing these newcomers how to dig for clams along the shore and roast them on beds of seaweed.

In 1618 the Dutch settlers established the Bergen Trading Station in the area now known as Jersey City Heights, on the bank of the Hudson River. Later, the Swedes arrived and colonized South Jersey along the Delaware River. The Dutch and the Swedes each occupied their own areas and co-existed amicably enough until their interests finally clashed. It was during these skirmishes that the English arrived in 1664 and settled all arguments by taking firm control over what is now New Jersey.

The settlers in the northern part of the state quickly discovered that shad was something of a delicacy. Though the season was short, it was anticipated each year and recipes and traditions for its preparation soon evolved.

As the population grew, church suppers became synonymous with good eating. Attendance was largely dependent upon the quality of the food with the best menus attracting the largest crowds. Fried oysters, chicken salad, and coleslaw (from the Dutch *"koolslaa"*) were the most popular dishes.

New Jersey quickly acquired its well-deserved nickname of "The Garden State." A journal published in Scotland in 1684 referred to the colony as the "Garden of the World." Today, New Jersey's tomatoes, corn, blueberries and peaches are famous, as is the rest of the bounty of vegetables and fruits grown in this small, yet fertile, state. In fact, it was a daring New Jersey gentleman farmer, who in 1820 gathered an audience on the steps of the Salem County Courthouse, and proceeded to shock the crowd by taking a bite of a here-to-fore considered poisonous tomato, establishing it at once as both edible and delicious.

The first settlers in New England were the Plymouth Pilgrims who landed on the shores of Massachusetts in December 1620. It was the worst time of the year to arrive—no shelter, no crops to harvest, no supplies remaining from their long voyage and no one to turn to for aid. The town-bred men were not skilled in hunting or fishing and the native fruits and berries were long past their season. By spring, more than half had died from starvation, disease and exposure. Yet they did not yield and when the Mayflower returned to England, not one hardy soul went with her. They had, in a few short months, learned quickly from the friendly Indians about corn and squash; about netting codfish in the spring and salting and drying them for the winter; about clams and lobsters and oysters; about using herring to fertilize the fields; about which berries and greens were edible; how to make spruce tea to ward off scurvy; how to tap maple trees and boil down the sap. Before winter closed in again, their little colony stood firmly on its feet. It was then, in the brilliance of a late New England autumn, that they gathered with their Native American mentors at a special feast to give thanks for a bountiful harvest, the first celebration of Thanksgiving Day. Turkey was prepared as the centerpiece of the meal, a tradition that continues in American homes today.

Life continued to be difficult for these persistent folk. Eventually the friendship with the Indians eroded, invasions and wars with the French and the English stretched out for more than 80 years, the weather was never friendly for very long, causing crops to fail and fishing to be unpredictable at best. Yet they never gave up or gave in. Thus, the "Yankee" personality began evolving—remarkably distinct from state to state, with waves of immigration from Ireland, Portugal, Eastern Europe, and every country of the Mediterranean, and yet remarkably homogenous in character. Adjectives such as "independent", "determined", "inventive", "self-reliant", "industrious", "frugal", "bold yet cautious", and "filled with dry humor" usually come to mind when one thinks of New Englanders.

Translated to the table, these characteristics were seen in bowls of hearty chowders and stews, filling crocks of baked beans, and slow-cooked meats and roasts.

An array of wild berries were gathered and their versatility employed as they appeared in pies, cakes, muffins, and griddle cakes; were dried; and were made into conserves and jams. Molasses was often substituted for sugar and corn meal for flour. And of course, everywhere and in every form: fish and seafood. There was no end to the variety of fish and recipes for preparing it. Potatoes were first introduced to the colony by the Irish immigrants who arrived in 1719. They quickly found favor as a commercial crop in New Hampshire, and continue to be grown in the Northeast corner of New England today.

Portuguese sailors soon found their way to the shores of Rhode Island and with them came the unique dishes and cooking methods of the Iberian Peninsula. To this day, the influence of the Portuguese appears in many local dishes, especially in seafood. Another specialty is their delicious, slightly sweet bread.

This is not to say that New England cookery was only of the homespun variety. With every state but Vermont having access to the sea, fishing and shipping dominated the early economy, with graceful clipper ships bringing rare objects and foreign customs from the Far East to New England shores. Seafaring men whose palates had been broadened by strange and new foods from the Orient brought the exotic flavors of lemons, kumquats, ginger, and rare wines to the New England table.

Today, the cooking of New England takes us back to the days when we were newcomers on this continent, forward through the years of our expansion and coming of age as a free country, and forward again to reflect the influence of the many cultures and customs that make up twenty-first century America.

The culinary traditions of Maryland are inexorably tied to its predominately English heritage and the natural bounty of the Chesapeake Bay, which divides the state into two distinct regions.

Created and fed by rivers in Pennsylvania and Virginia, the Chesapeake Bay waters range from sweet in the Upper Bay, brackish (salty-sweet) in the Middle Bay, to salty in the Lower Bay where it joins the Atlantic Ocean. The selection of available seafood varies with the changes in water characteristics. Freshwater fish are available in the northernmost reaches. Oysters and rockfish and the famous Maryland Blue Crab are delicacies of the central region. Ocean species such as bluefish and tuna are caught in the south. Early folklore describes shallow waters so full of crabs that bathers had to beware, and rivers so full of fish that men would row out with iron frying pans to kill the fish as they leapt from the water.

When the first colonists arrived in 1634, they followed the example of the native Algonquin in harvesting the riches of the Bay and cultivating corn for food. The Europeans immediately introduced tobacco as a cash crop as well. Experience, however, had shown that too much emphasis on tobacco and not enough on basic foodstuffs could prove disastrous. Thus, a law was enacted compelling the planting of two acres of corn for each acre of tobacco.

The bounties of land and water, augmented by a generally temperate climate, helped Maryland to be one of only three permanent English settlements to survive its early years without starvation, fire or massacre.

In 1650, Englishman Robert Brooke sailed for America with his large family, a retinue of servants, and his pack of hounds, thus introducing foxhunting to the Tidewater region. Tradition mandated an elaborate "hunt breakfast" following the morning hunt. A typical menu from the mid-1700's included steamed oysters, roast suckling pig, Maryland baked ham, roast turkey, Brunswick stew, sauerkraut, hominy, spoon bread, tomatoes, broccoli, spiced apples, pumpkin and minced meat pies, plum pudding, little sponge cakes, as well as coffee, fruit and nuts.

Another popular and thoroughly British form of entertainment was thoroughbred racing. Maryland was known for its fine horses bred from English and Arabian stock. The fall racing season was the liveliest period of the year in the provincial capital of Anne Arundel (present-day Annapolis). After a long day at the track, evening hours were filled with teas, lavish dinners and supper parties, balls and theatrical productions. Even George Washington frequently attended these social activities, which always featured a table literally "groaning" from the weight of game and seafood.

Life in early Maryland mirrored its British heritage in other ways. Gentlemen's clubs flourished in mid-eighteenth century Annapolis. Members of the famous Tuesday Club met weekly in the house of a member. Following several rounds of the punch bowl and a hearty supper consisting of courses such as wild duck, steak and kidney pie and roasted oysters, the order of the evening was unbridled fun in the form of wit, ridicule, caricature, songs and poetry. According to the unwritten rules, "discussions of a political nature shall be silenced by vociferous and roaring laughter."

The eastern peninsula of Maryland remained isolated from America's growing population and evolving customs that were being broadened by wave after wave of immigrants who brought their own culinary and social traditions with them. Instead, life on "The Eastern Shore" continued in the old ways with villages populated by "watermen" who earned their living from the waters of the Bay—crabs during the summer, oysters and clams in the winter, and fish in spring and fall. This way of life continued almost uninterrupted on the Eastern Shore for more than three centuries until the Chesapeake Bay Bridge was completed in 1952, linking it with the rest of the state. However, even today many of these small villages remain, where nearly the entire population (usually two or three extended families) still work "on the water." These watermen are fiercely independent and have resisted the homogenization so prevalent across the rest of the state. Local culinary traditions have also been carefully preserved. Recipes for crab cakes and oyster stew in Easton or Smith Island are quite different from the same dishes served in Baltimore or Annapolis. Indeed, not only the food but also the accents and colloquialisms of the inhabitants continue to maintain their unique, regional personalities.

Very Special Recognition To:

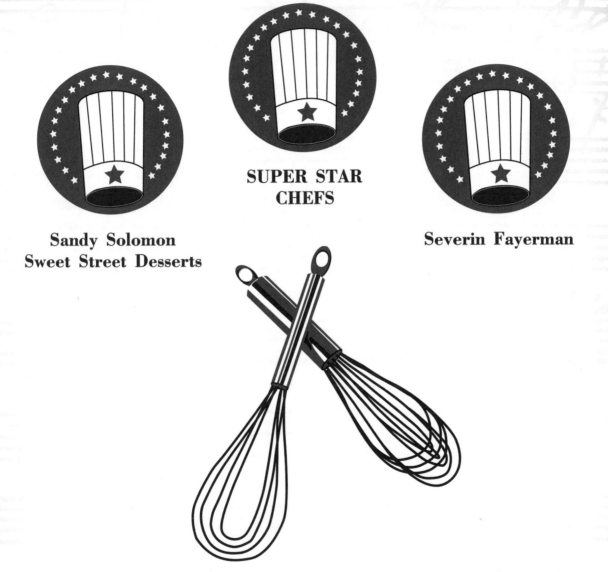

SUPER STAR CHEFS

Sandy Solomon
Sweet Street Desserts

Severin Fayerman

The musical score used on the cover, liner pages, and throughout Ode to Joyous Cooking is reproduced from Beethoven's handwritten manuscript of his **Ninth Symphony**. *We are grateful to Grover Batts, a friend and former curator of the Library of Congress, Washington, D.C., who generously provided the facsimile of this document.*

Table of Contents

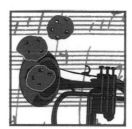

Cookbook Committee

EDITOR: Penny Proserpi

ASSISTANT EDITOR: Margaret Patch

TREASURER: Janice Barney

PUBLIC RELATIONS: Ginny Hand

RECIPE COORDINATORS: Francine Black   Tammy Black

SECTION CHAIRMEN:

Appetizers and Beverages—Margaret Patch

Meats—Nancy Russo

Breads, Muffins, and Brunch—Francine Black

Pasta, Potatoes, Rice, and Grains—Lenore Peloso

Soups and Stews—Caroline Dunford

Vegetables and Side Dishes—Margo Thomas

Salads and Dressings—Tammy Black

Desserts—Jane Cambria-Gill

Fish and Seafood—Penny Proserpi

From the Pantry—Margaret Patch

Poultry and Game—Florence Russo

Restaurants—Kathy Kleppinger

LIAISONS FROM THE READING SYMPHONY ORCHESTRA LEAGUE:

Jean Blickle, President   Margaret Patch

Caroline Dunford   Florence Russo

Carole Lusch   Nancy Russo

COPY EDITOR: Diana Tirion

EDITORIAL ASSISTANT: Kate Donohue

MEMBERS AT LARGE:

Carol Cohn   Angela Gesualdi

Anne DuFour   Stephanie Kahn

EX-OFFICIO: Richard Black   Stewart Dunford   James Fegley, Esq

SPECIAL EVENTS COORDINATORS:

Ginny Hand   Margaret Patch

Allyson McKechnie   Nancy Russo

RETAIL SALES CO-CHAIRMEN:

Jane Cambria-Gill   Nancy Russo

Caroline Dunford

WINE CONSULTANT: Frank Buttaro, Jr.

JUNIOR MEMBER: Isabelle Rose Stretka

MASCOTS: Razz, Miss Priss, Romeo and Tallulah

Appetizers & Beverages

COLD DIPS

COLD SPREADS

COLD APPETIZERS

PLATED DISHES

HOT APPETIZERS

MISCELLANEOUS

BEVERAGES

Appetizers & Beverages

SMOKED OYSTER DIP

Oysters are one of the bounties of the Chesapeake, and the early settlers smoked them to have on hand to eat during the "forbidden" months without an "r", when harvesting was prohibited.

1 (8-ounce) package cream cheese, softened

1½ cups mayonnaise

7 dashes Tabasco sauce or to taste

1 tablespoon lemon juice

1 (4-ounce) can chopped black olives, drained

2 (3¾-ounce) cans smoked oysters, drained and chopped

2-3 tablespoons chopped parsley for garnish

Melba toast or assorted crackers

1. Blend cream cheese, mayonnaise, Tabasco, and lemon juice in a food processor until smooth.

2. Add olives and oysters.

3. Pulse just enough to incorporate. Refrigerate until cold.

4. Sprinkle with parsley and serve with crackers.

Yield: 2 cups

Music is one of only two or three of the Arts where the creative process is never finished. For instance, in painting, literature, and sculpture the author has the definitive word. But music offers the opportunity to enlarge the idea, to merge with the creation, to comment on the composer's inspiration.

~ANONYMOUS

Appetizers & Beverages

SUZAN'S CHUTNEY DIP

This is an unusual dip that combines great creamy and crunchy textures with smokey and exotic flavors.

4 (3-ounce) packages cream cheese, softened
1 cup sour cream
3 tablespoons curry powder or to taste
1 cup dark raisins
1 teaspoon salt

1 (5-ounce) jar ginger or cranberry chutney, or choose one of our recipes in "From the Pantry"
1 cup chopped green onions
¼ cup smoked almonds
10 slices bacon, cooked, drained, and crumbled

1. Blend cream cheese, sour cream, and curry in a food processor until smooth.

2. Add raisins, salt, chutney, green onions and almonds.

3. Pulse briefly until mixture is a coarse texture. Place in a serving bowl.

4. Top with bacon before serving.

Yield: 8 servings

 Tip: May be prepared a day in advance. The flavors will develop even more.

"I not only like Mozart—I idolize him. It is thanks to Mozart that I have devoted my life to music."
~PETER ILYICH TCHAIKOVSKY

BABA GHANNOUJ

Exotic, mysterious, and healthy, too. Serve this wonderful eggplant dip with toasted pita wedges.

1 large eggplant
½ cup tahini (sesame seed paste)
1 garlic clove, minced
Juice of one lemon

Salt, to taste
2 tablespoons vegetable oil
Chopped parsley and tomato wedges for garnish
Toasted pita wedges

1. Preheat oven to 500 degrees. Cut 1-inch slits in eggplant to prevent splattering while baking.

2. Bake until fork tender.

3. Slice eggplant in half. Scoop out pulp with juices and transfer to a bowl. Mash eggplant.

4. Combine sesame seed paste, garlic, lemon juice, and salt in a separate bowl. Add water if mixture is too thick.

5. Add eggplant purée and mix well. Place in a serving bowl and drizzle with oil.

6. Garnish with parsley and tomato slices. Serve with toasted pita wedges.

Yield: 1½ cups

REALLY GREAT PÂTÉ

 Set the calorie counting aside for this outrageously rich spread. This silky pâté puts the commerical variety to shame.

1 pound chicken livers, rinsed and patted dry
4 tablespoons butter
1 tablespoon brandy
¼ cup Madeira
2 sticks unsalted butter, softened
½ cup dry breadcrumbs
½ cup milk
4 medium onions, minced
½ teaspoon ground cloves
⅛ teaspoon cayenne pepper

6 hard-cooked eggs, chopped
2 teaspoons dried parsley
½ teaspoon pepper
1 teaspoon dried basil
½ teaspoon dried marjoram
4 teaspoons Worcestershire sauce
2 teaspoons dry mustard
1 teaspoon ground nutmeg or ½ teaspoon freshly grated
Assorted crackers

1. Sauté livers in butter until pale pink. Transfer to food processor and purée. Remove to a bowl. Stir in brandy and Madeira. Cool to room temperature.

2. Combine butter, breadcrumbs, and milk. Add breadcrumb mixture, cloves and cayenne to liver mixture.

3. Process onions, eggs, parsley, pepper, basil, marjoram, Worcestershire sauce, mustard, and nutmeg in a clean food processor. Gently stir into liver mixture.

4. Serve at room temperature with crackers.

Yield: 15-20 servings

"When words leave off, music begins."
~HEINRICH HEINE

APRICOT-PEACH SPREAD

For unexpected company, keep the ingredients on hand for this delicious, quick, and zippy spread.

1 (16-ounce) jar premium apricot preserves
1 (16-ounce) jar premium peach preserves
2 tablespoons dry mustard

1 (5-ounce) jar prepared horseradish
1 (8-ounce) package cream cheese, softened
Assorted crackers

1. Combine preserves, mustard, and horseradish and mix until well blended.

2. Spread over cream cheese and serve with crackers.

Yield: 16 servings

Appetizers & Beverages

FRUIT AND CHEESE LOG

The versatile cranberry adds a chewy texture and a pleasantly bittersweet taste to this yummy, homemade cheese log.

1 (8-ounce) package cream cheese, softened
1 (8-ounce) package shredded Monterey Jack
    cheese, room temperature
2 tablespoons orange juice
1 teaspoon orange zest
½ cup chopped dried cranberries

⅓ cup golden raisins
⅓ cup chopped dried apricots or peaches
¼ teaspoon salt
Sliced almonds for garnish
Apple slices and crackers

1. Beat cream cheese, Jack cheese, orange juice, and zest with an electric mixer on low speed until smooth.
2. Stir in cranberries, raisins, apricots, and salt. Mix well.
3. Divide mixture in half. Shape each half into a log. Cover and refrigerate at least 4 hours or overnight.
4. Bring logs to room temperature. Roll in almonds. Serve with apple slices and crackers.

Yield: 12-15 servings

ROQUEFORT OR GINGER GRAPES

Nutty, sweet, and tangy as well, either version of this recipe will be a hit at any gathering.

1 (10-ounce) package pecans, chopped and lightly
    toasted
4 tablespoons crumbled Roquefort cheese

1 (8-ounce) package cream cheese, softened
2 tablespoons heavy cream
1 pound large, red seedless grapes

1. Grind pecans in a food processor. Remove to plate.
2. Blend Roquefort cheese, cream cheese, and cream in food processor.
3. Coat grapes in cheese mixture and refrigerate for 45 minutes.
4. Roll in pecans, coating well. Cover and refrigerate until ready to serve.

Yield: 10-12 servings

Variation: Substitute 3 tablespoons finely chopped crystallized ginger and 1 teaspoon ground ginger for Roquefort and add to cream cheese-cream mixture. Proceed as above with green seedless grapes. May also substitute crushed almonds for pecans.

"A good cook is like a sorceress who dispenses happiness."
~ELSA SCHIAPARELLI

PEAR AND PROSCIUTTO BRUSCHETTA

♫ *Say it correctly: "brew-sket-ah"—("che" in Italian is always pronounced as "K", not ssh)—and enjoy this delicious, open-faced variation of an Italian favorite.*

2 ripe Bosc or Bartlett pears, peeled, cored and chopped
¼ cup minced red onion
1 tablespoon extra virgin olive oil
1 tablespoon white balsamic vinegar

1 tablespoon chopped fresh thyme
⅔ cup crumbled bleu cheese, room temperature
5⅓ tablespoons unsalted butter, softened
32 crusty French baguette slices, ¼ inch thick
32 small thin slices Italian prosciutto

1. Combine pears, onions, oil, vinegar, and thyme. Marinate for 10 minutes, stirring occasionally.

2. Cream together bleu cheese and butter until smooth.

3. Place baguette slices in a single layer on a baking sheet. Bake at 400 degrees 8 to 10 minutes until crisp and lightly toasted. May prepare bread slices in advance and store in an airtight container.

4. Spread ½ tablespoon butter mixture on each bread slice. Top each toast with a prosciutto slice and a small spoonful of pear mixture. Serve immediately.

Yield: 32 slices

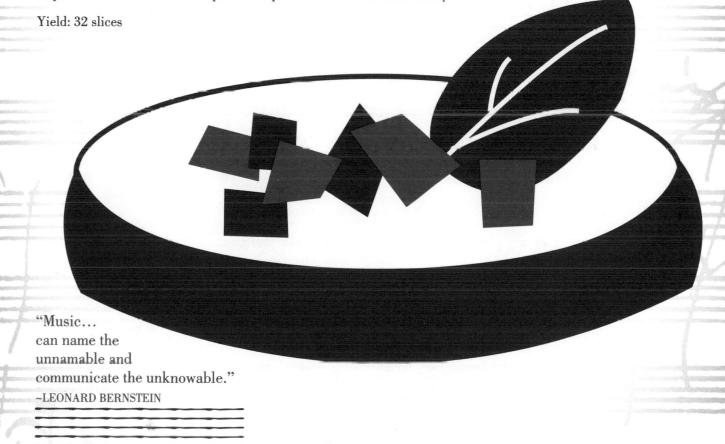

"Music…
can name the
unnamable and
communicate the unknowable."
~LEONARD BERNSTEIN

Appetizers & Beverages

ISLAND CHICKEN BALLS

These slightly exotic tidbits always get raves. This recipe should be made in advance so that the flavors have time to blend.

⅔ cup raisins

2 tablespoons rum or pineapple juice

1 (8-ounce) package cream cheese, softened

1 (3-ounce) package cream cheese, softened

3 tablespoons hot mango chutney

3 tablespoons mayonnaise

1 tablespoon teriyaki sauce

2 teaspoons curry powder or to taste

½ teaspoon ground ginger

½ teaspoon salt

¼ teaspoon cayenne pepper

4 boneless, skinless chicken breast halves, poached and shredded to equal 2 cups

1 cup sliced almonds, toasted

1½ cups flaked coconut

1. Mix raisins and rum in a small bowl. Set aside.

2. Blend cream cheese, chutney, mayonnaise, teriyaki sauce, curry, ginger, salt, and cayenne until smooth.

3. Drain raisins. Add raisins, chicken, and almonds to creamed mixture. Mix well.

4. Shape mixture into 1-inch balls. Roll in coconut. Cover and refrigerate.

Yield: 10-12 servings

Tip: May substitute a roasted chicken from the supermarket for cooked chicken breasts.

WEST INDIES CRAB

This is a delicious variation of crab cocktail and so easy to prepare.

1 pound lump crabmeat

1 medium onion, finely chopped

Salt and pepper, to taste

½ cup vegetable oil

⅓ cup cider vinegar

½ cup ice water

Mixed greens and crackers

1. Layer one-third crabmeat in a bowl. Top with one-third onions. Season with salt and pepper. Repeat layers two more times.

2. Mix together oil, vinegar, and water until well blended. Pour marinade over crabmeat layers.

3. Cover and refrigerate for 24 hours.

4. Drain marinade. Toss crabmeat mixture. Serve on a bed of mixed greens with crackers.

Yield: 6-8 servings

CRAB À LA CARMEN

The unique presentation makes this elegant appetizer a favorite at special dinners.

½ pound lump crabmeat

⅓ cup minced sweet red pepper, plus additional for garnish

2 tablespoons chopped green onions

1 tablespoon chopped fresh cilantro

1 tablespoon minced jalapeño pepper

Juice of one lime

Salt, to taste

4 long strips of seedless cucumber

Wasabi mayonnaise for garnish

Melba toast or toasted pita wedges

1. Combine crabmeat, peppers, onions, cilantro, jalapeño peppers, lime juice, and salt. Mix well.

2. Spray insides of four 3x1-inch ring molds with cooking spray. Place on serving plates.

3. Line each mold with a cucumber strip. Fill mold with crabmeat mixture. Cover and refrigerate 30 minutes.

4. Slip off mold and decorate each plate with wasabi mayonnaise and sprinkle with additional minced red peppers. Serve with Melba toast or pita wedges.

Yield: 4 servings

Tip: To improvise the ring mold, remove the top and bottom lids from tuna fish cans. Wash, dry and use as molds.

BAKED BRIE WITH MANGO-STRAWBERRY COULIS

Individual servings of baked Brie resting on a luscious pool of sauce will wow your guests.

1 cup strawberries, hulled

1 cup mango, peeled

½ cup sugar

Juice of one-half lemon

8 round crusty dinner rolls

1 pound Brie cheese, soft spreadable or regular, rind removed

½ cup toasted slivered almonds

Fresh mint for garnish

1. Combine strawberries, mango, sugar, and lemon juice in a saucepan. Bring to boil. Remove from heat and transfer to blender. Purée mixture until smooth. Cool mango-strawberry coulis in the refrigerator.

2. Slice off top of each roll and save. Hollow out the inside of each roll and fill with several chunks of Brie cheese. Sprinkle with almonds. Return tops on rolls. Place rolls on a baking sheet.

3. Bake at 350 degrees 10 to 12 minutes.

4. Ladle ¼ cup mango-strawberry coulis on eight individual salad or dessert plates. Place hot baked roll in center of sauce. Garnish with mint.

Yield: 8 servings

~STIRLING GUEST HOTEL, READING, PENNSYLVANIA~
~KAJ SKOV, OWNER~
~ANTHONY C. WELTMER, CHEF~

Appetizers & Beverages

ARTICHOKE CHEESE PUFFS

These delicious mouthsful can be made in advance and popped in the microwave just before serving.

4 (6-ounce) jars marinated artichoke hearts
2 small onions, chopped
2 garlic cloves, finely minced
8 eggs, beaten
½ cup fine dry breadcrumbs
½ teaspoon salt

¼ teaspoon pepper
½ teaspoon dried oregano
Tabasco sauce, to taste
2 (8-ounce) packages shredded Cheddar cheese
¼ cup minced fresh parsley

1. Preheat oven to 325 degrees.

2. Drain marinade from 2 jars of artichokes into a skillet. Drain other jars, discarding marinade, and dice all artichokes. Set aside.

3. Sauté onions and garlic in marinade until tender.

4. Combine onion mixture, eggs, breadcrumbs, salt, pepper, oregano, and Tabasco.

5. Stir in artichokes, cheese, and parsley.

6. Spoon mixture into greased mini muffin cups, filling three-quarters full.

7. Bake 30 to 40 minutes until golden brown and firm to the touch.

8. Cool puffs in pan. Rim edges of cups with a knife to remove with ease.

Yield: 120 puffs

~ADAPTED FROM THE
ELMS BED AND
BREAKFAST~
~FALMOUTH,
MASSACHUSETTS~

Tip: May substitute Swiss or Gouda cheese for Cheddar cheese. Recipe may be halved. Puffs may be made a day in advance, refrigerated and reheated in a 350 degree oven or microwave. Puffs may also be frozen up to two weeks.

HOT CRAB CURRY DIP

This rich and elegant dish is a wonderful complement to the sweet and delicate flavor of the blue crab.

2 (8-ounce) packages cream cheese, softened
2 tablespoons milk
2 tablespoons minced onion
1 teaspoon minced garlic
4 teaspoons curry powder or to taste

1 teaspoon salt
2 teaspoons pepper
1 pound lump or backfin crabmeat
2 tablespoons chopped parsley for garnish
Assorted crackers

1. Preheat oven to 350 degrees.

2. Heat cheese, milk, and onion in a microwave until soft. Add garlic, curry, salt, and pepper. Stir in crabmeat.

3. Spoon into an ovenproof dish.

4. Bake 20 minutes.

5. Top with parsley and serve with crackers.

Yield: 10-12 servings

~ADAPTED FROM THE STRAWBERRY INN~
~NEW MARKET, MARYLAND~

OYSTERS OXFORD

The Robert Morris Inn has been located at the edge of the Tred Avon River in Oxford, Maryland since 1710. With its location just off the Chesapeake Bay, Oxford was once Maryland's main port of entry for goods from England and a center of shipping activity. If the name Robert Morris is a familiar one, it is because his son was a friend of George Washington, helped finance the Revolutionary War, was a signer of the Declaration of Independence, the Articles of Confederation, and United States Constitution. The Inn's reputation for serving noteworthy food is well deserved and their menu includes many divine recipes for the bounties of the Bay. James Michner lived in the area while he researched and wrote **Chesapeake** *and proclaimed the Inn's crabcakes and other seafood dishes the best he had even eaten. Here is an adaptation of a favorite that combines two of the "best of the Bay" ingredients.*

2 tablespoons butter
⅓ cup all-purpose flour
1 tablespoon ground paprika
½ teaspoon garlic powder
½ teaspoon Old Bay seasoning
½ teaspoon white pepper

1 cup milk
2 tablespoons dry sherry
½ pound lump crabmeat
2 dozen shucked oysters, preferably with their shells
6 slices bacon, cut into 24 pieces

1. Preheat oven to 375 degrees. In a large saucepan over low heat, melt the butter and mix in the flour, paprika, garlic powder, Old Bay, and white pepper. Stir in the milk and whisk until smooth

2. Remove from the heat, add sherry and cool. Add the crabmeat.

3. Arrange the oysters in the shell on a bed of salt in a shallow roasting pan or in individual ramekins or baking shells. Top each with a tablespoon of the crab mixture and a slice of bacon.

4. Bake for 10-12 minutes, or until the bacon is crisp.

Appetizers & Beverages

VEGETABLE STUFFED BAKED BRIE

 The layer of vegetables adds a different twist to this popular dish.

2 (8-ounce) wheels Brie cheese
1 medium carrot, diced
¼ cup minced green onions
2 tablespoons minced shallots
½ cup sliced mushrooms (optional)
2 teaspoons minced garlic
4 tablespoons unsalted butter
Pinch of saffron

Pepper, to taste
3 tablespoons freshly grated Parmesan cheese
1 (17-ounce) package frozen puff pastry, thawed, separated into 2 sheets, and rolled out slightly
Egg wash made with 1 egg beaten with 1 tablespoon water
Paprika and chopped parsley for garnish

1. Place cheese in the freezer about 20 minutes until firm. Remove and slice both wheels in half horizontally.

2. Sauté carrot, green onions, shallots, mushrooms, and garlic in butter until tender.

3. Add saffron and pepper. Cool slightly. Fold in Parmesan cheese.

4. Place one layer Brie, rind side down, on one pastry sheet. Make sure pastry will cover entire wheel.

5. Spoon half of vegetable filling on top and press down. Stack second layer of Brie rind side up on top.

6. Brush cheese with egg wash. Pull pastry up over wheel. Pinch edges to seal. Brush pastry with egg wash.

7. Repeat steps with other cheese wheel, pastry sheet and remaining vegetable filling.

8. Sprinkle both with paprika and chopped parsley. Refrigerate 20 minutes.

9. Place cheese on a baking sheet. Bake at 350 degrees 15 minutes until puffed and browned.

Yield: 15-20 servings

BLACK OLIVE MUFFINS

Keep a batch of these in the freezer to have a quick appetizer on hand.

1 (6-ounce) can chopped olives, drained
½ cup chopped onion
1½ cups shredded sharp Cheddar cheese
½ cup mayonnaise

½ teaspoon curry powder
½ teaspoon salt
6 English muffins, split in half

1. Combine olives, onion, cheese, mayonnaise, curry, and salt.

2. Spread mixture on each muffin half. Place on a baking sheet. Broil until bubbly. Cool slightly.

3. Cut each muffin into quarters and serve. May also freeze muffin quarters on baking sheet, then pack in a zip-top plastic bag. Reheat in oven.

Yield: 48 pieces

♪ Variation: May substitute ½ pound lump crabmeat for olives and add curry powder to taste.

DICK'S FAVORITE STUFFED MUSHROOMS

Berks County, Pennsylvania is acknowledged by many to be the mushroom capitol of the country and most of the mushroom growers come from generations of Italian heritage. This delicious recipe blends these two factors into a winning and versatile dish that can be served as an appetizer, first course, vegetable or, when combined with a green salad, a light supper.

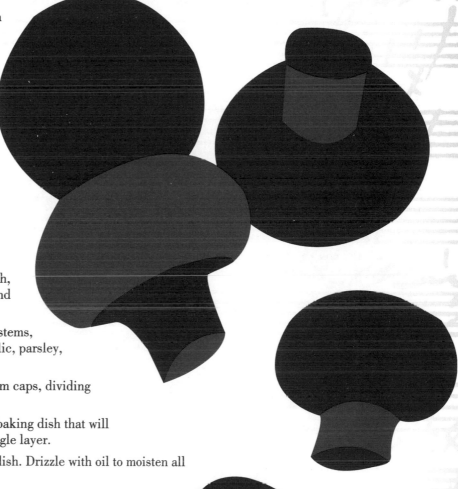

**3 pounds white mushrooms, each
    1½ to 2-inches in diameter**
**½ cup freshly grated Parmesan
    cheese**
**¾ cup Italian style dry
    breadcrumbs**
½ cup finely diced onions
2 garlic cloves, minced
3 tablespoons minced parsley
½ teaspoon dried oregano
Salt and pepper, to taste
⅓ cup virgin olive oil

1. Preheat oven to 350 degrees.

2. Clean mushrooms with a soft brush, but do not wash. Remove stems and finely chop. Reserve caps.

3. Mix together chopped mushroom stems, cheese, breadcrumbs, onions, garlic, parsley, oregano, salt, and pepper.

4. Stuff crumb mixture into mushroom caps, dividing equally.

5. Pour a small amount of oil into a baking dish that will accommodate all the caps in a single layer.

6. Arrange mushrooms in prepared dish. Drizzle with oil to moisten all mushrooms.

7. Bake about 25 minutes.

8. Serve hot or at room temperature as an antipasto, appetizer or vegetable.

Yield: 8-10 servings

INDONESIAN CHICKEN SATAY WITH PEANUT SAUCE

♫ *Even though there are several steps, this is an easy recipe that will excite the taste buds of everyone who eats it.*

PEANUT SAUCE

⅔ cup chunky peanut butter

1½ cups unsweetened coconut milk

¼ cup lemon juice

2 tablespoons soy sauce

2 tablespoons packed brown sugar

1 teaspoon grated fresh ginger

4 garlic cloves, minced

Cayenne pepper, to taste

¼ cup low sodium chicken broth

¼ cup heavy cream

1. Combine peanut butter, coconut milk, lemon juice, soy sauce, brown sugar, ginger, garlic, and cayenne. Cook over moderate heat, stirring constantly, 15 minutes until sauce thickens.

2. Transfer to blender and purée.

3. Add broth and cream and blend until smooth. Cool until ready to serve.

CHICKEN

2 tablespoons peanut butter

½ cup soy sauce

½ cup lime juice

1 tablespoon packed brown sugar

1 tablespoon curry powder

2 garlic cloves, minced

2 dried red chile peppers, crushed

6 boneless, skinless chicken breast halves, cut into long strips ½-inch wide

Wooden skewers

1. Combine peanut butter, soy sauce, lime juice, brown sugar, curry, garlic, and chile peppers in a glass dish.

2. Thread chicken strips onto skewers and place in marinade, tossing to coat. Refrigerate 2 hours or overnight.

3. Grill or broil chicken 6 to 8 minutes, basting with marinade, until crisp and fully cooked. Serve with Peanut Sauce.

Yield: 10 appetizer servings or 4 main courses

"Oh Mozart, immortal Mozart! What countless images of a brighter and better world thou hast stamped upon our souls."

~FRANZ SCHUBERT

PARMESAN-PESTO PINWHEELS

 They will think you worked for hours to create these easy and attractive appetizers.

PESTO

2 cups fresh basil leaves

½ cup olive oil

2 tablespoons pine nuts

2 garlic cloves, lightly crushed

1 teaspoon salt

½ cup freshly grated Parmesan cheese

2 tablespoons freshly grated Romano cheese

1. Blend basil, oil, pine nuts, garlic, and salt in a food processor, scraping down sides occasionally.

2. Transfer to a bowl. Add cheeses and mix by hand. Set aside.

PINWHEELS

4 (3-ounce) packages cream cheese, softened

1 cup freshly grated Parmesan cheese

2 green onions, cut in 1-inch pieces

¼ cup pesto, see recipe or use a 4 ounce jar of prepared pesto

1 (17-ounce) package frozen puff pastry, thawed

1. Blend cream cheese and Parmesan cheese in a food processor until smooth. Add onions and pesto and process until well blended.

2. Roll one pastry sheet on a floured surface to a 10x16-inch rectangle.

3. Spread half cheese mixture over pastry to ½-inch of edge. Roll up lengthwise. Wrap in plastic wrap and freeze.

4. Repeat with second pastry and remaining cheese mixture. Freeze.

5. Thaw logs 30 to 45 minutes. Cut rolls into ¼-inch slices. Place on ungreased baking sheet.

6. Bake at 375 degrees 10 to 13 minutes until flaky and golden brown.

Yield: 3 dozen

 Tip: The quantity of basil in most recipes is given in terms of whole leaves. American basil varies greatly in leaf sizes. Leaves pack differently in the measuring cup. For the sake of accurate measurement, tear all but the tiniest leaves into two or more small pieces. Be gentle not to crush the basil. This would discolor it and waste the first, fresh droplets of juice.

 Tip: Use leftover pesto and toss with your favorite pasta.

"I haven't understood a bar of music in my life, but I have felt it."
~IGOR STRAVINSKY

Appetizers & Beverages

ITALO'S CLAMS

Clams are abundant along the entire New England coastline, and are used in a variety of interesting dishes—from raw to fried to this terrific stuffed presentation.

3 tablespoons extra virgin olive oil

10-12 slices bacon, minced

3 garlic cloves, minced

¾ cup finely chopped celery

¾ cup finely chopped sweet red pepper

¾ cup finely chopped onion

2 quarts shucked hard-shell clams with juice, chopped or good quality canned clams

½ cup chopped parsley

2 tablespoons lemon juice

1 teaspoon dried oregano

Tabasco sauce, to taste

2 tablespoons Worcestershire sauce

1 stick unsalted butter, cut into 10 slices

6-8 cups panko (Japanese breadcrumbs) or fresh breadcrumbs

24-30 clean quahog shells, 3-4-inches across or 48 cherrystone clam shells

Paprika for dusting

Lemon wedges for garnish

1. Heat oil in a large skillet. Sauté bacon, garlic, celery, pepper and onion 10 to 15 minutes until bacon is crisp and vegetables are tender. Spoon off excess fat. Add clams, parsley, lemon juice, oregano, Tabasco and Worcestershire sauce. Bring to simmer. Reduce to low heat.

2. Add butter and 6 cups of breadcrumbs. Cook gently, stirring and adding more crumbs as needed to absorb most of the liquid. Mixture should hold its shape but not be dry.

3. Fill shells with a generous amount of clam mixture. Refrigerate until 30 minutes before serving. Stuffed clams may be frozen at this point.

4. Place clams on a baking sheet. Bake at 375 degrees 25 to 30 minutes or until heated through and lightly browned. Bake 45 minutes for frozen clams. Broil if need further browning.

5. Sprinkle with paprika and serve with lemon wedges.

Yield: 12-24 servings

~ADAPTED FROM FAIRFIELD BY THE SEA~
~GREEN HILL, RHODE ISLAND~

ALEXANDRA'S DELIGHT

Super fast and super popular at every party at which they are served

1 cup mayonnaise

1 cup finely diced onions

1 cup freshly grated Parmesan cheese

1 (16-ounce) loaf French bread, cut into ¼-inch slices

1. Combine mayonnaise, onions, and cheese. Spread a spoonful on each bread slice and place on a baking sheet.

2. Broil about 8 minutes on top oven rack until bubbly and browned.

3. Watch closely to not burn bread. Serve immediately.

Yield: 12-15 servings

CURRIED CHICKEN MINI-DRUMSTICKS

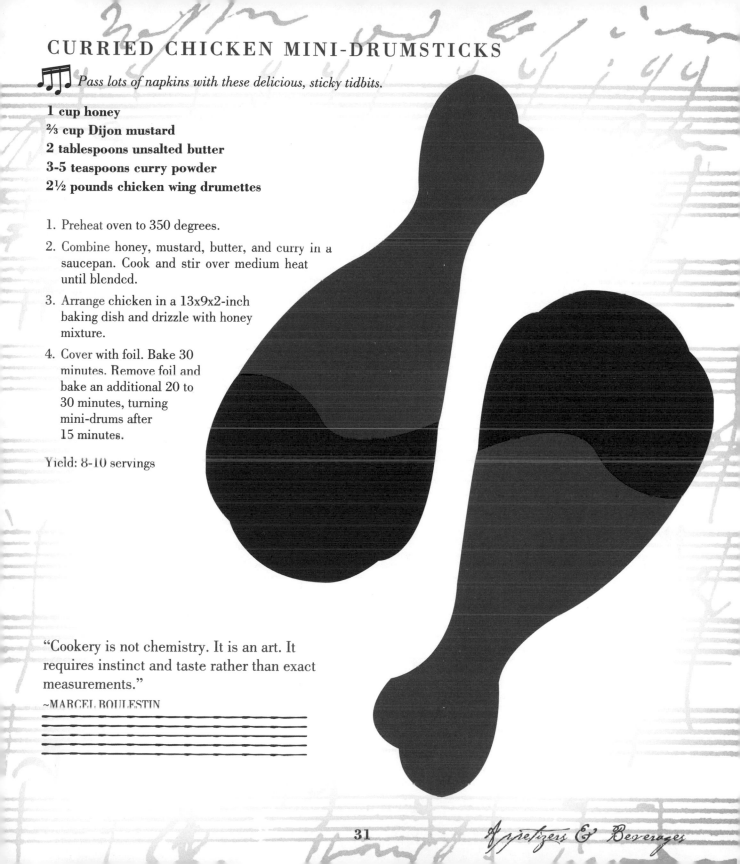

Pass lots of napkins with these delicious, sticky tidbits.

1 cup honey
⅔ cup Dijon mustard
2 tablespoons unsalted butter
3-5 teaspoons curry powder
2½ pounds chicken wing drumettes

1. Preheat oven to 350 degrees.

2. Combine honey, mustard, butter, and curry in a saucepan. Cook and stir over medium heat until blended.

3. Arrange chicken in a 13x9x2-inch baking dish and drizzle with honey mixture.

4. Cover with foil. Bake 30 minutes. Remove foil and bake an additional 20 to 30 minutes, turning mini-drums after 15 minutes.

Yield: 8-10 servings

"Cookery is not chemistry. It is an art. It requires instinct and taste rather than exact measurements."
~MARCEL BOULESTIN

Appetizers & Beverages

RUSTY'S GRILLED OYSTER BROCHETTES

Spicy hot and smokey too, this tasty variation of "angels on horseback" is a winner every time. A great dish to prepare ahead and pop on the grill at the last minute.

6-7 dozen shucked large oysters
1 (2-ounce) bottle Louisiana hot sauce
1 pound bacon

Wooden skewers, soaked in water for 30 minutes so they won't burn

1. Marinate oysters in hot sauce for about 1 hour in the refrigerator.

2. Cut bacon in half or thirds. Wrap bacon around the oysters and place on a skewer to secure bacon.

3. Place about a dozen oysters per skewer. Return to hot sauce and marinate for another hour. The longer oysters are in the marinade, the hotter the taste.

4. Grill over medium-high heat until bacon is cooked.

5. Slide oysters off the skewers and serve.

Yield: 6-7 dozen oysters

"Jack Benny played Mendelssohn last night. Mendelssohn lost."
~ANONYMOUS

SWEET AND SPICY NUTS

The flavor of these crunchy nuts can be varied from sweet to spicy to hot. Presented in a fancy tin, they make a great holiday gift.

1½ cups blanched almonds
2 egg whites
Dash of salt
1 cup sugar

2 cups walnuts
2 cups pecan halves
1 stick butter, melted

1. Toast almonds in a 325 degree oven until light brown.

2. Beat egg whites with salt until foamy. Gradually add sugar and beat until stiff peaks form.

3. Fold almonds, walnuts, and pecans into meringue. Pour butter into a 15x10x1-inch jelly roll pan. Spread nut mixture over butter.

4. Bake at 325 degrees 30 minutes, stirring every 10 minutes, until entire mixture is browned.

Yield: 12-15 servings

Variation: May add cinnamon, ground nutmeg and ground cloves to taste for spiced nuts. Add cayenne pepper to taste for a sweet-spicy flavor. You can also vary the selection of nuts.

SCREAMING PEANUTS

*Marcel Desaulniers, author of **Death By Chocolate**, has shared his special recipe for cocktail peanuts. You decide how loud a "scream."*

1-2 tablespoons peanut oil
1 tablespoon soy sauce
1 teaspoon sugar
3-4 teaspoons Tabasco sauce

1-2 dashes chili oil
1 cup unsalted peanut halves
Salt, to taste

1. Preheat oven to 325 degrees.

2. Heat 1 tablespoon oil in a nonstick skillet. When hot, remove from heat and whisk in soy sauce, sugar, Tabasco, and chili oil.

3. Add peanuts and toss to coat. Spread peanuts in a single layer on a nonstick baking sheet.

4. Bake 12 minutes. Transfer peanuts to a paper towel lined baking sheet. Season with salt while peanuts are warm. Cool completely and store in an airtight container.

Yield: 1 cup peanuts

~TRELLIS RESTAURANT, WILLIAMSBURG, VIRGINIA~
~MARCEL DESAULNIERS, CHEF/OWNER~

BOURBON OR BRANDY SLUSH

Think adult "snow-cone" and you will have an idea of the special treat in store when you try either version of this festive recipe.

1 cup sugar
2 cups very strong hot tea, made with four tea bags
1 (12-ounce) can frozen orange juice concentrate, undiluted

1 (12-ounce) can frozen lemonade concentrate, undiluted
7 cups water
2½ cups bourbon or brandy
Mint leaves or maraschino cherries for garnish

1. Dissolve sugar in hot tea. Add orange juice, lemonade, water, and bourbon or brandy. Mix well.

2. Pour mixture into several containers and freeze.

3. Scrape shavings of slush into glasses and garnish with mint leaves or cherry.

Yield: 12-15 servings

Tip: Slush may be diluted with either grapefruit or lemon-lime soda.

Appetizers & Beverages

CHAMPAGNE FREEZE

♫♪♫ *Serve this light, lemony apéritif at a brunch for a delicious change from traditional tomato and orange juice based drinks.*

4 scoops lemon sorbet
¼ cup chilled citrus vodka or limoncello

¼ cup sparkling wine or champagne
Fresh mint sprigs for garnish

1. Blend sorbet on low speed. Pour in vodka in a slow stream.

2. Stir in champagne. Pour into chilled martini glasses or flutes and garnish with mint sprigs.

Yield: 2 servings

"So long the human spirit thrives on this planet, music in some living form will accompany and sustain it and give it expressive meaning."
~AARON COPLAND

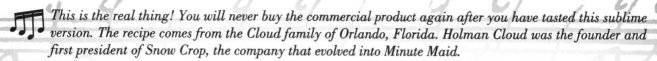

EGGNOG

This is the real thing! You will never buy the commercial product again after you have tasted this sublime version. The recipe comes from the Cloud family of Orlando, Florida. Holman Cloud was the founder and first president of Snow Crop, the company that evolved into Minute Maid.

3 dozen eggs

2¼ cups sugar

2¼ cups whiskey or brandy

½ gallon premium vanilla ice cream

1 pint heavy cream (optional)

1. Separate egg yolks and egg whites into two bowls. Beat egg yolks until pale yellow. Gradually beat in sugar until smooth.

2. Beat egg whites until stiff. Stir in whiskey. Fold egg white mixture into egg yolks.

3. Place ice cream in a large punch bowl. Pour egg mixture over ice cream and stir gently. Stir in cream.

Yield: 36 cups

WHITE WINE SANGRÍA

For a change, try this light, fruity, Spanish white wine beverage on a hot, sultry day.

1 ripe peach, thinly sliced

1 ripe nectarine, thinly sliced

3 ripe apricots, thinly sliced

⅔ cup peach brandy, chilled

1 (750 ml) bottle white wine or champagne, chilled

1 cup peach nectar, chilled

Sugar to sweeten, to taste

Fruit slices for garnish

1. Combine peach, nectarine, and apricots in a pitcher. Add peach brandy. Refrigerate at least 1 hour, stirring once or twice.

2. Add wine and nectar prior to serving. Add sugar to desired taste.

3. Serve in glasses with a slice of fruit.

Yield: 6-8 servings

"I play the notes no better than many other pianists. But the pauses between the notes—ah, that is where the art resides."
~ARTUR SCHNABEL

Appetizers & Beverages

LIMONCELLO

Although available commercially, many Tuscans have their own family recipe for limoncello. It is often a closely guarded secret, passed on from generation to generation. This one comes to us from Franco DePlano, father of Marco DePlano of the DePlano Group, NYC, the designers of Ode to Joyous Cooking.

8 lemons, smooth skinned and heavy for their size **1 quart water**
1 quart grain alcohol or 90+ proof vodka **5 cups sugar**

1. Peel rind from lemons being careful not to cut into bitter white pith. Place rind in alcohol for 3 to 4 days, stirring several times each day.

2. Bring water to boil, add sugar and cook until sugar is dissolved. Cool syrup and add to alcohol-lemon mixture.

3. Let sit eight more days. Strain and rebottle. Store in refrigerator or freezer. Serve very cold.

Yield: 24-30 servings

Breads, Muffins

&

Brunch

BREAKFAST/BRUNCH DISHES

QUICHES AND SAVORIES

MUFFINS AND BREADS

"It may be a good thing to copy reality, but to invent reality is much, much better."
~GIUSEPPE VERDI

COTTAGE CHEESE PANCAKES

♪♪♪ *Requests for this recipe have come as late as 3:00 a.m.*

5 eggs, separated
2 (12-ounce) containers small curd cottage cheese
   (do not use low-fat)
½ cup whole wheat flour
1 teaspoon cinnamon
1 tablespoon honey
Vegetable oil for cooking
Warm maple syrup

"Music is enough for a lifetime, but a lifetime is
not enough for music."
~SERGEI RACHMANINOV

1. Mix egg yolks, cottage cheese, flour, cinnamon, and honey by hand until smooth.

2. Beat egg whites until stiff peaks form. Fold into cottage cheese mixture.

3. Heat a lightly oiled griddle or large skillet to medium. Using a ⅓ cup measure, pour batter onto griddle. Turn pancakes when bubbles appear. Serve with warm maple syrup or honey.

Yield: 4-6 servings

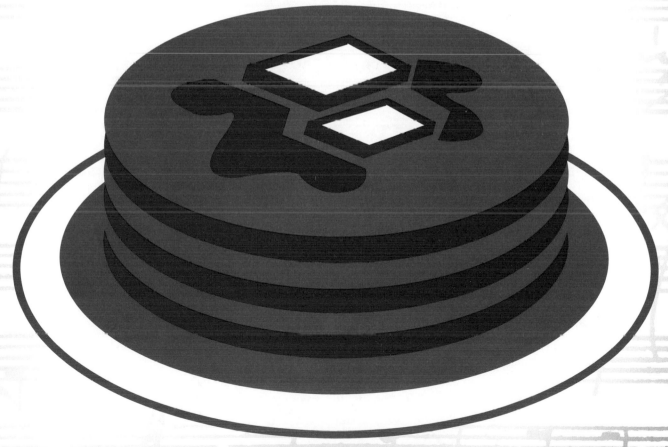

GRAND MARNIER FRENCH TOAST

A delicious addition to an elegant breakfast buffet.

**8 slices French bread, ¾-inch thick, cut on
    diagonal**
4 eggs
1 cup milk
¼ cup Grand Marnier
1 tablespoon sugar
½ teaspoon vanilla
¼ teaspoon salt
2 tablespoons butter
Powdered sugar for dusting

"No one who cooks, cooks alone. Even at her most solitary, a cook in the kitchen is surrounded by generations of cooks past, the advice and menus of cooks present, the wisdom of cookbook writers."

~LAURIE COLWIN

1. Arrange bread in a single layer in a 12x8x2-inch baking dish.

2. Beat eggs with milk, Grand Marnier, sugar, vanilla, and salt until well blended. Pour egg mixture over bread, turning to coat. Cover and refrigerate overnight.

3. Melt butter in a skillet. When hot, sauté bread 4 minutes each side until golden brown. Sprinkle with powdered sugar.

Yield: 4 servings

~ADAPTED FROM THE INN AT MITCHELL HOUSE~
~CHESTERTOWN, MARYLAND~

OUTRAGEOUS STUFFED FRENCH TOAST

 Rich, elegant and it lives up to its name. A real treat.

1 (8-ounce) package cream cheese
¼ cup crushed pineapple, drained
½ cup chopped pecans
1 (16-ounce) loaf unsliced French bread
4 large eggs

1 cup heavy cream
½ teaspoon vanilla
1 teaspoon ground ginger
1 (12-ounce) jar apricot preserves
½ cup orange juice

1. Beat cream cheese and pineapple at medium speed until light and fluffy. Stir in pecans.

2. Cut bread into 12 slices, 1½-inches thick. Cut a pocket in each slice. Stuff pocket with cheese mixture.

3. Beat eggs with cream, vanilla, and ginger. Dip bread into egg mixture letting it absorb some of the liquid. Cook 3 minutes per side on a slightly greased hot griddle.

4. Combine preserves and orange juice in a saucepan. Cook over low heat, stirring constantly, until preserves melt and are slightly thickened. Serve fruit sauce on the side with French toast.

Yield: 8-12 servings

APPLE PUFF PANCAKE

Enjoy the warm, homey flavor of apples and cinnamon in this great oven baked pancake.

10 eggs
2⅓ cups plus 2 tablespoons milk
⅓ cup sugar
2 teaspoons vanilla
1⅔ cups all-purpose flour

¾ teaspoon salt or to taste
½ teaspoon cinnamon
2 tablespoons butter
4-5 apples, peeled and sliced
⅓-½ cup packed brown sugar

1. Beat eggs and milk until well blended. Add sugar, vanilla, flour, salt and cinnamon. Mix well.

2. Melt butter in a 13x9x2-inch baking dish in a 350 degree oven. Add apple slices and return to oven. Cook until butter sizzles.

3. Pour batter over apples. Sprinkle with brown sugar.

4. Bake 20 to 30 minutes until puffed and browned. Watch closely.

Yield: 8-10 servings

~ADAPTED FROM THE RED LION INN~
STOCKBRIDGE, MASSACHUSETTS~

SMOKED SALMON POTATO CRÊPES

An absolutely delicious and amazing accompaniment to eggs prepared your favorite way. Garnish with grape tomatoes and fresh herbs.

2 large eggs
1 medium onion, diced
2 tablespoons all-purpose flour
1 tablespoon chopped parsley

¼ teaspoon kosher salt
¼ teaspoon white pepper
3 ounces smoked salmon, diced
4 large potatoes, grated, pressed in a towel to dry

1. Beat eggs until frothy. Add onion, flour, parsley, salt, and pepper and mix well. Stir in salmon and potatoes.

2. Heat oil in a non-stick skillet. Add 1 large tablespoon (enough to make half-dollar sized crêpes about ¼ inch thick) of batter to pan. Cook until set and browned on one side; turn and cook other side. Repeat with remaining batter. Keep warm until ready to use.

Yield: 8 servings

~GREEN HILLS INN, READING, PENNSYLVANIA~
~JAY SCHAEFFER, OWNER~

 Tip: Serve Crêpes with poached eggs and hollandaise sauce.

NORMANDY OMELET

 Enjoy the unbeatable combination of Roquefort and apple in this unusually good omelet.

5 large eggs
3 tablespoons freshly grated Parmesan cheese
Salt and freshly ground pepper, to taste
2 tablespoons unsalted butter

1 Granny Smith apple, peeled, quartered and cut
  into thin slices
2 ounces crumbled Roquefort cheese

1. Beat eggs with Parmesan cheese. Season with salt and pepper. Set aside.

2. Melt one tablespoon butter in a 12-inch omelet pan. Sauté apples about 1 minute. Remove apple slices and set aside.

3. Add remaining tablespoon butter to pan. Heat until foamy. Add egg mixture. As soon as eggs are set, add apple slices and Roquefort cheese. Fold over and serve immediately.

Yield: one large omelet, serving 2-3 people

"There is only one rule of music: if it sounds good, it is good."

~ANONYMOUS

JAM NOODLE KUGEL

The word "kugel" means pudding in Yiddish. You do not have to be Jewish to make or enjoy this traditional dish. It is extremely versatile and can be served hot or cold, at any meal and for any course.

1 (3-ounce) package cream cheese, softened
3 eggs
½ cup sugar
¾ cup apricot preserves
¾ cup milk
6 tablespoons unsalted butter, melted

8 ounces wide noodles, cooked al dente and
  drained
1-1½ cups crushed cornflakes
¼ cup sugar
1 teaspoon cinnamon
6 tablespoons unsalted butter, melted

1. Preheat oven to 350 degrees. Blend cream cheese, eggs, sugar, preserves, milk, and butter. Mix well. Stir in noodles.

2. Pour mixture into a greased 13x9x2-inch baking dish.

3. Combine crushed cornflakes, sugar, cinnamon, and butter. Sprinkle over noodle mixture. May refrigerate at this point and bake the next day.

4. Bake 45 to 60 minutes or until firm and browned.

Yield: 8-10 servings

EGGS IN PURGATORY

♪♪♪ *Enjoy this dish with as much "heat" as you like or can stand.*

4-6 green onions, sliced
1 (8-ounce) package sliced mushrooms
Butter
2 tablespoons all-purpose flour
4 large tomatoes, peeled, seeded and chopped or
    1 (15-ounce) can diced tomatoes, drained

½ teaspoon dried basil
1-2 garlic cloves, minced
½ teaspoon dried tarragon
4 eggs
Tabasco sauce, to taste
Freshly grated Parmesan cheese

1. Preheat oven to 350 degrees. Sauté onions and mushrooms in butter. Stir in flour until well blended. Add tomatoes, basil, garlic and tarragon and mix well.

2. Divide vegetable mixture among four buttered shallow 8-ounce ramekins. Break an egg into each ramekin. Season with Tabasco. Top generously with Parmesan cheese.

3. Bake 15 minutes for soft eggs or 17 to 18 minutes for firm eggs.

Yield: 4 servings

"For breakfast I always have a 3-minute boiled egg. Do you know how I time it? I bring it to a boil and then I conduct the *Overture to Marriage of Figaro*. Three minutes exactly."
~SIR JOHN BARBIROLLI, BRITISH CONDUCTOR

CRUSTLESS QUICHE

Easy and elegant, this amazing quiche will please your palate.

½ pound fresh mushrooms, thinly sliced
2 tablespoons butter
4 eggs
1 cup sour cream
1 cup small curd cottage cheese
½ cup freshly grated Parmesan cheese
¼ cup all-purpose flour
2 teaspoons grated onion
¼ teaspoon salt
4 drops Tabasco sauce
1 (8-ounce) package or
    2 cups shredded Monterey
     Jack cheese
8 ounces slivered ham

> "All our hens lay fresh eggs."
> ~FROM A SIGN OUTSIDE THE CACKLE
> AND CROW HENNERY NEAR GROTON,
> MASSACHUSETTS

1. Preheat oven to 350 degrees. Sauté mushrooms in butter. Drain on paper towels.

2. Combine eggs, sour cream, cottage cheese, Parmesan cheese, flour, onion, salt, and Tabasco in a blender. Blend until thoroughly mixed.

3. Pour cream mixture into a large bowl. Add mushrooms, Monterey Jack cheese, and ham.

4. Pour mixture into a greased 10-inch quiche dish or 10-inch pie plate.

5. Bake 45 minutes or until knife comes out clean. Let stand 5 minutes before cutting. May be prepared in advance and refrigerated. Bring to room temperature before baking.

Yield: 6-8 servings

Variation: May substitute 1 pound lump or backfin crabmeat for ham. A combination of vegetables can also be used. It is your chance to be creative!

Tip: Serve with a green salad and crusty French bread.

SYMPHONY OF SEAFOOD PIE

A savory rich quiche. Great served at a brunch buffet or as a light dinner with a green salad.

1 (9-inch) pie crust, unbaked, see Basic Pie Crust
    recipe, page 200
½ cup mayonnaise
2 tablespoons all-purpose flour
2 eggs, beaten
⅓ cup thinly sliced celery
⅓ cup thinly sliced green onions

½ pound sliced mushrooms
2 tablespoons butter
¼ cup white wine or sherry
1 cup lump crabmeat
1 cup shrimp, peeled and deveined
⅔ cup bay scallops
1 (8-ounce) package shredded Swiss cheese

1. Preheat oven to 350 degrees. Combine mayonnaise, flour, and eggs. Blend well.

2. Sauté celery, onions, and mushrooms in butter 3 to 5 minutes. Add wine and cook until liquid is reduced.

3. Stir in crabmeat, shrimp, scallops, mushroom mixture, and cheese. Pour into pie crust.

4. Bake 55 to 60 minutes.

Yield: 6-8 servings

~ADAPTED FROM~
~TOLLGATE HILL INN AND RESTAURANT~
~LITCHFIELD, CONNECTICUT~

POTATO AND ONION TORTILLA

Some cultures have latkes, some have potato pancakes, and Spain has this tasty tortilla. Serve hot or cold anytime of day.

1 cup olive oil
2-3 medium Yukon Gold or Red Bliss potatoes,
    peeled and thinly sliced

1 large Spanish onion, thinly sliced
6 eggs
Salt and freshly ground pepper, to taste

1. Heat oil in a 12-inch cast iron skillet. Add potatoes and onion. Cover and cook over medium heat 15 minutes until soft.

2. Beat eggs in a large bowl. Using a slotted spoon, transfer potatoes and onion to eggs. Season with salt and pepper.

3. Pour most of oil from skillet. Heat until remaining oil is very hot.

4. Pour in egg mixture, spreading and pressing potatoes and onion as flat as possible. Cook 3 to 5 minutes or until mixture begins to set. Do not stir.

5. Place skillet under broiler and cook until golden brown but slightly moist in the center.

6. Cut into wedges and serve hot or at room temperature with a tomato salad.

Yield: 6 servings

Breads, Muffins & Brunch

ONION PIE

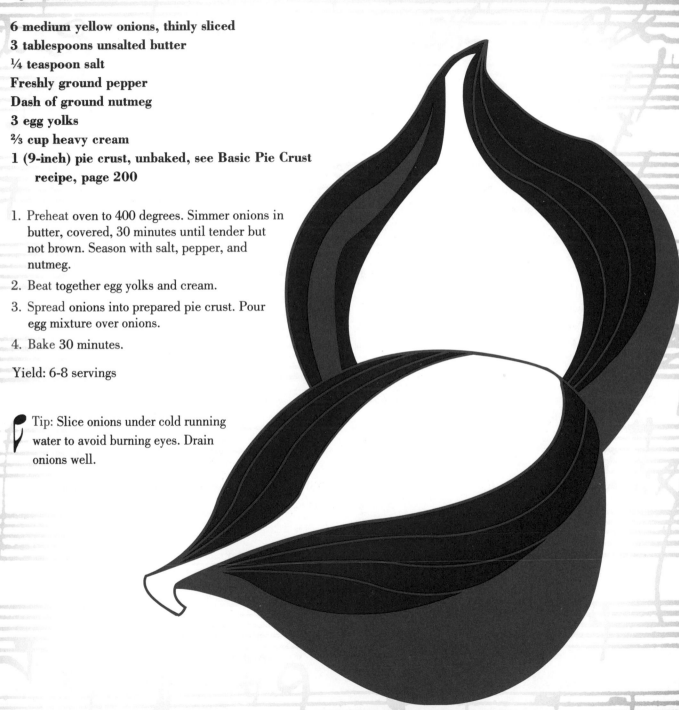

This savory custard will satisfy even the heartiest appetite when served with a crusty bread and fresh sliced tomato salad.

6 medium yellow onions, thinly sliced
3 tablespoons unsalted butter
¼ teaspoon salt
Freshly ground pepper
Dash of ground nutmeg
3 egg yolks
⅔ cup heavy cream
1 (9-inch) pie crust, unbaked, see Basic Pie Crust recipe, page 200

1. Preheat oven to 400 degrees. Simmer onions in butter, covered, 30 minutes until tender but not brown. Season with salt, pepper, and nutmeg.

2. Beat together egg yolks and cream.

3. Spread onions into prepared pie crust. Pour egg mixture over onions.

4. Bake 30 minutes.

Yield: 6-8 servings

Tip: Slice onions under cold running water to avoid burning eyes. Drain onions well.

CREAMY GRITS WITH FONTINA FONDUTA AND SAUTÉED MUSHROOMS

Southern grits with an Ivy League education!

FONDUTA

4 ounces fontina cheese, shredded

¼ cup whole milk

⅔ cup heavy cream

½ cup freshly grated Parmesan cheese

Salt and pepper, to taste

1 egg yolk

1. Combine fontina cheese with milk in a stainless bowl. Let stand 30 minutes.

2. Combine cream and Parmesan cheese in a saucepan. Cook over low heat, stirring constantly, until cheese melts. Season with salt and pepper. Remove from heat, but keep warm.

3. Set bowl with fontina cheese over a pan of simmering water, stirring constantly, to melt cheese into threads.

4. Transfer fontina cheese mixture and Parmesan cheese mixture to a blender. Add egg yolk and blend until smooth. Return to saucepan and keep warm.

MUSHROOMS

6 teaspoons extra virgin olive oil

8 ounces assorted mushrooms, cut into ¼-inch slices

Salt and pepper, to taste

2 shallots, minced

3 garlic cloves, minced

1 tablespoon chopped thyme

1. Heat 2 teaspoons oil in a large skillet. Sauté mushrooms and season with salt and pepper. Transfer to a plate.

2. Add remaining 4 teaspoons oil to skillet. Cook shallots and garlic 3 minutes. Return mushrooms to skillet, cover and cook 4 minutes. Stir in thyme. Keep warm.

GRITS

Quick grits

1 teaspoon salt

1-2 tablespoons cold butter

2 cups cabbage, shaved paper thin

Freshly ground pepper

1. Prepare four servings of grits according to package directions. Add salt, butter, and pepper.

2. Divide cabbage among 4 warm plates. Top with a spoonful of grits. Pour fonduta over grits. Top with mushrooms.

3. Sprinkle with pepper and serve immediately.

Yield: 4 servings

~THE RIALTO, CAMBRIDGE, MASSACHUSETTS~

CHOCOLATE SOUR CREAM CRUMB CAKES

Get on the road and going in the right direction with these appetite soothing, sour cream enhanced chocolate cupcakes. Rather than an irritating ride, you will drive into cinnamon and walnut flavored crumbs at breakneck speeds. What a way to start your day with these treats created especially for Ode to Joyous Cooking by Marcel Desaulniers.

CINNAMON WALNUT CRUMB TOPPING

½ cup all-purpose flour

½ cup walnut halves, toasted and coarsely chopped

¼ cup packed brown sugar

4 tablespoons unsalted butter, cut into pieces

⅛ teaspoon cinnamon

¼ teaspoon salt

1. Combine flour, walnuts, brown sugar, butter, cinnamon, and salt in a bowl. Beat on low-medium speed until mixture resembles coarse crumbs. Set aside.

CHOCOLATE SOUR CREAM CAKE BATTER

1½ cups all-purpose flour

¼ cup unsweetened cocoa powder

1 teaspoon baking powder

1 teaspoon baking soda

½ teaspoon salt

1 cup sugar

1 stick unsalted butter, cut into pieces

2 large eggs

2 ounces semi-sweet baking chocolate, melted

1 cup sour cream

1 teaspoon vanilla

1. Preheat oven to 350 degrees. Sift together flour, cocoa, baking powder, baking soda, and salt. Set aside.

2. Beat sugar and butter with an electric mixer until smooth and fluffy. Add eggs, one at a time, beating well after each addition. Beat in chocolate for 15 seconds. Add sour cream and beat 2 minutes on medium speed until smooth. Scrape down sides of bowl.

3. Add dry ingredients in batches and mix at low speed. Add vanilla. Mix by hand until thoroughly combined.

4. Spoon 2 heaping tablespoons of batter into 18 foil-lined muffin cups.

5. Sprinkle 1 heaping tablespoon of cinnamon walnut crumb topping over batter in each muffin cup.

6. Bake 25 to 27 minutes. Rotate muffin pans 180 degrees halfway through baking.

7. Cool cakes in muffin pans 15 minutes. Remove cupcakes from muffin pans and serve immediately.

Yield: 18 crumb cakes

~MARCEL DESAULNIERS~
~AUTHOR OF DEATH BY CHOCOLATE~

Tip: The crumb cakes are best when served warm. However, cakes may be stored up to 48 hours at room temperature in a zip-top plastic bag. Microwaving is not recommended.

RHUBARB NUT MUFFINS

Rhubarb grows in abundance in the fertile farmlands of New Jersey as well as in the southeastern portion of Pennsylvania where the Amish refer to it as "pie plant." Its sour edge provides a perfect foil for strawberries, and strawberry-rhubarb pie is often seen on roadside stands in the region. Another marriage made in heaven is rhubarb sweetened with the slightly caramel flavor of brown sugar. These muffins bring those two partners together in a morning breakfast muffin that is tart, sweet, tangy, and moist.

MUFFINS
1½ cups all-purpose flour
¾ cup packed brown sugar
½ teaspoon baking soda
½ teaspoon salt
⅓ cup vegetable oil

1 egg
½ cup buttermilk
1 teaspoon vanilla
1 cup fresh or frozen rhubarb, diced
   (frozen must be drained)
½ cup chopped walnuts or pecans

TOPPING
½ cup packed brown sugar
½ cup chopped walnuts or pecans

1 teaspoon cinnamon

1. Preheat oven to 375 degrees. Combine flour, brown sugar, baking soda, and salt. In a separate bowl, mix together oil, egg, buttermilk, and vanilla. Stir liquid ingredients into dry ingredients, just until moistened.

2. Fold in rhubarb and nuts. Spoon batter into paper-lined muffin cups, filling two-thirds full.

3. Mix brown sugar, nuts, and cinnamon. Sprinkle over tops.

4. Bake 20 to 25 minutes or until muffins test done.

5. Cool in pans 10 minutes before removing to wire rack to cool completely.

Yield: 12 muffins

Variation: May substitute ½ cup whole wheat flour for ½ cup all-purpose flour.

SPICED CRANAPPLE NUT MUFFINS

Have you even wondered how cranberries got their name? The Pequots, a Cape Cod tribe of Native Americans, mixed together cranberries which they called "ibimi"—bitter berry—with animal fat and dried deer meat to make "pemmican," an early form of jerky, that was high in nutritional value and could be stored indefinitely due to the high acidity of the berries. When the European settlers came, they saw the beautiful flowers on the berry's low growing bushes and thought they resembled the head and bill of a crane—thus giving the berry its common name.

The story of the pairing of the tart cranberries with sweet apples is lost to us, but we can be indebted to the person who first made the felicitous discovery.

4 tablespoons unsalted butter, melted and cooled

1 large egg

½ cup sugar

½ cup fresh orange juice

Zest of one orange

1 cup all-purpose flour

1 teaspoon baking powder

½ teaspoon baking soda

1 teaspoon cinnamon

½ teaspoon ground nutmeg

½ teaspoon ground allspice

¼ teaspoon ground ginger

¼ teaspoon salt

1-2 medium apples, peeled and coarsely chopped to equal 1¼ cups

1 cup fresh or dried cranberries

½ cup chopped walnuts

Powdered sugar for dusting

1. Preheat oven to 350 degrees. Whisk egg in a bowl. Blend in butter. Add sugar, orange juice, and zest and mix well.

2. In a separate bowl, sift together flour, baking powder, baking soda, cinnamon, nutmeg, allspice, ginger, and salt. Make a well in center. Pour egg mixture into well. Stir until just blended.

3. Add apples, cranberries, and nuts. Spoon batter into paper-lined or greased muffin cups, filling three-fourths full.

4. Bake 25 to 30 minutes until tops spring back. Dust with powdered sugar.

Yield: 12 muffins

Variation: Use whole wheat flour for a denser muffin. Increase orange juice by 2 tablespoons.

Tip: Try this wonderful butter sauce with these muffins. Combine 1 cup sugar, 4 tablespoons butter, ½ cup heavy cream, and 1 teaspoon vanilla in a saucepan. Cook and stir over low heat until sugar dissolves and butter melts.

"There are two golden rules for an orchestra: start together and finish together. The public doesn't give a damn what goes on in between."
~SIR THOMAS BEECHAM

BLUEBERRY WALNUT BREAD

Blueberries are indigenous to New England, where early settlers found them growing wild on low, dense bushes. They were difficult to harvest and highly perishable, but were an anticipated treat during the short season. Today blueberries are widely cultivated throughout the Mid-Atlantic States where their taller bushes make them easier to pick and refrigeration extends their shelf life. New Jersey berries are particularly sought after for their delicious flavor and super-large size. Pies, muffins, jams and breads are the most common usage, but this versatile fruit now appears on the tables of imaginative cooks in salads, salsas, and beverages as well. The Inn at Jackson in Jackson, New Hampshire serves them in this wonderfully moist bread.

4 sticks unsalted butter, softened	1 tablespoon baking powder
3 cups sugar	½ teaspoon salt
6 large eggs	1 cup milk
2 teaspoons lemon extract or zest of two lemons	2½ cups fresh blueberries
4 cups unbleached all-purpose flour	1 cup chopped walnuts

1. Preheat oven to 350 degrees. Beat butter and sugar until light and fluffy. Add eggs, one at a time, beating well after each addition. Stir in lemon extract. Set aside.

2. Sift together all but 2 tablespoons flour, baking powder, and salt. Add dry ingredients alternately with milk into the creamed mixture, starting and ending with flour mixture.

3. Toss blueberries with remaining 2 tablespoons flour. Fold blueberries and walnuts into batter.

4. Grease an 8x4-inch loaf pan and a 12-cup Bundt pan. Pour 2 cups batter into loaf pan and remaining batter into Bundt pan.

5. Bake 45 minutes for loaf pan. Bake 1 hour, 5 minutes for Bundt pan. Test for doneness. Cool in pans on wire racks 10 minutes. Invert and unmold bread. Cool completely on wire racks.

Yield: 1 loaf and 1 Bundt cake

~ADAPTED FROM THE INN AT JACKSON~
~JACKSON, NEW HAMPSHIRE~

"Take a music bath daily, and you will find that it is to the soul what the water bath is to the body."
~OLIVER WENDELL HOLMES

TASTY LEMON BREAD

Sweet and tart with the crunch of pecans, this loaf is lovely with tea.

1 stick unsalted butter, softened

1 cup sugar

2 eggs, slightly beaten

1¼ cups sifted all-purpose flour, sifted

1 teaspoon baking powder

½ teaspoon salt

½ cup milk

½ cup finely chopped pecans

Zest of one lemon

¼ cup sugar

Juice of one lemon

1. Preheat oven to 350 degrees. Cream butter and sugar. Stir in eggs until well blended.

2. Sift together flour, baking powder, and salt. Add dry ingredients alternately with milk into the creamed mixture. Stir in pecans and zest. Pour batter into a greased 9x5-inch loaf pan.

3. Bake 1 hour. Test for doneness.

4. Combine sugar and juice in a saucepan. Cook and stir over low heat until sugar dissolves. Set aside to cool.

5. Remove bread from oven and pierce top with a fork. Pour lemon sauce over top of hot bread.

Yield: 1 loaf

"The smell of good bread baking, like the sound of lightly flowing water, is indescribable in its evocation of innocence and delight…
[Breadmaking is] one of those almost hypnotic businesses, like a dance from some ancient ceremony. It leaves you filled with one of the world's sweetest smells…there is no chiropractic treatment, no Yoga exercise, no hour of meditation in a music-throbbing chapel that will leave you emptier of bad thoughts than this homely ceremony of making bread."
~M.F.K. FISHER

GRANDMOTHER'S GINGERBREAD

The original English colonists are credited with putting gingerbread on the American table where it found particular favor in the Southern states such as Maryland. The costal colonies, from New England to Georgia, were acquainted with many exotic ingredients and flavors due to the active shipping trade with the Far East. Ginger was just such a flavor and when combined with other spices and the sweetening properties of molasses, produced gingerbread—dense, moist, and with a long shelf life—making it an ideal "snack" to have on hand.

1 stick unsalted butter, softened	1 teaspoon ground ginger
½ cup sugar	½ teaspoon ground cloves
1 egg, beaten	½ teaspoon salt
2½ cups all-purpose flour	1 cup molasses
1½ teaspoons baking soda	1 cup hot water
1 teaspoon cinnamon	Whipped cream for garnish

1. Preheat oven to 350 degrees. Cream butter and sugar. Add egg and mix well.

2. Combine flour, baking soda, cinnamon, ginger, cloves, and salt.

3. Stir together molasses and hot water until blended. Add dry ingredients alternately with molasses into the creamed mixture, beating well after each addition. Pour batter into a greased 9x9x2-inch square baking dish.

4. Bake 45 minutes. Garnish with whipped cream.

Yield: 12 servings

Tip: When measuring sticky substances like molasses, honey or corn syrup, coat the measuring cup first with non-stick cooking spray.

"Bread is the warmest, kindest of words. Write it always with a capital letter, like your own name."
~RUSSIAN CAFÉ SIGN

BANANA BREAD WITH CHOCOLATE MORSELS

Remember chocolate covered bananas? Here we have those two wonderful flavors combined in a delicious, moist bread. May prepare as a cake, frost it and take to a summer picnic. Yum!!

1½ sticks unsalted butter, softened
⅔ cup sugar
⅔ cup packed brown sugar
2 cups all-purpose flour
½ teaspoon salt
½ teaspoon baking powder

½ teaspoon baking soda
1 egg
3 ripe bananas
1 teaspoon vanilla
1 cup chocolate morsels

1. Preheat oven to 350 degrees. Cream butter, sugar, and brown sugar until light and fluffy.

2. Combine flour, salt, baking powder, and baking soda. Set aside

3. Add egg, bananas, and vanilla to creamed mixture. Mix well.

4. Stir in dry ingredients and mix until well blended. Add chocolate morsels.

5. Grease either a 13x9x2-inch baking dish or 9x5-inch loaf pan. Pour batter into prepared pan.

6. Bake 30 to 35 minutes for cake or 55 to 60 minutes for loaf until golden brown. Test with cake tester.

7. If prepared as a loaf, slice and serve with breakfast or as an afternoon snack. If prepared as a cake, frost with your favorite butter or cream cheese frosting.

Yield: 10-12 servings

"Never eat more than you can lift."
~MISS PIGGY (AMERICAN PUPPET)

CINNAMON SOUR CREAM COFFEE CAKE

Chocolate morsels are the special addition to this delicious cake at The Farmhouse at Nauset Beach, East Orleans, Massachusetts.

2 sticks unsalted butter, softened
1¼ cups sugar
2 eggs
1 cup sour cream
2 cups all-purpose flour
½ teaspoon baking soda

1½ teaspoons baking powder
1 teaspoon vanilla
¾ cup finely chopped walnuts
1 teaspoon cinnamon
3 tablespoons sugar
6 ounces chocolate morsels (optional)

1. Beat butter, sugar, and eggs with an electric mixer until light and fluffy. Blend in sour cream.

2. Sift together flour, baking soda, and baking powder. Gradually stir into creamed mixture. Add vanilla.

3. Spoon half of the batter into a buttered and floured 9-inch tube pan. Batter will be quite thick.

4. Combine walnuts, cinnamon, sugar, and chocolate morsels. Sprinkle half over batter. Spoon in remaining batter and top with remaining cinnamon mixture.

5. Place in a cold oven. Bake at 350 degrees 45 to 55 minutes. Test for doneness. Serve warm or room temperature.

Yield: 12-15 servings

GERMAN BEER BRÖT

You will enjoy this easy loaf served with a rich soup of beans or lentils.

3 cups self-rising flour
12 ounces beer
2 tablespoons sugar

1. Preheat to 400 degrees.

2. Combine flour, beer, and sugar. Mix well. Shape dough into a loaf and place in a 9x5-inch buttered loaf pan.

3. Bake 1 hour.

Yield: 1 loaf

"Cooking is at once one of the simplest and most gratifying of the arts, but to cook well one must love and respect food."
~CRAIG CLAIBORNE

~ADAPTED FROM NESTLENOOK FARM BED AND BREAKFAST~
~JACKSON, NEW HAMPSHIRE~

Breads, Muffins & Brunch

SWEET BREAD DOUGH

The Portuguese heritage of Rhode Island is in evidence in this delicious, basic sweet bread with a chameleon-like ability to change into many wonderful variations.

1 package active dry yeast	2 large eggs
¼ cup warm water (110 degrees)	1½ teaspoons vanilla
½ cup warm milk (110 degrees)	1 teaspoon salt
⅓ cup sugar	3½ cups unbleached all-purpose flour
4 tablespoons unsalted butter	

1. Sprinkle yeast over water. Let stand 5 to 10 minutes until foamy.

2. Combine milk, sugar, butter, eggs, vanilla, salt, and yeast mixture. Add 2 cups flour and beat 4 minutes, scraping bowl often. Add remaining dough ½ cup at a time, beating well after each addition until a soft dough forms.

3. Turn dough out onto a lightly floured surface and knead 5 to 10 minutes until smooth and elastic. Place dough in a greased bowl. Cover and let rise in a warm place 1 hour, 30 minutes or until doubled in size.

4. Shape dough into any of the following four variations:

   A. For wonderful plain rolls, pull of 2-inch dough pieces and place 2 inches apart on a buttered baking sheet.

   B. Roll dough into a 10x30-inch rectangle for cinnamon bread. Spread with butter. Sprinkle with brown sugar and cinnamon. Roll up and divide into 3 loaves. Place in buttered loaf pans.

   C. Roll bread into a 10x30-inch rectangle to make a fancy nut roll. Combine 5⅓ tablespoons softened butter, ⅓ cup packed brown sugar, ⅓ cup all-purpose flour, 2 teaspoons vanilla. 1½ teaspoons cinnamon and 1½ cups finely chopped nuts. Spread mixture over dough. Roll up. Cut roll lengthwise in half and twist. Shape into a ring.

   D. Stir golden raisins soaked in rum and toasted almonds into dough. Place dough in a buttered fluted Bundt pan.

5. Cover dough and let rise 1 hour in a warm place. Bake at 375 degrees 15 to 20 minutes for rolls and longer for breads.

Yield: 2 dozen dinner rolls, 3 cinnamon loaves, 1 large nut roll or 1 Bundt cake

Tip: May double recipe.

"All sorrows are less with bread."
~SPANISH PROVERB

Soups

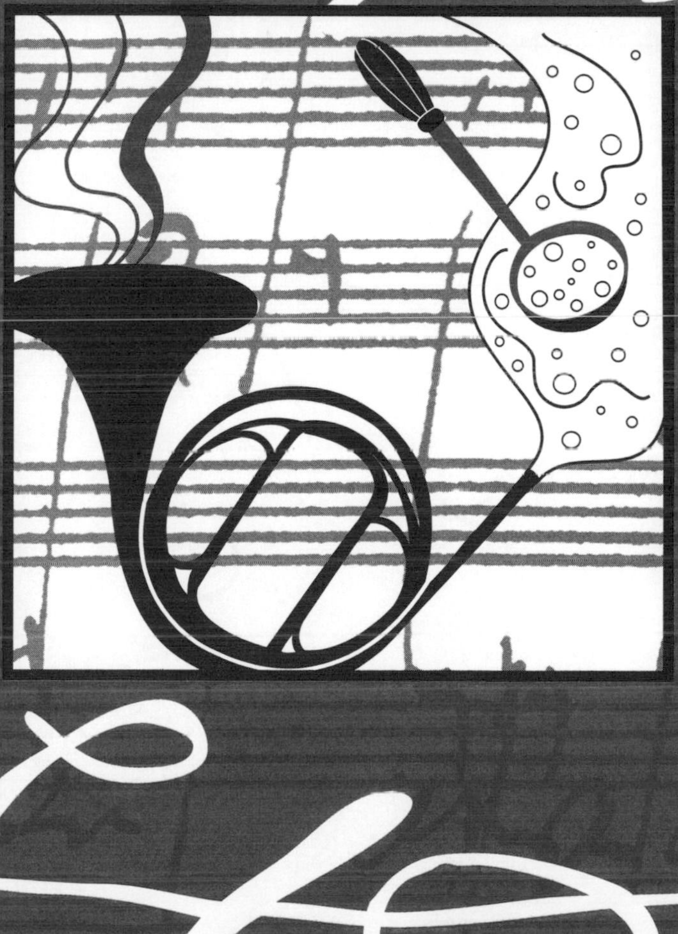

& Stews

HOT SOUPS

COLD SOUPS

FRUIT SOUPS

CHILI

STEWS

"If I had a son who was ready to marry, I would tell him, 'Beware of girls who don't like wine, truffles, cheese, or music.'"
~COLETTE

Soups & Stews

APPLE AND BUTTERNUT SQUASH SOUP

New Englanders relied on winter squash from the 1750's on because of its extended shelf life and fine taste. The Hubbard was the favored variety in earlier times, a specimen often tipping the scales at more than twelve pounds. Today, the butternut fills that role and has become one of the most favored and versatile squashes available. Its smooth, thin skin and string-free flesh makes it a popular choice for many delicious dishes. Given their similar seasonal availability, it was only a matter of time until the wonderful culinary marriage between the squash and the apple took place. This delicious soup that highlights this pairing is a beloved menu favorite throughout New England, its silky texture and slightly sweet taste warming the palate on the coldest night. The ingredients in each recipe are similar, and the recipe featured below is a variation of one from The Stonebridge Inn in Hillsborough, New Hampshire.

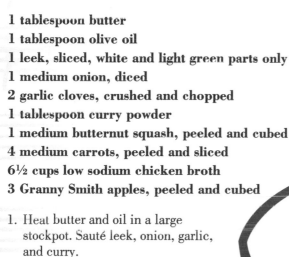

1 tablespoon butter
1 tablespoon olive oil
1 leek, sliced, white and light green parts only
1 medium onion, diced
2 garlic cloves, crushed and chopped
1 tablespoon curry powder
1 medium butternut squash, peeled and cubed
4 medium carrots, peeled and sliced
6½ cups low sodium chicken broth
3 Granny Smith apples, peeled and cubed

¾ cup light cream or sour cream
Salt and pepper, to taste
Sour cream for garnish

1. Heat butter and oil in a large stockpot. Sauté leek, onion, garlic, and curry.

2. Add squash and carrots and mix well. Add broth and bring to boil. Reduce heat, add apples and simmer 35 minutes.

3. Purée mixture in batches in a blender. Return to stockpot and keep warm. Add cream prior to serving. Season with salt and pepper. Ladle into soup bowls. Garnish with a dollop of sour cream.

Yield: 4-6 servings

Tip: May freeze soup before adding cream.

Tip: When choosing a squash, pick one with a long neck and small bulb. It will yield the most flesh and the fewest seeds.

Soups & Stews

WILD RICE SOUP WITH BACON

 Hearty and rich, this soup is perfect to warm you on a chilly winter day.

2-3 slices thick bacon, diced
⅔ cup wild rice, rinsed
½ cup chopped onion
½ cup chopped carrot
½ cup chopped celery
4½ cups low sodium chicken broth

1 cup heavy cream
1 tablespoon butter, softened
1 tablespoon all-purpose flour
Salt and pepper, to taste
2 tablespoons minced parsley

1. Cook bacon until crisp in a stockpot. Remove and reserve bacon. Drain and reserve 2 tablespoons drippings. Sauté rice, onion, carrot, and celery 5 minutes in drippings. Return bacon to pot.

2. Add broth and bring to boil, stirring constantly. Reduce heat. Cover and simmer, stirring occasionally, 40 minutes until rice is tender.

3. Stir in cream. Combine butter and flour. Whisk into soup. Cook and stir 1 minute until soup thickens. Add up to 1 cup more of broth, if a thinner soup is desired. Season with salt and pepper. Sprinkle with parsley prior to serving.

Yield: 4 servings

Tip: To store bacon in useable sized quantities, roll 3 or 4 slices together into tight cylinders. Store the cylinders in a zipper lock bag in the freezer.

BOWERS HOTEL POTATO SOUP

This creamy, elegant soup can start a meal, or be the centerpiece of a supper when paired with crusty bread, a robust salad, and a delicious sweet.

4-6 slices bacon, diced
½ onion, diced
2 stalks celery, diced
6 potatoes, peeled and sliced

3-4 cups low sodium chicken broth
¾-1 cup milk or cream
Salt and pepper, to taste
¼ bunch parsley, chopped

1. Sauté bacon in a saucepan until crisp. Remove bacon and set aside. Add onion and celery to bacon drippings and sauté until tender. Add potatoes and broth. Bring to boil. Cook until potatoes are tender. Cool slightly.

2. Purée mixture in batches in a blender. Process until smooth. Return soup to saucepan.

3. Stir in milk and season with salt and pepper. Add bacon and parsley when ready to serve.

Yield: 10 servings

~BOWERS HOTEL~
~BOWERS, PENNSYLVANIA~

CREAM OF GARLIC SOUP

♪♪♪ *You have to taste this to believe it!*

2 pounds onions, coarsely chopped, about 4 cups
2 cups garlic cloves, peeled and chopped
2 tablespoons olive oil
2 tablespoons butter
6 cups low sodium chicken broth
1 bouquet garni (parsley stems, thyme sprigs and
**   bay leaf tied in a cheesecloth bag)**
2 cups stale French bread, torn into ½-inch pieces
1 cup half-and-half
Salt and pepper, to taste

1. Combine onions, garlic, oil, and butter in a 1-gallon stockpot. Cook, stirring frequently, about 30 minutes over medium heat until a deep golden brown.

2. Add broth and bouquet garni. Bring to boil. Reduce heat and add bread cubes. Simmer 10 minutes until bread is soft.

3. Remove bouquet garni. Cool soup slightly. Purée mixture in batches in a blender. Strain soup and return to stockpot. Heat and add more broth if too thick. Stir in half-and-half. Season with salt and pepper.

Yield: 8 servings

♩ Tip: A coffee filter can be used instead of cheesecloth for bouquet garni. Simply place the herbs in the filter (cone shaped ones work best) and tie with a long piece of string. Secure the other end of the string to the handle of the pot for easy removal.

What love is to man, music is to the arts and to mankind. Music is love itself.
~CARL MARIA VON WEBER

Soups & Stews

New Englanders are quite vociferous when it comes to the preparation of one of their signature dishes—clam chowder. The raging controversy, which has continued for generations, centers on the use of tomatoes as an ingredient in its preparation. The upper states—Maine, New Hampshire, Vermont and Massachusetts would never consider putting them in their chowder kettle, but the housewives of Rhode Island and Connecticut endorse its inclusion. One theory is that Italians and other Mediterraneans were among the largest number of immigrants to the Rhode Island and Connecticut shores and brought the culinary tradition of using tomatoes frequently in their food preparation. We offer both versions for your consideration so that you may be the judge.

CLAM CHOWDER (NORTHERN NEW ENGLAND)

3½ pounds hard-shelled clams, well scrubbed

¾ cup water

2 cups bottled clam juice

¼ cup diced pancetta (Italian, non-smoked bacon)

2 tablespoons unsalted butter

2 small leeks, including some of the tender green
   tops, diced

2 small celery stalks, thinly sliced

1 clove garlic

1 teaspoon chopped fresh thyme

½ pound red potatoes, unpeeled, diced

salt and pepper to taste

1½ cups heavy cream

1 cup fresh or frozen white corn

2 tablespoons minced fresh chives

1. Combine the clams and water in a heavy pot with a tight lid and bring to a boil. Cook, shaking the pot occasionally, until the clams open, about 3 minutes. Remove the clams from their shells and set aside. Strain the liquid through a fine-mesh sieve and add enough to the bottled juice to equal 3 cups.

2. Rinse the soup pot and sauté the pancetta over medium heat until crisp. Remove with a slotted spoon and reserve. Add butter to the pot and sauté the leeks and celery until tender. Add garlic and thyme and cook until fragrant.

3. Stir in the potatoes, the reserved clam broth and the cream. Bring to a boil over high heat; reduce heat and simmer gently until potatoes are tender, about 10 minutes.

4. Chop the reserved clams into coarse pieces and add to the soup along with the pancetta and corn. Heat through, taste and adjust the seasoning.

5. Serve in warmed bowls, sprinkled with chives.

Yield: 6 servings

"Recipe for making canaries sing: feed them hemp seed."

~FROM AN 18TH CENTURY NEW ENGLAND COOKBOOK

3-inch cube fat salt pork, diced
3 onions, sliced
4 cups peeled, cubed potatoes
1 quart shucked clams, hard parts chopped, soft
     part reserved
1 cup clam juice
1 cup water

1 cup stewed tomatoes
½ teaspoon baking soda
1 cup milk, scalded
1 cup cream
2 tablespoons unsalted butter
Salt and pepper, to taste

1. Cook pork in a heavy pot until crisp; remove bits and discard. Sauté onions in fat until lightly browned and remove from pot.

2. Add potatoes to fat and cook over low flame 10 minutes. Add chopped clams pieces, any liquid from the clams, clam juice, water and onions and simmer until potatoes are nearly done.

3. Stir in tomatoes, baking soda, and soft part of clams and simmer for about 30 minutes.

4. Add milk, cream, butter and seasonings when ready to serve.

Yield: 8 servings

VELVET OYSTER BISQUE

Over the top, sinfully rich, special occasion soup! You will find versions of this wonderful dish along the coastal waters of Connecticut and Rhode Island and in the Chesapeake Bay area as well. Perfect for a holiday meal.

2 sticks unsalted butter
½ cup all-purpose flour
8 cups seafood broth or oyster liquor, or a
     combination
5 cups heavy cream
1½ teaspoons cayenne pepper
1½ pounds ripe Brie cheese, rind removed and
     diced (To facilitate this, briefly freeze cheese
     for about 20 minutes)

2½ cups brut Champagne
4 dozen shucked oysters
1 cup finely chopped green onions
2 tablespoons finely chopped shallots
1 tablespoon clarified butter
Salt and pepper, to taste
Chopped chives

1. Melt butter in a saucepan. Whisk in flour, stirring constantly, to make a thick roux. Add broth in a steady stream, whisking constantly, until well blended. Bring to boil. Reduce heat and simmer 10 minutes.

2. Add cream and simmer 5 minutes, stirring constantly.

3. Add cayenne and cheese. Stir until cheese melts and is smooth.

4. Blend in Champagne, oysters, and onions. Cover and turn off heat.

5. Sauté shallots in butter until translucent. Add to soup. Season with salt and pepper. Garnish with chives.

Yield: 10-12 servings

~OLD NEW ENGLAND RECIPE~

Soups & Stews

CRAB-CORN CHOWDER

This soup has become a signature dish at the Canal Street Restaurant and a sought-after favorite of our regular guests.

2 sticks unsalted butter
2 cups all-purpose flour
1 medium carrot, chopped
2 stalks celery, chopped
¼ onion, chopped
2 cups heavy cream
8 cups water
2 tablespoons lobster base or 4 fish bouillon cubes
1 small bay leaf

1 tablespoon Old Bay seasoning
1 teaspoon white pepper
1½ teaspoons Tabasco sauce
1 teaspoon Worcestershire sauce
1 (10-ounce) package frozen white corn, thawed
1 pound claw crabmeat
¼ cup roasted red peppers, chopped
2 tablespoons chopped parsley

1. Melt all but 2 tablespoons butter in a large stockpot. Whisk in flour until smooth and bubbly. Purée carrots, celery, and onions and sauté in remaining 2 tablespoons butter until tender.

2. Combine water and lobster base and mix well. Add to stockpot.

3. Add bay leaf, Old Bay seasoning, pepper, Tabasco, Worcestershire sauce, and corn.

4. Bring to boil. Reduce heat and simmer 15 minutes. Remove bay leaf.

5. Add crab, red peppers and parsley. Heat through.

Yield: 10-12 servings

~CANAL STREET RESTAURANT, READING, PENNSYLVANIA~
~JAKE BAUSHER, CHEF/OWNER~

Tip: This soup is also hearty enough to serve in a hollowed bread boule making it the perfect meal.

"If a man does not keep pace with his companions, perhaps it is because he hears a different drummer. Let him step to the music he hears, however measured and far away."
~HENRY DAVID THOREAU

ROASTED RED PEPPER SOUP

Tangy Parmesan cheese and sweet roasted peppers make this soup flavorful and satisfying.

2 tablespoons olive oil
1 stalk celery, chopped
⅓ cup chopped onion
1 garlic clove, minced
2 sweet red peppers, roasted, peeled, seeded, and chopped

1½ cups low sodium chicken broth
⅓ cup heavy cream
Salt and pepper, to taste
¼ cup freshly grated Parmesan cheese

1. Heat oil in a large skillet until hot but not smoking. Sauté celery, onion, and garlic 5 minutes until tender, stirring occasionally.

2. Add roasted peppers and broth. Bring to boil, reduce heat and simmer 3 minutes. Transfer mixture to a blender.

3. Add cream and season with salt and pepper. Process about 45 seconds, until smooth.

4. Ladle soup into two serving bowls and sprinkle with Parmesan cheese.

Yield: 2 servings

Tip: Broil peppers until skins are blackened, turning every 5 minutes. Place peppers immediately into a brown paper bag and seal for 20 minutes. Peppers will be easier to peel.

CURRIED SWEET POTATO AND LEEK SOUP

This heavenly soup is sure to warm the hearts and stomachs of all who eat it.

3 leeks, white and light green parts only, thinly sliced and rinsed
3 garlic cloves, chopped
½ cup orange juice
4 cups vegetable or low-sodium chicken broth
2½ cups water

3 large sweet potatoes, peeled and cubed
1 Granny Smith apple, peeled and chopped
2 teaspoons curry powder or to taste
2 teaspoons lemon juice
½ teaspoon ground cumin
Salt and pepper, to taste

1. Combine leeks, garlic, and orange juice in a stockpot. Cook 4 to 5 minutes until leeks soften.

2. Add broth, water, potatoes, apple, curry, lemon juice, and cumin. Bring to boil. Reduce heat to medium-low. Simmer, partially covered, 20 minutes or until sweet potatoes are tender.

3. Purée soup in batches in a blender until smooth. Return to stockpot and season with salt and pepper. Warm over low heat, do not boil.

Yield: 6 servings

Variations: Try any of these with this soup: 1) Add a shot of Madeira to soup when reheating. 2) Add ½ cup heavy cream or half-and-half when reheating. 3) Substitute a large, sweet red onion in place of the leeks.

Soups & Stews

NEW ENGLAND CHEDDAR SOUP

Calling all cheese lovers! This soup is for you.

6 cups low sodium chicken broth
5⅓ tablespoons unsalted butter
½ onion, chopped
1 garlic clove, minced
⅔ cup all-purpose flour
½ teaspoon finely chopped thyme
1 bay leaf

Salt and pepper, to taste
8 ounces shredded sharp Cheddar
  cheese
½ cup grated carrots
½ cup minced celery
1 cup half-and-half
½ cup heavy cream

1. Bring broth to boil. Keep warm. Melt butter in heavy stockpot, sauté onion and garlic until tender. Stir in flour and cook 15 minutes over low heat.

2. Whisk in one-third of broth at a time until smooth. Add thyme, bay leaf, salt, pepper, and cheese. Cook over low heat, stirring constantly, until cheese melts and soup is smooth and creamy.

3. Steam carrots and celery until tender. Drain well. Add to soup.

4. Stir in half-and-half and cream. Warm over low heat. Do not overheat. Remove bay leaf before serving.

Yield: 8-10 servings

"Only the pure of heart can make good soup."
~LUDWIG VAN BEETHOVEN

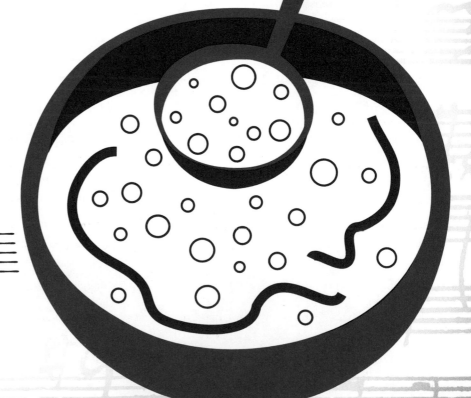

PHILADELPHIA PEPPER POT SOUP

Just in case you want to step back in time and sample Philadelphia's famous Pepper Pot Soup, here is a recipe to satisfy your historical and culinary curiosity.

1 pound tripe, cut into ½-inch cubes

1 extra meaty veal shank, sawed into several pieces

2 quarts water

4-6 whole black peppercorns

1 teaspoon salt

4 tablespoons unsalted butter

1 cup finely chopped onion

½ cup finely chopped celery

½ cup finely chopped green pepper

3 tablespoons all-purpose flour

2 medium-sized boiling potatoes, peeled and cut into ½-inch dice

Crushed dried red pepper

Freshly ground black pepper

1. Combine tripe, veal shank and water in a heavy stock pot. The water should cover the meat by several inches; if necessary add more. Bring to a boil, add the peppercorns and salt, and cook, covered, for two hours or until tripe is tender. Skim the foam from time to time.

2. Transfer the tripe and the veal to a plate. Remove the meat from the bones and cut into ½-inch pieces. Strain the cooking liquid through a fine sieve and reserve 6 cups. Add water, if necessary, to reach that amount.

3. Melt the butter in the same pot and lightly sauté the onion, celery, and pepper until the vegetables are soft but not brown.

4. Sprinkle the flour over the vegetables and mix well. Add the reserved liquid in a slow steady stream and cook until the mixture thickens.

5. Add the potatoes, tripe and veal, reduce the heat to low and simmer, covered, for about an hour. Taste for seasoning, adding more salt and a generous amount of the two peppers to give the dish a distinctively peppery flavor.

Yield: 6-8 servings

SUMMER HARVEST SOUP

 Cooking the fresh vegetables first adds dimension to the flavors of this cold summer soup.

1 onion, chopped

1 bell pepper, chopped

1 sweet red pepper, chopped

2 jalapeño peppers, seeded and chopped

1 tablespoon olive oil

Corn kernels from 4 ears of cooked corn

1 pint grape tomatoes

1 (14-ounce) can low sodium chicken broth

Basil leaves and chopped parsley, to taste

Salt and pepper, to taste

1. Combine onion, bell pepper, red pepper, jalapeño peppers and olive oil and "sweat" until vegetables are wilted and soft.

2. Add corn and cook another 2 to 3 minutes.

3. Add tomatoes, basil, parsley and broth and cook another 10 minutes. Cool slightly.

4. Purée soup in batches. Strain and refrigerate.

5. Serve cold and garnish with basil. Season with salt and pepper.

Yield: 2 servings

Soups & Stews

CHILLED SWEET PEPPER SOUP

The cream cheese is a surprise ingredient that gives this soup added richness.

2 tablespoons unsalted butter
2 medium carrots, peeled and chopped
1 large onion, chopped
2 yellow peppers, diced
3-4 cups low sodium chicken broth

1 (8-ounce) package cream cheese, softened and cubed
Dash of cayenne pepper
Dash of grated nutmeg or to taste
Milk or half-and-half
Finely chopped chives for garnish

1. Melt butter in a stockpot. Sauté carrots and onion about 5 minutes. Add peppers and enough broth to cover vegetables. Bring to boil and reduce heat. Cover and simmer 45 minutes.

2. Whisk in cream cheese, cayenne and nutmeg. Stir in remaining broth. Cook another 10 minutes over medium heat.

3. Purée soup in small batches in the blender until smooth. Refrigerate at least 4 hours or overnight for better flavor.

4. Add milk, half-and-half, or more broth when ready to serve if soup is too thick. Garnish with chives.

Yield: 4 servings

ROASTED PEAR SOUP
WITH GORGONZOLA AND WALNUTS

The sweetness of the roasted pears contrasts with the sharpness of Gorgonzola. The crunchiness of the walnuts plays against the silky texture of the pears. Sensational!

12 pears, peeled and halved
1 onion, diced
2 tablespoons unsalted butter
1 sprig rosemary
1 cup white wine

¼ cup port wine
4 cups low sodium chicken broth
Salt and pepper, to taste
1 cup crumbled Gorgonzola cheese
¼ cup toasted walnuts

1. Place pear halves on a baking sheet. Spray pears with cooking spray. Bake at 350 degrees 25 minutes.

2. Sauté onion in butter in a Dutch oven until tender. Stir in rosemary and cook 2 minutes.

3. Add wine and port and cook until liquid is reduced by one-third. Stir in broth and bring to boil.

4. Add pears and reduce heat. Simmer 30 minutes. Cool slightly. Purée mixture in batches in a blender. Strain soup and place in a saucepan. Season with salt and pepper. Warm over low heat.

5. Garnish individual servings with Gorgonzola cheese and walnuts.

Yield: 8 servings

Tip: May be served cold in the summer.

STRAWBERRY AND BURGUNDY SOUP

A perfect summer soup which also can be served as dessert on a hot summer night.

3 pints strawberries, rinsed, hulled and quartered
1 cup water
½ cup sugar
¼ cup all-purpose flour
2 cups Burgundy

2 cups orange juice
3 cups sour cream
1 cup milk or light cream
Sliced strawberries and mint leaves for garnish

1. Cook strawberries and water over low heat 10 minutes.

2. Combine sugar and flour in a separate saucepan. Stir in wine and orange juice. Bring to boil, whisking constantly, for 10 minutes. Add to strawberries and cool.

3. Purée mixture in a blender. Add sour cream and milk. Blend until smooth. Refrigerate.

4. Garnish individual servings with sliced strawberries and mint leaves.

Yield: 6 servings

~THE INN AT DUCK CREEKE~
~WELLFLEET, MASSACHUSETTS~

Soups & Stews

VEGETARIAN CHILI

 Do not be intimidated by the long list of ingredients. Most items are on every cook's shelf. And you will never miss the meat because bulgur takes its place. This is a very satisfying dish, especially on a frosty day.

⅓ cup olive oil
2 cups finely chopped onions
¾ cup chopped celery
1 cup chopped bell pepper
1 cup chopped carrots
2 cups sliced mushrooms
2 large garlic cloves, minced
¼ teaspoon crushed red pepper
1 tablespoon ground cumin
¾ teaspoon dried basil
2 tablespoons chili powder
¾ teaspoon dried oregano
Salt and pepper, to taste
2 cups tomato juice
¾ cup bulgur wheat
2 cups chopped tomatoes or 1 (15-ounce)
     can diced tomatoes, undrained

1 (20-ounce) can kidney beans, undrained
Dash of Tabasco sauce or to taste
2 tablespoons lemon juice
3 tablespoons tomato paste
1 tablespoon Worcestershire sauce
¼ cup red wine
2 tablespoons chopped canned green chilies or
     1-2 jalapeño peppers, seeded and chopped

1. Heat oil in a large Dutch oven. Add onions, celery, bell peppers, carrots, mushrooms, garlic, red pepper, cumin, basil, chili powder, oregano, salt, and pepper. Cook 3 to 5 minutes over high heat, stirring constantly.

2. Add tomato juice, bulgur wheat, tomatoes, beans, Tabasco, lemon juice, tomato paste, Worcestershire sauce, wine, and green chilies. Bring to boil briefly. Reduce heat and simmer 20 to 25 minutes. Chili may be thinned with additional tomato juice. For a hotter taste, add more Tabasco.

Yield: 6 servings

"Wish I had time for just one more bowl of chili."
~THE DYING WORDS OF KIT CARSON

CHICKEN CHILI

Chunks of delicate chicken provide a great contrast to the spicy chili sauce.

4 split chicken breasts, bone in, skin on, and rubbed with olive oil
Salt and pepper, to taste
3 onions, chopped, about 4 cups
¼ cup olive oil
4 garlic cloves, minced
2 sweet red peppers, seeded and cut in large dice
2 sweet yellow peppers, seeded and cut in large dice
1 teaspoon chili powder or to taste

1 teaspoon ground cumin
¼ teaspoon crushed red pepper
¼ teaspoon cayenne pepper or to taste
2 teaspoons kosher salt
2 (28-ounce) cans whole peeled tomatoes in purée, crushed and undrained
¼ cup minced fresh basil leaves
Chopped green onions, sour cream, shredded Cheddar cheese, tortilla chips for garnish

1. Place chicken on a baking sheet. Sprinkle generously with salt and pepper. Roast at 350 degrees 35 to 40 minutes until just cooked. Cool slightly. Skin, remove meat from bones and cut into ¾-inch chunks. Set aside.

2. Sauté onions in oil in Dutch oven 15 minutes until translucent. Add garlic and cook 1 minute. Stir in red peppers, yellow peppers, chili powder, cumin, crushed red pepper, cayenne and salt. Cook 1 minute.

3. Add tomatoes and basil. Bring to boil. Reduce heat and simmer, partially covered, 30 minutes, stirring occasionally.

4. Add chicken and simmer an additional 20 minutes. Serve with onions, sour cream, cheese or tortilla chips.

Yield: 8 servings

BLANQUETTE DE VEAU

This delicate veal stew is elegant enough for company, but why wait for a special occasion to enjoy it?

8 tablespoons unsalted butter, divided
4½ pound leg or breast of veal, cut into 1½-inch pieces
Salt and pepper, to taste
1 cup finely chopped onion
2 garlic cloves, crushed
4 tablespoons chopped, fresh dill

½ cup all-purpose flour
1 teaspoon fresh grated nutmeg
1½ cups low sodium chicken broth
1½ cups water
3 carrots, sliced
2 leeks, sliced, white part only
1 cup heavy cream

1. Melt 4 tablespoons butter in an ovenproof stockpot. Add veal, salt, pepper, onion, garlic and half of dill. Cook, stirring constantly, 5 minutes without browning.

2. Sprinkle with flour and nutmeg. Pour in broth and water. Bring to boil.

3. Cover and place in a 350 degrees oven for 1 hour.

4. Melt remaining butter in a saucepan. Cook carrots and leeks until tender but not browned.

5. Add vegetables to veal mixture. Stir in cream and bring to boil. Remove from heat.

6. Ladle stew into bowls and garnish with remaining dill.

Yield: 8-10 servings

Soups & Stews

BISTRO BEEF BURGUNDY

A French classic that will never lose its popularity.

3 pounds well-marbled stewing beef, cut into
    1-inch cubes

2 tablespoons olive oil

Salt and pepper, to taste

2 teaspoons dried thyme

½ cup dry red wine for deglazing

6 slices bacon, diced

2 small onions, diced

2 garlic cloves, finely minced

2 tablespoons tomato paste

2 tablespoons packed brown sugar

⅓ bottle dry red wine

1 teaspoon salt

2 bay leaves

3 (10-ounce) cans low-sodium beef broth

½ pound mushrooms, halved

3 carrots, peeled and cut into ½-inch slices

1 pound potatoes, cut into thick batons

1. Heat a portion of oil in skillet. Brown beef on all sides in small batches, seasoning with salt and pepper. Sprinkle a bit of thyme and add a small amount of wine. Deglaze the pan with wine. Reserve beef and deglazing liquid. Repeat two or three more times until all beef is browned.

2. Cook bacon over low heat in an ovenproof stockpot. Add onions and sauté until translucent and bacon is cooked but not crisp. Add garlic, tomato paste, and brown sugar. Cook and stir 2 to 3 minutes.

3. Stir in wine, salt, bay leaves, remaining thyme, browned beef and deglazing liquid, and beef broth. Bring to boil. Immediately cover pot and place in preheated 350 degree oven. Bake 1 hour.

4. Remove pot from oven and skim accumulated fat from top of liquid. Add mushrooms, carrots, and potatoes. Return pot to oven. Bake an additional 30 minutes or until meat is tender, and vegetables are cooked.

5. Remove bay leaves. Thicken stew if necessary with a mixture of cornstarch and water.

6. Ladle into soup bowls and serve with a mixed green salad and warm bread.

Yield: 6-8 servings

~JUDY'S ON CHERRY, READING, PENNSYLVANIA~
~JUDY HENRY, PROPRIETRESS~

 Only a French Burgundy will do.

"Music is a moral law. It gives soul to the universe, wings to the mind, flight to the imagination, a charm to sadness, gaiety and life to everything."
~PLATO

VEGETABLE-BEEF STEW IN PUMPKINSEED SAUCE

In Africa, toasted pumpkinseeds have long been ground and stirred into soups and stews. Here, they add body and a subtle, nutty flavor. Serve this stew with mashed sweet potatoes or over rice.

2 tablespoons roasted salted pumpkinseed kernels

1 teaspoon ground cumin

½ teaspoon ground coriander

½ teaspoon ground allspice

¼ teaspoon ground cloves

¼ teaspoon cinnamon

¼ teaspoon salt

¼ teaspoon pepper

2 teaspoons vegetable oil

1 (8-ounce) boneless sirloin steak, cut into 1-inch cubes

1 cup chopped onions

½ cup chopped sweet red pepper

2 teaspoons finely chopped, seeded pickled jalapeño pepper

1½ cups sliced carrots, ¼-inch thick

1½ cups canned crushed tomatoes, undrained

2 tablespoons molasses

1 (10½-ounce) can low-sodium beef broth

1½ cups cut green beans

2 cups thinly sliced kale or spinach

Whole pumpkin seeds for garnish

1. Cook pumpkinseeds in a Dutch oven over medium-high heat 3 minutes or until kernels are toasted and pop. Remove from heat and cool. Place kernels in coffee grinder or mortar and pestle and crush until fine. Set aside.

2. Combine cumin, coriander, allspice, cloves, cinnamon, salt, and pepper. Set aside.

3. Heat 1 teaspoon oil in a pan. Sauté beef cubes 3 minutes until browned. Remove beef from pan.

4. Add remaining oil to pan. Sauté onions, red pepper, and jalapeño pepper 4 minutes. Add ground kernels and cumin mixture and cook 1 minute. Stir in beef, carrots, tomatoes, molasses, and broth. Bring to boil. Reduce heat, partially cover and simmer 15 minutes.

5. Add beans and simmer 30 minutes or until beef is tender. Add kale or spinach and cook 4 minutes until wilted. Sprinkle individual servings with whole pumpkinseeds.

Yield: 6 servings

Tip: Pumpkinseeds are available at health food stores.

"Never pay attention to what the critics say. A statue has never been erected in honor of a critic."
~JEAN SIBELIUS

Soups & Stews

SCOTCH BROTH

Barley and split peas are the characteristic ingredients of this delicious lamb-based stew that hails from Scotland.

2 pounds boned leg of lamb, cut into 1-inch cubes
2 cups leeks, thinly sliced, white part only
½ cup uncooked pearl barley
¼ cup yellow or green split peas
8 cups low sodium chicken broth

1 pound turnips, peeled and cubed
1 cup celery, chopped
1 pound carrots, peeled and sliced
1 teaspoon salt
¼ teaspoon pepper

1. Brown lamb cubes in batches in a greased non-stick skillet. Transfer to a 6-quart Dutch oven.

2. Add leeks, barley, and peas to skillet. Toss to coat in lamb drippings. Stir in 1 cup broth, mixing well. Transfer mixture to the Dutch oven.

3. Add remaining broth. Bring to boil. Reduce heat, cover and simmer 45 minutes.

4. Add turnips, celery, and carrots. Raise heat slightly until mixture simmers. Cook an additional 45 minutes. Add salt and pepper.

Yield: 8-10 servings

"My tongue is smiling."
~ABIGAIL TRILLIN

CHICKEN "STU"

 An entire meal in a single dish. Notice the unusual trick of roasting the vegetables before they are added to the chicken-broth-wine mixture.

2 tablespoons olive oil

1½ teaspoons chopped thyme or ½ teaspoon dried

¾ pound small white onions, peeled, about 12

2½ pounds chicken pieces on the bone, your choice, thighs preferred

Salt and pepper, to taste

2 cups parsnips, peeled and cut into 1-inch chunks

1 cup turnip or rutabaga, peeled and cut into 1-inch chunks

2 cups red potatoes, cut into 1-inch chunks

1 cup carrots, peeled and cut into 1-inch chunks or baby carrots

3 teaspoons herbes de Provence

2 (14-ounce) cans low sodium chicken broth

1 (10½-ounce) can low sodium beef consommé

2 cups white wine

2 tablespoons balsamic vinegar

1. Preheat oven to 450 degrees. Heat oil in a Dutch oven until hot. Add thyme and onions and cook until browned. Transfer onions to a plate.

2. Rinse, pat dry and season chicken with salt and pepper. Brown on all sides in the same pot. Transfer to a plate.

3. Add parsnips, turnips, potatoes, carrots and reserved onions to pot with chicken drippings and oil. Stir to thoroughly coat vegetables. Transfer to a roasting pan, distributing them in a single layer. Place in hot oven and roast 20 minutes, stirring occasionally.

4. Return chicken to pot with oil and thyme. Add herbes, broth, consommé, wine, and vinegar. Mix well and bring to boil. Reduce heat, cover and simmer 45 minutes.

5. Add roasted vegetables to chicken mixture. Cover and simmer an additional 15 minutes. Remove cover and raise heat to a slow boil to thicken stew. May also whisk in a small amount of cornstarch and water mixture.

Yield: 6-8 servings

 Tip: This heart-healthy meal may be made in advance and reheated. Do not microwave.

"My doctor told me to stop having intimate dinners
for four—unless there are three other people."
~ORSON WELLES

Soups & Stews

LAMB ROGAN JOSH

Is it curry? or just exotic? This fragrant stew will perfume your kitchen and whet your appetite.

¼ cup all-purpose flour

2 teaspoons salt

2 teaspoons ground cumin

2 teaspoons ground coriander seed

1 tablespoon turmeric

1 tablespoon chili powder

Dash of ground nutmeg

1 teaspoon smoked hot paprika

½-¾ teaspoon cayenne pepper or to taste

3 pounds lamb cubes

3 tablespoons butter

3 onions, large dice

3 sweet red peppers, large dice

7 garlic cloves, finely minced

¼ cup cardamom pods, flattened with the side of a knife

2 teaspoons salt or to taste

2-inch piece fresh gingerroot, peeled and finely minced

3 cups diced Roma plum tomatoes

3 (14-ounce) cans low sodium chicken broth or sufficient to cover

1. Combine flour, salt, cumin, coriander, turmeric, chili powder, nutmeg, paprika and cayenne in a bowl. Add lamb cubes and toss to coat. Reserve extra flour.

2. Brown lamb in butter in a large stockpot. Add onions, peppers, garlic, and cardamom pods. Cook and stir until onions are tender. Blend in remaining flour mixture until well combined. Stir in salt, ginger, and tomatoes.

3. Cover lamb mixture with chicken broth. Simmer, covered, 2 hours or until lamb is tender.

4. Add additional salt and pepper to desired taste. Ladle into soup bowls and serve with jasmine or basmati rice and a good fruit chutney (refer to page 229).

Yield: 6-8 servings

~THE SPECKLED HEN~
~READING, PENNSYLVANIA~
~JUDY HENRY, PROPRIETRESS~

"Without music, life is a journey through a desert."
~PAT CONROY

Salads & Dressings

BABY ROMAINE WITH PEARS, ROQUEFORT AND TOASTED ALMONDS IN ORANGE–BASIL VINAIGRETTE

This refreshing salad offers interesting contrasts of flavor, texture and color. It is great as a side salad or as a light luncheon entrée.

ORANGE-BASIL VINAIGRETTE

½ cup white vinegar

½ cup Mandarin orange segments

2 teaspoons chopped basil

1 tablespoon sugar

½ teaspoon salt

⅛ teaspoon pepper

1 cup olive oil

1. Combine vinegar, oranges, basil, sugar, salt and pepper in a blender. Process until well mixed.

2. Add oil in a steady stream and blend 2 minutes until oil is incorporated. May prepare in advance and refrigerate.

SALAD

8 cups baby red romaine or spring greens, chopped

1 Bartlett pear, diced in ½-inch pieces

6 red cherry tomatoes, halved

6 yellow cherry tomatoes, halved

¾ cup Roquefort cheese, crumbled

½ cup almond slivers, toasted

1. Toss lettuce and pears with vinaigrette to coat. Divide onto four salad plates. Place tomatoes halves around perimeter in alternating colors. Top each salad with cheese and almonds.

2. Drizzle with dressing as desired.

Yield: 4 servings

~DANS RESTAURANT, READING, PA~
~DAN GALLAGHER AND DAN SMITH, OWNERS~

A Semillon from Washington state or Australia or a Viognier from California would be a nice complement to this salad.

Salads & Dressings

WATERCRESS SLAW WITH TOASTED COCONUT

The delicate Thai flavors in this salad provide a delightful counterpoint to the peppery bite of the watercress.

3 tablespoons mayonnaise	2 bunches watercress, leaves and tender sprigs only
3 tablespoons olive oil	½ red onion, thinly sliced
1 tablespoon lime juice	1 sweet red pepper, thinly sliced
½ teaspoon hot chili oil	½ cup unsweetened shredded coconut
1 teaspoon kosher salt	½ cup chopped basil
Pepper, to taste	½ cup chopped mint

1. Whisk together mayonnaise, olive oil, lime juice, chili oil, salt and pepper until well blended. Set aside.

2. Mix watercress, onion, and pepper in a bowl. Pour mayonnaise mixture over vegetables. Toss to coat and refrigerate at least 30 minutes.

3. Heat a small skillet over medium heat. Cook coconut, shaking skillet, 2 to 3 minutes until lightly browned. Remove coconut and cool.

4. Toss salad with basil and mint when ready to serve. Garnish with toasted coconut.

Yield: 4 servings

> "I never use a score when conducting my orchestra...Does a lion tamer enter a cage with a book on how to tame a lion?"
> ~DIMITRI MITROPOLIS

CELERY GORGONZOLA COLESLAW

Here is an updated version of the original Dutch "Koolslaa" with its New Jersey origins. Gorgonzola adds a burst of flavor to this incredibly creamy and colorful coleslaw.

2 tablespoons sugar	4 cups shredded green cabbage
½ cup cider vinegar	⅓ cup shredded red cabbage
1 cup mayonnaise	⅓ cup shredded carrots
2 tablespoons celery seeds	1 cup Gorgonzola cheese, crumbled

1. Blend sugar, vinegar, and mayonnaise until smooth. Add celery seeds.

2. Combine green cabbage, red cabbage, carrots, and Gorgonzola cheese in a bowl. Mix in mayonnaise mixture until evenly distributed.

3. Refrigerate at least 1 hour, mixing every 15 minutes.

Yield: 4-6 servings

GREEN SALAD WITH APPLES, SIZZLED WALNUTS AND SHERRY VINAIGRETTE

♫ *The hot oil and sizzled walnuts are a surprise addition to this elegant salad.*

SHERRY VINAIGRETTE

2 tablespoons minced shallots
2 tablespoons sherry vinegar
2 tablespoons lemon juice

½ teaspoon sugar
⅓ cup olive oil
Salt and pepper, to taste

1. Combine shallots, vinegar, juice, sugar, oil, salt and pepper and mix well. Set aside.

GREEN SALAD

6 cups mixed baby greens
1 Gala apple, quartered, cored and thinly sliced
1 Granny Smith or Golden Delicious apple, quartered, cored and thinly sliced

⅔ cup bleu cheese, crumbled
3 tablespoons walnut oil
⅔ cup walnuts

1. Mix greens, apples, and cheese in a large bowl. Toss with vinaigrette.

2. Heat oil in a small skillet. Cook walnuts, stirring constantly, 2 to 3 minutes. Watch closely not to burn nuts.

3. Pour hot oil and walnuts over salad. Toss well and serve immediately.

Yield: 4 servings

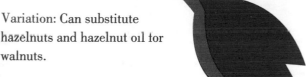

♪ Variation: Can substitute hazelnuts and hazelnut oil for walnuts.

Salads & Dressings

MARINA BAY SALAD WITH MANGO CHUTNEY VINAIGRETTE

Renowned chef Jean-Maurice Jugé, from the Reading Country Club, has shared his signature salad recipe.

MANGO CHUTNEY VINAIGRETTE

6 tablespoons balsamic vinegar

⅓ cup Major Grey mango chutney

2 tablespoons Dijon mustard

2 tablespoons honey

2 garlic cloves, minced

¼ cup olive oil

1. Prepare the dressing by combining all the ingredients (except for the olive oil) in a small saucepan and heat.

2. Remove from heat and whisk in the olive oil. Whirl briefly in blender, still leaving small bits of fruit intact. Serve at room temperature.

SALAD

1 small can artichoke hearts, rinsed, drained, and halved

1 small can hearts of palm, rinsed, drained, and sliced on the bias

1 small can Mandarin oranges (fresh oranges, tangerines, blood oranges may be substituted), drained

1 tomato, seeded and diced

1 ounce slivered almonds, slightly toasted

6 cups Boston Bibb lettuce, torn into bite-sized pieces or other baby greens

Leeks, julienned and quickly fried as garnish

1. Toss all ingredients with enough vinaigrette to lightly coat the salad. Place salad in middle of plate and garnish with fried leeks, if preferred.

~ THE READING COUNTRY CLUB, READING, PENNSYLVANIA~

~JEAN-MAURICE JUGÉ, EXECUTIVE CHEF ~

~MITCH MARRON, GENERAL MANAGER~

TABBOULEH

Healthy, refreshing, and unique, this salad is a favorite dish in Middle Eastern countries and is growing in popularity in the United States.

3 bunches parsley, finely chopped

½ bunch mint, finely chopped

1 medium onion, finely chopped

3 medium tomatoes, diced

2 tablespoons refined bulgur

Juice of one lemon, or more to taste

6 tablespoons olive oil

Salt and pepper, to taste

1. Combine parsley, mint, onion, tomatoes, and bulgur in a bowl.

2. Pour in lemon juice and oil. Season with salt and pepper and mix well. Chill briefly before serving.

Yield: 2-4 servings

~SAHARA RESTAURANT, READING, PENNSYLVANIA~

♪ Variation: TORTELLINI SALAD: Cook a (9-ounce) package fresh cheese tortellini according to package directions. Drain and toss with 2 tablespoons olive oil. Cool. Add to the Tabbouleh for a luncheon dish.

BLUE RIBBON POTATO SALAD

This potato salad is appropriately named. The cooked dressing is deliciously smooth, and cooking the potatoes in the microwave is quick and easy!

½ cup sugar

1 tablespoon cornstarch

1 teaspoon dry mustard

¼ cup water

¾ cup vinegar

2 eggs

1 cup mayonnaise

3 pounds red bliss or Yukon gold potatoes, enough to yield 6 cups cubed potatoes

5 hard-cooked eggs, chopped

¼ cup grated onion

Chopped parsley for garnish

1. Combine sugar, cornstarch, mustard, water, vinegar, and eggs in a saucepan. Cook and stir until thickened. Cool slightly. Stir in mayonnaise.

2. Place potatoes in microwave. Cook in batches until tender. Cool slightly, peel and dice. Add to mayonnaise mixture. Stir in onion and eggs. Toss gently to coat. Sprinkle with parsley.

Yield: 8 servings

ZITI SALAD

A refreshingly different and delicious pasta salad!

1 (16-ounce) package ziti, cooked al dente, drain well

2-4 tablespoons extra virgin olive oil

¼ cup milk

½ cup sour cream

1½ cups mayonnaise

2 packets George Washington brown bouillon powder

1 teaspoon dill weed

½ teaspoon salt

Dash of pepper

1 red onion, chopped

2 tomatoes, chopped

6 sweet pickles, chopped

2 small bell peppers, chopped

1 large shallot, minced

Dash of red wine vinegar

1 tablespoon pickle juice

Chopped dill for garnish

1. Toss cooked ziti with oil and milk. Whisk together sour cream and mayonnaise until smooth. Add bouillon powder, dill weed, salt and pepper. Pour over ziti and gently mix.

2. Reserve 1 tablespoon each of onion, tomatoes, pickles, and peppers. Add remaining onion, tomatoes, pickles, peppers and shallots to ziti. Stir in vinegar and pickle juice. Mix well.

3. Top with reserved onion, tomatoes, pickles, and peppers. Garnish with dill. Refrigerate until cold.

Yield: 8-10 servings

Salads & Dressings

ORZO SALAD

Fresh ginger and orange zest lend an exotic note to orzo. Delicious with grilled meats or alone as a light meal.

DRESSING

1 teaspoon salt

¾ cup corn oil

¼ cup sesame oil

½ cup rice vinegar

2 tablespoons rice wine or dry sherry

½ teaspoon orange zest

1 teaspoon thinly sliced green onions

1 teaspoon minced fresh ginger

½ teaspoon minced garlic

¼ teaspoon crushed red pepper

1 teaspoon pepper

1 tablespoon sugar

1. Combine salt, corn oil, sesame oil, vinegar, wine, orange zest, onions, ginger, garlic, red pepper, pepper, and sugar in a food processor. Process until well blended. Set aside.

SALAD

1 pound orzo

1 tablespoon sesame oil

3 cups julienned carrots

2 cups raisins

1 cup pine nuts, toasted

1 tablespoon minced parsley

1. Cook orzo in boiling water 7 to 10 minutes. Rinse under cold water and drain well. Toss with sesame oil and cool completely.

2. Combine orzo, carrots, raisins, and pine nuts just before serving. Pour on dressing and mix well. Serve in a serving bowl or on individual salad plates with lettuce leaves. Garnish with parsley.

Yield: 8 servings

CONFETTI RICE SALAD

This salad gets its name from the colorful veggies that are sprinkled throughout. Furthermore, you can use any combination of ingredients to vary the taste.

1 double recipe Fool-Proof Fluffy, Steamed Rice (see page 168)

2 cups Versatile Vinaigrette (see page 97)

⅔ cup mayonnaise

1 cup chopped green onions

¾ cup peeled, seeded, thinly sliced cucumber

1 cup chopped parsley

1 cup thinly sliced radishes

1 cup thinly sliced carrots

1 bell pepper, diced

1 (9-ounce) can tuna fish, drained and mashed

3 cups cooked medium shrimp, peeled, deveined and cut in half lengthwise

2 cups cubed smoked ham

½ cup chopped sweet pickles

Salt and pepper, to taste

Lettuce leaves

1. Transfer cooked rice to a serving bowl. Do not pack down. Whisk together Versatile Vinaigrette and mayonnaise. Pour over rice and toss gently.

2. Add onions, cucumber, parsley, radishes, carrots, pepper, tuna, shrimp, ham, and pickles. Season with salt and pepper. Cool completely. Serve over a bed of crisp greens.

Yield: 8 servings

Salads & Dressings

PANZANELLA

Summer's bounty is showcased in this classic Tuscan salad in which bread cubes absorb all of the delicious dressing and juices. Stop at a roadside stand in New Jersey and buy the wonderful fresh ingredients for this salad.

3-4 large ripe tomatoes, peeled, seeded and cut into bite-size chunks
2 large cucumbers, peeled, halved, seeded and cut into ¼-inch slices
1 large yellow pepper, cut into julienne strips
1 large onion, red or Vidalia, cut into thin rings
2 tablespoons capers, rinsed and blotted dry
½ cup Italian black olives
Salt and pepper, to taste
⅔ cup extra virgin olive oil
¼ cup balsamic vinegar or to taste
5 cups coarsely cubed, day old French, peasant or ciabatta bread
½ cup shredded basil leaves

> "Music produces a kind of pleasure
> which human nature cannot do without."
> ~CONFUCIOUS

1. Combine tomatoes, cucumbers, peppers, onions, capers, olives, salt and pepper in a large bowl. Whisk together oil and vinegar. Pour over vegetables and mix well. Marinate 30 minutes at room temperature.

2. Add bread cubes and basil to vegetables. Toss to coat well. Let stand 1 hour so that bread can absorb the oil mixture. If salad seems dry, drizzle with more oil. Serve at room temperature.

Yield: 6-8 servings

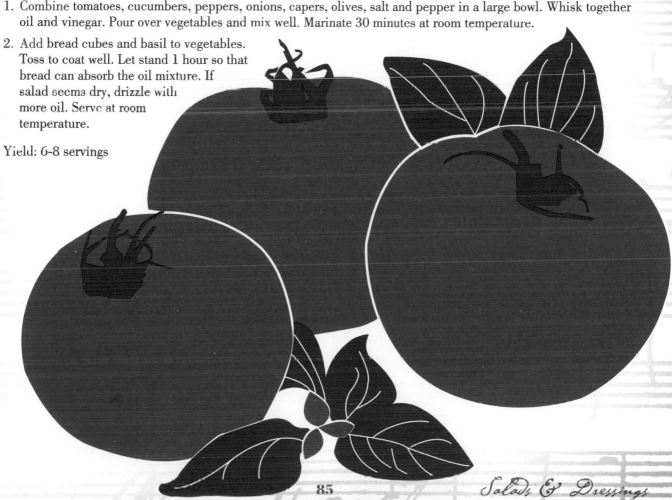

Salads & Dressings

CITRUS-MARINATED SHRIMP

The marriage of shrimp and citrus flavors is always a happy one, particularly when served with a rich, zesty sauce.

LOUIS SAUCE

1 (12-ounce) jar chili sauce

2 cups mayonnaise

2 tablespoons grated onion

2 tablespoons lemon zest

3 tablespoons lemon juice

1 tablespoon prepared horseradish

1½ teaspoons Greek seasoning

1½ teaspoons Worcestershire sauce

¼ teaspoon cayenne pepper

½ teaspoon Tabasco sauce

1. Whisk together chili sauce, mayonnaise, onion, zest, lemon juice, horseradish, seasoning, Worcestershire sauce, cayenne, and Tabasco until well blended. Cover and refrigerate until ready to serve.

CITRUS-MARINATED SHRIMP

2 lemons, halved

2 limes, halved

Half an orange

1 tablespoon crushed red pepper flakes

4 pounds large shrimp, peeled and deveined, leave tails intact

2 cups fresh orange juice

2 cups grapefruit juice

2 cups pineapple juice

½ cup fresh lemon juice

½ cup fresh lime juice

1 lemon, sliced

1 orange, sliced

1 lime, sliced

1 grapefruit, sliced

1 teaspoon crushed red pepper flakes

Lettuce leaves

Citrus fruit slices for garnish

1. Combine lemons, limes, and orange with 1 tablespoon red pepper in a Dutch oven. Pour in salted water to cover. Bring to boil. Add shrimp and cook 2 to 3 minutes or until shrimp turn pink. Don't overcook. Plunge shrimp into ice water to stop cooking. Drain well.

2. Combine orange, grapefruit, pineapple, lemon, lime juices, lemon, orange, lime, grapefruit slices and 1 teaspoon red pepper in a zip-top plastic bag. Add shrimp. Seal and refrigerate 25 minutes or up to 2 hours.

3. Drain marinade. Arrange shrimp on lettuce leaves, garnish with fruit slices and serve with Louis Sauce.

Yield: 8-10 servings, 3 cups sauce

Tip: For the best and juiciest citrus fruit, always pick fruit that has the smoothest skin. Avoid those with coarse, thick skin. Select fruit that seems heavy for its size. You can learn to judge by weighing several pieces, one at a time. This rule applies to all citrus: lemons, limes, oranges, and grapefruit. Additionally, when extracting juice, 15 to 20 seconds in the microwave will increase the yield as will rolling them back and forth on the counter using moderate pressure from the heel of your hand. One final tip: a sprinkle of salt will dramatically sweeten a grapefruit half.

SNAP-PEA AND JICAMA SALAD WITH SEA SCALLOPS

The silky scallops from off of the Rhode Island coast contrast beautifully with the crunchy vegetables in this delectable salad.

VINAIGRETTE

½ cup coarsely chopped basil
½ cup coarsely chopped mint
3 tablespoons lime juice
½ cup olive oil

½ teaspoon sugar
1½ teaspoons salt
⅛ teaspoon pepper

1. Combine basil, mint, and lime juice in a blender. Process, scraping down sides, until combined. With blender running, slowly pour in oil.

2. Add sugar, salt, and pepper. Blend until smooth. Set aside.

SALAD

¾ pound snap peas
1 small jicama, peeled and cut into 2-inch matchstick-sized batons
1½ cups fresh bean sprouts
18 large sea scallops, sliced in half horizontally and patted dry
1 teaspoon kosher salt
2 tablespoons unsalted butter
Thinly sliced basil leaves and thinly sliced mint leaves for garnish

1. Cook snap peas in salted boiling water 2 minutes until crisp tender. Plunge into ice water and drain well. Combine with jicama and sprouts. Set salad aside.

2. Sprinkle scallops with salt. Melt butter in a heavy skillet. Add scallops and cook 1½ minutes per side until browned.

3. Toss salad with half vinaigrette. Place on a serving platter or individual salad plates. Top with scallops and drizzle with remaining vinaigrette. Sprinkle with basil and mint leaves.

Yield: 4-6 servings

Salads & Dressings

SALAD NIÇOISE

A classic, timeless salad, it is appropriate for almost any informal occasion.

VINAIGRETTE

3 tablespoons cider vinegar
1 tablespoon Dijon mustard
1 cup plus 2 tablespoons olive oil
1 shallot, minced
2 garlic cloves, crushed
2 cups flat leaf parsley, loosely packed, minced
¾ cup minced fresh tarragon and chervil leaves

"Dining is and always was a great artistic opportunity."
~FRANK LLOYD WRIGHT

1. Whisk together vinegar and mustard. Add oil in a steady stream, whisking constantly. Blend in shallots, garlic, parsley, tarragon and chervil.

SALAD

2 pounds fresh tuna
1 tablespoon olive oil
Salt and pepper, to taste
1 pound green beans, trimmed
1 pound yellow beans, trimmed
2 pounds tiny new potatoes, cleaned

1 sweet red pepper, thinly sliced
20 anchovy fillets
5 hard-cooked eggs, quartered
6 medium tomatoes, quartered
1 cup niçoise olives

1. Rub tuna on all sides with oil. Grill or sear in a skillet 5 to 7 minutes per side. Transfer to a plate and season with salt and pepper. Cool.

2. Bring 4 cups water to boil. Cook beans in two batches 5 minutes each. Drain and cool.

3. Cook potatoes in salted boiling water 15 minutes or until tender. Drain and place in a bowl. Pour one-third vinaigrette over potatoes and toss to coat.

4. Combine beans and pepper slices. Add enough vinaigrette to moisten vegetables. Arrange in the center of a serving platter. Top with anchovies. Place eggs and tomatoes in an alternating fashion around bean mixture. Drizzle with 3 tablespoons vinaigrette.

5. Place potatoes on another serving platter. Break tuna into large pieces and layer on top. Sprinkle with olives. Drizzle with remaining vinaigrette. Serve immediately.

Yield: 8-10 servings

ORANGE BLUSH LOBSTER SALAD

An elegant luncheon dish. Lobster never looked so pretty and tasted so good.

2 pounds cooked lobster meat, cut into 1-inch pieces

3 cups cantaloupe balls

1¼ pounds papaya, peeled, seeded and diced into ½-inch pieces, about 2 cups

6 plum tomatoes, seeded and diced into ¼-inch pieces, about 2 cups

¼ cup fresh orange juice

2 tablespoons red wine vinegar

1 teaspoon Dijon mustard

1 tablespoon freshly grated ginger

Salt and pepper, to taste

½ cup extra virgin olive oil

1 teaspoon finely grated orange zest

¼ cup snipped chives

2 heads radicchio, rinsed and patted dry

1. Combine lobster, cantaloupe, papaya, and tomatoes in a large bowl. Gently mix with a spatula. Set aside.

2. Whisk together orange juice, vinegar, ginger, mustard, salt, and pepper. Add oil in a steady stream, whisking constantly, until mixture thickens. Stir in zest.

3. Combine lobster mixture, chives and ½ cup dressing just prior to serving. Arrange lobster mixture in the center in a serving platter surrounded by radicchio leaves. May also serve salad on individual plates on bed of radicchio leaves. Serve extra dressing on the side.

Yield: 12 servings

POACHED SCALLOPS WITH BLUEBERRY MAYONNAISE

Blueberries are a surprising addition to sweet scallops and tangy mayonnaise.

1 egg

2 egg yolks

1 tablespoon Dijon mustard

¼ cup blueberry vinegar

2 cups olive oil

Salt and pepper, to taste

Fresh blueberries

1½ pounds scallops

Belgium endive

Additional blueberries and fresh mint for garnish

1. Combine egg, egg yolks, mustard, and vinegar in the bowl of a food processor; blend until creamy.

2. Add olive oil in a very slow stream, blending until all the oil is incorporated. Set aside.

3. Place scallops in a medium-sized pan and cover with salted water; bring to a simmer and poach for 1 minute. Remove from heat and let cool to room temperature. Drain and pat dry.

4. Arrange four or five leaves of endive in a star pattern on individual serving plates and place the scallops in the center of each. Fold several tablespoons of fresh blueberries into mayonnaise and spoon over scallops. Garnish with fresh blueberries and fresh mint.

Yield: 4 to 6 servings

Variation: You can use 1-2 cups prepared mayonnaise, to which you have added several tablespoons of blueberry vinegar, several tablespoons of olive oil, and several tablespoons fresh blueberries.

~PENN SQUARE CATERING, READING, PENNSYLVANIA~

~MARIA LINDENMUTH-DICECCO, PROPRIETOR~

Salads & Dressings

CHICKEN SALAD: THEME AND VARIATIONS

 *Chicken Salad continues to be one of the most popular in the entire repertoire of salad recipes. The following ten recipes expand the flavors and variety considerably. For the first eight, we suggest beginning with a pre-roasted chicken that is readily available at most supermarkets today—a great time saver. However, you may certainly cook the chicken in your preferred way at home. Each recipe begins after the chicken has been cooked, deboned, and cut into bite-sized chunks. You should have 3 to 4 cups of meat. The final two recipes feature hot, grilled chicken combined with interesting dressings and accompaniments.*

FESTIVE CHICKEN SALAD

The unusual combination of flavors and textures is not only festive to behold but tasty as well. A meal in a single bowl.

3 cups shredded cooked chicken

2 cups cooked Fool-Proof Fluffy Rice (see page 168)

¾ cup seedless grapes, halved

¾ cup chopped celery

½ cup pineapple tidbits, drained

½ cup Mandarin oranges

½ cup mayonnaise

1 cup ranch dressing

½ cup toasted slivered almonds for garnish

1. Combine chicken, rice, grapes, celery, pineapple, and oranges in a serving bowl.

2. Whisk together mayonnaise and dressing. Pour over chicken mixture and mix. Refrigerate at least an hour.

3. Top with almonds prior to serving.

Yield: 6-8 servings

"I feel a recipe is only a theme, which an intelligent cook can play each time with a variation."

~MADAME BENOIT

RAMEN CHICKEN SALAD

 This version combines an Oriental twist of flavors with interesting textures.

1 tablespoon toasted sesame seeds

½ cup toasted sliced almonds

½ head medium cabbage, shredded

4 green onions, chopped

½ cup olive oil

3 tablespoons rice vinegar

1 package chicken-flavored ramen soup mix

3 cups chopped cooked chicken

Ramen noodles, crushed

1. Mix sesame seeds, almonds, cabbage, onions, oil, vinegar, and flavor packet from soup mix in a bowl.

2. Add chicken and marinate overnight in refrigerator.

3. Toss in noodles 2 to 3 hours prior to serving. Refrigerate.

Yield: 6-8 servings

CHICKEN, MANGO AND AVOCADO SALAD

This wonderful summer dish is a perfect marriage of sweet, tart and creamy fruits. Be sure to use perfectly ripe mangoes and avocados for optimal results.

1½ cups cooked Fool-Proof Fluffy Rice (see page 168)
4 cups shredded cooked chicken
¾ cup finely chopped red onion
3 mangoes, peeled and diced
3 ripe avocados, peeled and diced

¼ cup lime juice
½ cup chopped cilantro
2 tablespoons olive oil
Salt and pepper, to taste

1. Combine rice, chicken, onion, mangoes, avocados, lime juice, cilantro, oil, salt, and pepper and mix well.
2. Refrigerate at least 1 hour.

Yield: 6-8 servings

> "There is nothing more notable in Socrates than that he found time, when he was an old man, to learn music and dancing, and thought it was time well spent."
> ~PLUTARCH

CHUTNEY CANTALOUPE CHICKEN SALAD

Here is an interesting version that places the emphasis on an unusual dressing.

3 tablespoons mango chutney, chopped
2 tablespoons apple juice
½ cup mayonnaise
¼ cup minced green onions, white and
   pale green parts only

3 cups chopped cooked chicken
1 tablespoon minced parsley
1⅓ cups bite-size cantaloupe chunks

1. Blend chutney, apple juice, mayonnaise, and green onions.
2. Add chicken, parsley, and cantaloupe and mix well, Serve immediately.

Yield: 6-8 servings

Tip: The washing machine has several uses: it can be pressed into service as a spare ice cooler for a large party. Just fill the washtub with cubes and nestle in the bottles and cans. Clean-up is a cinch—when the party is over, let the ice melt and run the spin cycle of the machine to whisk the water away.

Salads & Dressings

MOROCCAN CHICKEN SALAD

A main dish with a wonderful list of ingredients that combine for great texture and flavor.

1½ cups chicken broth
1 cup chopped dried plums
1 teaspoon curry powder
1 cup dry couscous
½ cup chopped green onions
¼ cup olive oil

¼ cup white vinegar
Salt and pepper, to taste
2 cups chopped cooked chicken
⅔ cup chopped tomato
½ cup toasted sliced almonds

1. Combine broth, dried plums, and curry in a saucepan. Bring to boil. Add couscous and onions. Remove from heat. Cover and let stand 5 minutes. Fluff with a fork and cool.

2. Whisk together oil, vinegar, salt and pepper. Pour over couscous.

3. Add chicken, tomatoes, and almonds and mix well.

Yield: 6-8 servings

"If ya ain't got it in ya, ya can't blow it out."
~LOUIS ARMSTRONG

CHICKEN DELIGHT

This chicken salad variation is indeed a delight, with its sweet and tart combination of flavors, as well as the lovely rosy color.

1 small onion, finely chopped
1 tablespoon tomato paste
½ teaspoon curry paste
2 tablespoons lemon juice

2 tablespoons apricot preserves
1 cup mayonnaise
3 cups chopped cooked chicken

1. Combine onion, tomato paste, curry paste, lemon juice, and preserves in a saucepan. Cook and stir until onions are tender.

2. Purée mixture in a food processor. Refrigerate.

3. Whisk together tomato mixture and mayonnaise. Add to chicken and toss to coat. Serve cold.

Yield: 4-6 servings

AMAZING CHICKEN SALAD

♫ *This main-dish salad satisfies all taste buds—sweet, crunchy, tangy, and creamy.*

6-8 stalks celery, thinly sliced

3 apples, cored and cut into bite-sized pieces

2 cups pineapple, bite-size pieces, fresh or canned, and drained

1 cup golden or dark raisins

1 cup red or green seedless grapes, halved

1 (8-ounce) can sliced water chestnuts, drained

1 cup toasted pecan halves

4 cups chopped cooked chicken

½ cup mayonnaise

½ cup sour cream

½ cup plain yogurt

1. Combine celery, apples, pineapple, raisins, grapes, water chestnuts, pecans, and chicken in a bowl.

2. Whisk together mayonnaise, sour cream, and yogurt. Add to chicken mixture and mix well.

Yield: 8-10 servings

SUNSET SALAD

♫ *The rosy sauce mixed with shredded cabbage hints at how this salad received its name.*

1½ cups shredded cooked chicken

1½ cups julienne smoked tongue or smoked ham

1½ cups shredded cabbage

½ cup chopped watercress

3 tablespoons olive oil

1½ tablespoons white vinegar

2 tablespoons chili sauce

Salt, to taste

1. Combine chicken, smoked tongue, cabbage, and watercress in a bowl.

2. Blend oil, vinegar, chili sauce, and salt. Pour over chicken mixture and toss to coat.

Yield: 4-6 servings

"We cannot expect you to be with us all the time, but perhaps you could be good enough to keep in touch now and again."

~SIR THOMAS BEECHAM *(to a musician during a rehearsal)*

Salads & Dressings

GRILLED CHICKEN SALAD
WITH RASPBERRY VINAIGRETTE

 The smokey flavor of the grilled chicken, and the addition of vegetables, along with the unusual dressing, make this salad unique.

½ cup olive oil

Juice of one-half lemon

2 tablespoons raspberry vinegar

1 teaspoon Dijon mustard

Salt and pepper, to taste

8 small red potatoes, cooked and quartered

½ pound asparagus or green beans, cooked crisp-tender

4 boneless, skinless chicken breast halves

Boston lettuce leaves, torn

Black olives and orange slices for garnish

1. Blend together oil, lemon juice, vinegar, mustard, salt, and pepper. Set vinaigrette aside.

2. Marinate cooked potatoes and asparagus in some of the vinaigrette for 1 hour at room temperature.

3. Grill chicken until done, about 4 minutes per side. Cut on a bias into thin strips.

4. Arrange lettuce among four salad plates. Drain vegetables from marinade. Divide among the four salad plates. Top with warm chicken strips and drizzle with vinaigrette. Garnish with olives and oranges.

Yield: 4 servings

 Tip: The washing machine has several uses: it can be turned into a giant salad spinner. Wash the leaves and arrange them in a single layer on a large opened beach towel. Roll up the towel like a giant jelly roll and place it in the tub of the washer in a circle. Set the cycle to spin and voilá—salad for a crowd, washed and dried.

BLEU CHEESE CHICKEN SALAD

Check out the interesting combination of ingredients in this variation.

6 cups romaine lettuce leaves, torn

1 medium cucumber, peeled and thinly sliced

1 small bell pepper, cut into thin rings

2 thin slices red onion, rings separated

2 tablespoons olive oil

1 tablespoon Dijon mustard

1 tablespoon balsamic vinegar

1 tablespoon grated onion

2 boneless, skinless chicken breast halves

1 tablespoon olive oil

Crumbled bleu cheese and tomato wedges for garnish

1. Preheat oven to 400 degrees.

2. Combine lettuce, cucumber, pepper, and onion rings.

3. Blend oil, mustard, vinegar, and grated onion. Pour over salad and toss to coat. Divide among four salad plates.

4. Brown chicken in oil 30 seconds per side. Bake chicken 10 minutes and cut on a bias into thin slices. Arrange on bed of greens. Garnish with bleu cheese and tomato wedges.

Yield: 4 servings

Salads & Dressings

WINTER CITRUS SALAD

 This incredible salad makes a lovely first course served on a bed of greens or a tangy accompaniment to grilled chicken.

FRUIT

3 blood oranges, peeled, seeded and sectioned

1 pink grapefruit, peeled, seeded and sectioned

1 lime, peeled, seeded and sliced

1 navel orange, peeled, seeded and sectioned
   (4 oranges if blood oranges are not available)

2 tangerines, peeled, seeded and sliced

1 lemon, peeled, seeded and thinly sliced

1. Combine blood oranges, grapefruit, lime slices, navel oranges, tangerines, and lemon slices in a bowl. Cover and refrigerate.

VINAIGRETTE

¼ cup citrus juice from fruit trimmings

1 teaspoon balsamic vinegar

⅛ teaspoon salt

Pepper, to taste

½ teaspoon chopped oregano

2 tablespoons extra virgin olive oil

½ cup small salt-cured Italian olives

Pinch of sugar, if needed

1. Whisk together citrus juice, vinegar, salt, pepper, and oregano. Add oil in steady stream and mix until smooth. Soak olives in 1 tablespoon vinaigrette.

2. Spoon remaining vinaigrette over fruit. Scatter olives on top. Serve very cold.

Yield: 6 servings

MAKE-AHEAD ORIENTAL SALAD

Whenever this salad is served to guests, someone always requests the recipe.

1 package frozen baby peas, thawed

1 (14-ounce) can bean sprouts, rinsed and drained

1 (12-ounce) can white shoepeg corn, drained

1 (8-ounce) can sliced water chestnuts, drained

1 (4½-ounce) jar sliced mushrooms, drained

1 (4-ounce) jar chopped pimientos, drained

1 large bell pepper, thinly sliced

1 cup sliced celery

1 cup sugar

1 cup vegetable oil

½ cup white vinegar

½ cup water

2 tablespoons red wine vinegar

1 tablespoon soy sauce

1 teaspoon dry mustard

½ teaspoon salt

½ teaspoon paprika

¼ teaspoon pepper

1 garlic clove, crushed

1. Combine peas, sprouts, corn, water chestnuts, mushrooms, pimientos, pepper, and celery in a large bowl.

2. Whisk together sugar, oil, vinegar, water, wine vinegar, soy sauce, mustard, salt, paprika, pepper, and garlic. Mix until well blended.

3. Pour marinade over vegetables, stirring gently. Cover and refrigerate overnight. Drain vegetables or serve with a slotted spoon.

Yield: 12-15 servings

Salads & Dressings

HOLIDAY FRUIT SALAD
WITH LEMON POPPY SEED DRESSING

Those multitalented cranberries make a cameo appearance in this colorful salad, which is sure to be popular year-round.

LEMON POPPY SEED DRESSING

½ cup sugar

½ cup lemon juice

1 teaspoon Dijon mustard

2 teaspoons diced shallots

Salt and pepper, to taste

⅔ cup olive oil

1 tablespoon poppy seeds

1. Combine sugar, lemon juice, mustard, shallots, salt, and pepper in a blender. Process until well blended.

2. Add oil in a steady stream while blender is running. Blend until thick and smooth. Add poppy seeds and process a few seconds to mix. Set aside.

FRUIT SALAD

1 head romaine lettuce, torn into bite-size pieces

4 ounces shredded Asiago cheese

1 cup cashews

¼ cup dried cranberries

1 apple, peeled and diced

1 pear, peeled and sliced

1. Combine lettuce, cheese, cashews, cranberries, apples and pears in a large bowl.

2. Pour dressing over salad prior to serving. Toss to coat.

Yield: 12 servings

PICKLED RED BEETS AND RED BEET EGGS

The Pennsylvania Dutch are known for their "sweets and sours." Somewhere between a salad and a side dish, they add zest to any meal. These two recipes are easy to prepare and go well together.

PICKLED RED BEETS

1 (14-ounce) can sliced red beets

1 cup cider vinegar

½ cup sugar

1 teaspoon salt

4 whole cloves

2-inch stick cinnamon

1. Drain and measure juice from beets. Add enough water to make 1 cup and place in a saucepan.

2. Add vinegar, sugar, salt, cloves and cinnamon. Bring to boil. Pour hot marinade over beets. Refrigerate 24 hours.

RED BEET EGGS

6-8 hard-cooked eggs, cooled and peeled

Red beet marinade, drained from beets

1. Place eggs in beet marinade. Refrigerate in marinade 8 to 12 hours so flavor penetrates the eggs. Cut eggs in half and arrange on a platter.

Yield: 1 pint beets and 16 egg halves

"Our times need mighty spirits to lash into action these timid, beggarly human souls."

~LUDWIG VAN BEETHOVEN

VERSATILE VINAIGRETTE

Use this wonderful dressing on the Confetti Rice Salad (page 84), grilled vegetables or sliced cold roast beef.

⅓ cup finely chopped pimientos

¼ cup capers, rinsed, drained and patted dry

1 garlic clove, minced

2 teaspoons salt

½ teaspoon pepper

½ teaspoon dried dill

½ teaspoon dried tarragon

1¾ cups olive oil

¾ cup wine vinegar

1. Combine pimientos, capers, garlic, salt, pepper, dill, tarragon, oil, and vinegar in a jar.

2. Seal lid tightly and shake 2 to 3 minutes. Store at room temperature. Shake before serving.

Yield: 3 cups

Variation: Blend ¾ cup vinaigrette with 2 tablespoons chopped parsley and ½ hard-cooked egg, chopped. Add chopped sweet pickles if desired.

Salads & Dressings

PENNSYLVANIA DUTCH PEPPER CABBAGE

This colorful, crunchy dish is standard Pennsylvania Dutch fare, much loved for its sweet and sour flavors.

2 pound cabbage head, rinsed and finely grated
2 bell peppers, finely diced (sweet red or yellow pepper can also be used)
1 cup vinegar

1 cup water
1 cup sugar
½ tablespoon salt

1. Combine cabbage and peppers in a bowl. Whisk together vinegar, water, sugar and salt. Pour over cabbage.
2. Place in refrigerator and marinate at least 24 hours. Stir and serve.

Yield: 8 servings

DIJON VINAIGRETTE

This vinaigrette goes beyond basic to special. You will want to keep a bottle on hand at all times.

⅓ cup rice vinegar
⅓ cup white vinegar
⅓ cup Dijon mustard
1 tablespoon crushed garlic
¾ cup sugar
1 cup olive oil
1¾ cups vegetable oil

1. Combine rice vinegar, white vinegar, mustard, garlic, sugar, olive oil and vegetable oil in a jar.
2. Seal lid tightly and shake well. Refrigerate.

Yield: 4 cups

~LATITUDE 38, OXFORD, MARYLAND~

"God tells me how the music should sound, but you stand in the way."
~ARTURO TOSCANINI TO A TRUMPET PLAYER

Around 1970, after a long period of testing, the Department of Fisheries in Canada developed what has come to be known as the Canadian Cooking Theory for Fish. The basic principle is that the fish is measured at its thickest point, that is its depth, not across the fish and that it be cooked, no matter how, at exactly 10 minutes per inch of thickness. This applies to filets, whole fish, and steaks. It applies to all methods of preparation: baking, broiling, grilling, braising, sautéing, frying, poaching, and steaming. When cooking rolled, stuffed filets, measure the diameter after you have rolled it. When poaching, wait until the water returns to the simmering point to begin your timing. When baking, use a 450 degree oven. When frying, heat oil to 375 degrees. For sautéing and grilling, use a fairly high temperature. When broiling, place the fish 3 to 4 inches from the heating unit. If the fish is frozen, do not thaw it, but merely double the time to 20 minutes per inch. The timings for cooking fish in the recipes in this section are based on this theory.

FISH

SEAFOOD

SAUCE

CHARLIE MARG'S FISH CAKES

Pick your favorite catch of the day and make these wonderful cakes.

2 large carrots, diced
1 onion, diced
1 stalk celery, diced
4-5 large mushrooms, diced
⅓ bunch parsley, chopped
Olive oil
2 pounds fresh fish
   (flounder, cod, tilapia, trout or catfish)

3 eggs, separated
1 cup heavy cream
1½ cups mashed potatoes
   (use instant potatoes as a shortcut)
1 pound shrimp, cleaned, slightly cooked and chopped
1 teaspoon sugar
Dry breadcrumbs
Juice of one lemon

1. Sauté carrots, onion, celery, mushrooms, and parsley in small amount of oil until lightly browned. Remove from heat and cool.

2. Remove bones from fish. Wet fish and place in a plastic bag. Cook 5 to 6 minutes in microwave. Remove fish from bag reserving juices. Flake the fish.

3. Combine egg yolks, cream, and potatoes. Slowly add flaked fish and some of fish juice. Mix fish batter with vegetables and remaining fish juice. If too runny, do not add any more juice.

4. Stir in chopped shrimp. Refrigerate at least 30 minutes.

5. Whip egg whites with sugar. Fold into fish batter prior to cooking. Shape batter into balls. Roll in breadcrumbs until well coated.

6. Place balls on a greased and foil-lined baking sheet. Flatten slightly. Broil 8 to 10 minutes each side. May also pan fry in olive oil. Drizzle with lemon juice before serving.

Yield: 12-15 cakes, depending on size

Go to the trouble of finding a Sémillon from Australia. You will be rewarded with a perfect partner.

Entrées ~ Fish & Seafood

These two recipes use a similar cooking technique, but the flavor of each is quite distinct. Why not try them both?

HORSERADISH CRUSTED SALMON

5 slices day old white bread, crusts trimmed

1 small shallot, minced

2 tablespoons chopped fresh dill or 2 teaspoons dried

½ cup grated horseradish, not creamed

6 (6-ounce) salmon filets, skin removed

Olive oil

Salt, to taste

Dash of white pepper

1. Preheat oven to 400 degrees. Process bread until coarse crumbs form. Add shallot, dill, and horseradish. Pulse lightly until combined.

2. Brush bottom and sides of filets with oil. Place in a shallow baking dish, 2-inches apart. Sprinkle with salt and pepper. Pat breadcrumb mixture on top of each filet.

3. Bake 6 to 7 minutes at 8 to 12-inches from heat source. Turn on broiler and cook 2 minutes until tops are golden brown.

Yield: 6 servings

 Find a crisp Chardonnay with high acidity.

HONEY-MUSTARD SALMON WITH CAPERS

4 tablespoons unsalted butter, melted

3 tablespoons Dijon mustard

1½ teaspoons honey

¼ cup breadcrumbs

4 teaspoons chopped parsley

1 (16-ounce) salmon filet

Salt and pepper, to taste

Capers, to taste

Lemon slices for garnish

"It is easy to play a musical instrument: all you have to do is touch the right key at the right time and the instrument will play itself."

~JOHANN SEBASTIAN BACH

1. Preheat oven to 400 degrees. Whisk together butter, mustard, and honey.

2. Combine breadcrumbs and parsley in another bowl.

3. Brush salmon with honey mixture. Season with salt and pepper. Sprinkle with breadcrumb mixture. Top with capers.

4. Bake 12 to 15 minutes or until fish flakes with a fork. Garnish with lemon slices.

Yield: 4 servings

 A very light Pinot Noir is a surprise pairing with this zingy dish.

MARINADE FOR SALMON

♫ *The unusual combination of ingredients gives this marinade an exotic flavor that marries well with salmon.*

1 teaspoon grated gingerroot
2 shallots, minced
1 garlic clove, minced
2 tablespoons Tamari
2 tablespoons sesame oil
¼ cup vinegar
1 cup olive oil
Juice of one lemon
Juice of one lime
Salt and pepper, to taste
1 bunch cilantro, discard large
    stems and chop leaves
Sesame seeds for garnish

1. Combine ginger, shallots, garlic, Tamari, sesame oil, vinegar, olive oil, lemon juice, lime juice, salt, pepper, and cilantro. Stir until well blended.

2. Pour over salmon and marinate for several hours. Bake in marinade using Canadian Cooking Theory. Garnish with sesame seeds.

Yield: 2 cups

"Beethoven can write music, thank God, but he can do nothing else on earth."
~LUDWIG VAN BEETHOVEN

FISH BARNETTI

The late Ken Barnett, chef and owner of a restaurant in Philadelphia, gave this recipe to me. I had nicknamed him "Barnetti," hence the name of the recipe. When I serve this fish, my guests can never guess the ingredients in the topping, but always rave about the taste.

TOPPING

2-3 fresh Kaiser rolls

6-8 large scallops

3 tablespoons unsalted butter, melted

Salt and pepper, to taste

½ teaspoon Italian seasoning

1. Break rolls into pieces and place in a food processor. Process until coarse crumbs form. Transfer to a bowl.

2. Pulse scallops in food processor. Do not overprocess or scallops will get sticky. Add to breadcrumbs.

3. Stir in butter, salt, pepper, and seasoning. Set aside

FISH

1 tablespoon unsalted butter, melted

2 pounds haddock, cod or other white firm-fleshed
   fish, rinsed and patted dry

Salt, to taste

1. Preheat oven to 425 degrees. Drizzle butter in bottom of 13x9x2-inch baking dish. Place fish in dish.

2. Mound breadcrumbs on top of fish.

3. Bake 10 minutes per inch of fish. If crumbs are not browned, place under broiler 1 to 2 minutes. Be careful not to burn breadcrumbs.

Yield: 4-6 servings

Go with the delicate scallop flavor and pick a delicate wine with lots of fruity notes.

"If music be the food of love, play on: give me
excess of it…"

~WILLIAM SHAKESPEARE, *Twelfth Night*

STUFFED SHAD

Shad and shad roe are two eagerly awaited delicacies each spring in Pennsylvania and New Jersey. It is worth the annual wait to eat this unusual dish that combines them both.

1 roe set, medium to large
3 tablespoons unsalted butter, melted
1½ tablespoons minced onion
2 teaspoons lemon juice
1½ tablespoons chopped parsley
½ cup fresh breadcrumbs
Salt and pepper, to taste
2 shad filets
All-purpose flour
Butter slices
Paprika, to taste
⅓ cup white wine
Lemon wedges and chopped parsley for garnish

1. Preheat oven to 450 degrees. Scald roe in boiling water. Remove membrane. Add butter, onion, lemon juice, parsley, breadcrumbs, salt and pepper.

2. Dredge 1 piece of shad in flour and place in oiled 13x9x2-inch baking dish. Spread breadcrumb-roe mixture on top. Dredge second piece of shad in flour. Place on top of breadcrumb mixture.

3. Tie fish together in 3 to 4 places using cotton string or unwaxed dental floss. Top with butter and paprika.

4. Bake 25 to 35 minutes. After 10 minutes cooking time, pour in wine. Remove string before serving.

5. Garnish with lemon wedges and parsley. Serve with boiled potatoes tossed with salt, pepper, butter, and parsley.

Yield: 6-8 servings

Choose a Viognier because it has the weight of a Chardonnay with floral notes not unlike a Riesling.

Entrées ~ Fish & Seafood

BROILED FISH WITH SOUFFLÉ TOPPING

This versatile and easy recipe can be used to enhance many types of fish including salmon, New Jersey blue fish, shad, rockfish, cod and sea trout. It also makes a most attractive presentation.

FISH

1½ sticks unsalted butter, melted

1 large shallot, minced

2 tablespoons minced fresh tarragon or
   1 tablespoon dried

1 tablespoon minced fresh dill or
   ½ tablespoon dried

2 tablespoons minced chives

6 fish filets

1. Preheat broiler. Combine butter, shallot, tarragon, dill and chives.

2. Place filets on broiler pan. Brush with herb butter.

3. Broil 10 minutes or until fish is firm.

SOUFFLÉ TOPPING

1½ cups mayonnaise

2 tablespoons minced fresh tarragon or
   1 tablespoon dried

1 tablespoon minced fresh dill or ½ tablespoon dried

2 tablespoons minced chives

2 egg whites, stiffly beaten

1. Combine mayonnaise, tarragon, dill, and chives. Fold in stiff egg whites. Spread mixture over filets.

2. Broil 2 to 3 minutes until puffy and browned.

Yield: 6 servings

Variation: Add ¼ cup freshly grated Parmesan cheese to topping. Either recipe can be prepared in oven using Canadian Cooking Theory which is baking at 425 degrees 10 to 12 minutes per inch thickness of fish. Soufflé topping can be put on fish for entire baking time.

This rich dish needs a crisp white wine like Sauvignon Blanc as a contrast.

One story of how the lowly cod became the "sacred cod" is worth telling. It is said that it was the fish that Christ used when He multiplied the fish and fed the multitudes and even today the fish bears the mark of His thumb and forefingers. The Devil was standing by, observing this miracle and said he, too, could multiply fish and feed the multitudes. He reached for one of the wriggling fish but it slid through his red-hot fingers, burning two black stripes down its sides, thus differentiating the haddock from the sacred cod. These two fish make up a great portion of the catch off New England waters and indeed are similar in taste and texture. They can often be used interchangeably in recipes.

BOUILLABAISSE

 Everyone in Zino Francescatti's family played the violin and loved to cook. His father was the only pupil of Camillo Sivori, who was the only pupil of Paganini. Before college, I lived with them in Marseilles and we traveled together when Zino performed. It was a time of wonderful memories revolving around music and cooking. Marseilles is famous for this fish soup and the locals all said that Madame Francescatti's closely guarded secret recipe was the very best. Here it is, just as she told it to me.

5 pounds of assorted firm fish such as red snapper, halibut, monkfish, rockfish. Ask fish monger for several large heads and bones as well.

1 carrot, sliced

1 onion, chopped

1 bay leaf

1 sprig thyme

7 cups water

1 large lobster, boiled and meat removed

½ pound lump crabmeat

¼ cup olive oil

¾ cup finely chopped onion

3 shallots, finely chopped

3 garlic cloves, finely minced

½ sweet red pepper, finely chopped

1 large tomato, peeled and finely chopped

3 stalks celery, finely chopped

1 two-inch slice fennel, finely chopped

¼ cup olive oil, divided

3 sprigs thyme

1 bay leaf

2 whole garlic cloves

Dash of orange zest

Dash of pepper

¼ teaspoon powdered saffron

1 (16-ounce) loaf French bread, sliced

1. Cut fish flesh into 1-inch cubes and set aside. Place heads of at least 2 large fish and fish bones together with carrot, onion, bay leaf, and thyme sprig. Cover with water and bring to boil. Skim top and cover, boil until reduced by half.

2. Mash mixture through a sieve with potato masher or wooden spoon. This is the fish purée. Set aside.

3. Keep lobster body meat separate from claw meat. Heat crabmeat, lobster claw meat, and 2 tablespoons oil in a large stockpot. Cook until slightly browned. Add onion, shallots, garlic, pepper, tomato, celery, and fennel. Toss to coat in oil.

4. Add remaining oil, thyme, bay leaf, garlic, orange zest, and pepper. Add fish purée and bring to boil. Cook, covered, 3 minutes.

5. Add reserved fish cubes in the following manner: first, put in the slower cooking fish and cook, uncovered, 5 minutes. Stir in faster cooking fish and lobster body meat. Boil, uncovered, 5 minutes.

6. Remove 5 tablespoons broth and mix with saffron. Pour mixture back into pot. Remove all leaves and sprigs. Serve hot in large bowls over sliced French bread, giving each person an assortment of fish.

Yield: 4-6 servings

~CHRISTOPHER COLLINS LEE~

~CONCERTMASTER OF THE READING SYMPHONY ORCHESTRA~

 Choose a Pouilly-Fumé with a strong character.

"Mozart is sweet sunshine."

~ANTONIN DVORAK

GRILLED TROUT WITH PINEAPPLE RUM SAUCE

The title says it all. This is a wonderfully flavored exotic dish!

4 tablespoons unsalted butter
½ cup packed brown sugar
½ cup dark rum
⅓ cup cornstarch

2¼ cups pineapple juice
8 trout filets
1 fresh pineapple, cut into chunks
Toasted almonds for garnish

1. Melt butter and sugar in a saucepan. Cook and stir until caramelized. Stir in rum. Set aside.

2. Dissolve cornstarch in ½ cup pineapple juice. Bring remaining juice to boil in a saucepan. Whisk in cornstarch mixture and cook until sauce thickens.

3. Blend in rum mixture. For a darker sauce, add more brown sugar. Set sauce aside.

4. Spray grill with salted water. Heat until grill turns white to prevent fish from sticking. Grill filets skin side up 4 minutes. Turn filets and grill until flaky and browned. Place pineapple chunks on skewers. Grill until golden browned.

5. Top grilled trout with pineapple rum sauce. Sprinkle with almonds and serve with grilled pineapple.

Yield: 8 servings

~ STIRLING GUEST HOTEL, READING, PENNSYLVANIA~
~KAJ SKOV, OWNER~
~ANTHONY G. WELTMER, CHEF ~

"Don't bother to look. I've composed all this already."
~GUSTAV MAHLER TO BRUNO WALTER,
who had stopped to admire mountain scenery in rural Austria.

SAUTÉED SCALLOPS

Scallops are found in the calm waters that border Rhode Island and Massachusetts, but most New Englanders agree that the best scallops are harvested just off Nantucket Island. Commercial scallopers are joined by locals who gather their equipment and set off at low tide in search of the treasured shellfish. This quick and easy recipe emphasizes the natural sweetness of the scallop without overwhelming it.

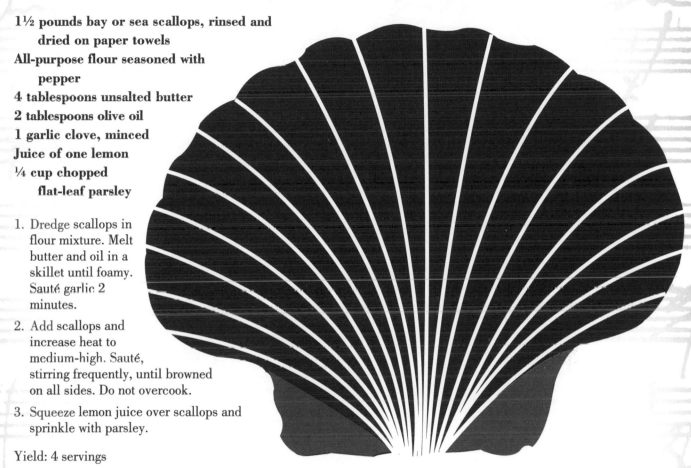

1½ pounds bay or sea scallops, rinsed and
    dried on paper towels
All-purpose flour seasoned with
    pepper
4 tablespoons unsalted butter
2 tablespoons olive oil
1 garlic clove, minced
Juice of one lemon
¼ cup chopped
    flat-leaf parsley

1. Dredge scallops in flour mixture. Melt butter and oil in a skillet until foamy. Sauté garlic 2 minutes.

2. Add scallops and increase heat to medium-high. Sauté, stirring frequently, until browned on all sides. Do not overcook.

3. Squeeze lemon juice over scallops and sprinkle with parsley.

Yield: 4 servings

♪ Variation: Once scallops are browned, remove to a serving platter and keep warm. Do not use lemon juice. Deglaze the skillet with ½ cup white wine, scraping browned bits. Cook and stir until slightly reduced. Pour sauce over scallops and serve.

Try a Chardonnay from the Russian River region of California.

HANGTOWN FRY

 Many stories about how it received its name accompany this recipe which dates back to the gold rush days in the West. The most popular, and by far the most interesting, is that it was the favorite choice as the last meal of a condemned man before going to the gallows. It combines two of the great delicacies of the time, oysters and fresh eggs.

6 eggs	**½ teaspoon garlic powder**
⅓ cup milk	**¼ teaspoon onion powder**
½ teaspoon salt	**Dash of salt and pepper**
½ cup all-purpose flour	**12 medium-size oysters**
1 teaspoon paprika	**2 tablespoons unsalted butter**

1. Beat together eggs, milk, and salt in a bowl. Set aside.

2. Combine flour, paprika, garlic powder, onion powder, salt, and pepper in a plastic bag. Add oysters and gently turn bag until heavily coated.

3. Melt butter in a skillet. Add oysters and cook over medium-high until edges begin to curl and they are golden brown. Pour in egg mixture. Cook until eggs begin to set on bottom and sides. Lift and fold with a wide spatula.

4. Cook 4 to 5 minutes until eggs are cooked throughout but still moist. Serve immediately.

Yield: 3-4 servings

 A delicate fruity Sauvignon Blanc would be perfect.

"When I hear music, I fear no danger. I am invulnerable. I see no foe. I am related to the earliest times, and to the latest."
~HENRY DAVID THOREAU

TUCKERNUCK LOBSTER CAKES

Tuckernuck is a little island off of Nantucket that has a well-guarded secret. It is where the natives trap their lobsters, swearing that they are the sweetest and most succulent. These cakes are a local specialty and the most delicious are the ones from Bluefin Restaurant.

1½ teaspoons Dijon mustard
1½ teaspoons whole grain mustard
1 tablespoon lemon juice
2 dashes of Tabasco sauce
Kosher salt and pepper, to taste
¾ cup panko (Japanese breadcrumbs)
½ cup mayonnaise
1 tablespoon finely chopped flat leaf parsley
1½ teaspoons Worcestershire sauce
1 egg
1 tablespoon finely chopped shallot
1 pound cooked lobster meat, cut into small chunks
Canola oil

1. Combine Dijon mustard, grain mustard, lemon juice, Tabasco, salt, pepper, some of the breadcrumbs, mayonnaise, parsley, Worcestershire sauce, egg, and shallot and mix well. Reserve some breadcrumbs until fully mixed. Add lobster meat. Shape ½ cup mixture into four round cakes. Refrigerate until cold.

2. Heat oil in a skillet. Sear cakes on each side. Finish baking at 375 degrees 10 minutes.

Yield: 4 servings

~ BLUEFIN RESTAURANT~
~NANTUCKET, MASSACHUSETTS~
~JONAS BAKER, CHEF/OWNER ~

Entrées ~ Fish & Seafood

EASTERN SHORE DELUXE CRAB CAKES

There are as many recipes for crab cakes as there are chefs in Maryland. The premise is to create a cake that holds the fragile lumps together without being too heavy; enhances but does not overwhelm the delicate crab flavor, and adds a regional touch that makes it unique. This recipe has taken fifteen years to perfect, by tasting crab cakes throughout the state and incorporating the best elements of each into a single recipe.

3-4 cups diced whole wheat bread, crusts removed
¼ cup chopped chives
¼ cup chopped parsley
1 tablespoon unsalted butter
¼ cup finely chopped green onions
¼ cup finely chopped sweet red pepper
1 garlic clove, finely chopped
2 tablespoons all-purpose flour
½ cup heavy cream

3 tablespoons minced fresh basil
2 large egg yolks
1 tablespoon Dijon mustard
2 teaspoons lemon juice
1½ teaspoons hot chili sauce, (Sriracha, often found in the ethnic food section, is best)
Salt, to taste
2 pounds backfin crabmeat
4 tablespoons unsalted butter, melted

1. Preheat oven to 450 degrees. Process bread cubes, chives, and parsley in a food processor into crumbs. Set aside.

2. Melt butter in a heavy skillet. Sauté onions, pepper, and garlic 2 to 4 minutes until tender. Whisk in flour and cook 1 minute. Add cream, stirring constantly, until thickened. Remove from heat.

3. Add basil, egg yolks, mustard, lemon juice, chili sauce, and salt. Fold in crabmeat, taking care not to break up lumps. Stir in just enough breadcrumbs to hold mixture together.

4. Pour enough melted butter into a 15x10x2-inch baking sheet to coat bottom. Shape cakes by placing a handful of breadcrumbs in the palm of one hand. Using a standard measure to suit the size of the cake you desire, scoop up ¼ to ½ cup of mixture and flip it over into the crumbs. Press additional crumbs onto the top of the cake. Place it on the buttered sheet. Work gently as the cakes will just hold together. Shape 8 to 10 crab cakes in the same manner. Drizzle the tops with additional melted butter.

5. Bake 10 to 12 minutes or until browned.

Yield: 10-12 crab cakes

Tip: Crab cakes may be made appetizer size with additional breadcrumbs to hold them together.

Pick a zesty New Zealand Sauvignon Blanc.

"Assassins!"
~ARTURO TOSCANINI TO HIS ORCHESTRA

CRAB IMPERIAL

 A delicious version of the all-time classic crabmeat dish. Look for the secret ingredient that gives it wonderful texture.

1 tablespoon unsalted butter
1 tablespoon all-purpose flour
½ cup milk
1 teaspoon minced onion
1½ teaspoons Worcestershire sauce (optional)
2 slices premium white sandwich bread,
    crusts removed and cubed
½ cup mayonnaise

1 tablespoon lemon juice
1 teaspoon salt
3 dashes of pepper
2 tablespoons unsalted butter
1 pound jumbo lump crabmeat, cartilage removed
Paprika for garnish

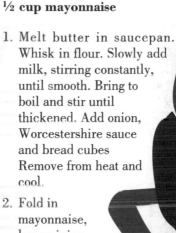

1. Melt butter in saucepan. Whisk in flour. Slowly add milk, stirring constantly, until smooth. Bring to boil and stir until thickened. Add onion, Worcestershire sauce and bread cubes Remove from heat and cool.

2. Fold in mayonnaise, lemon juice, salt, and pepper.

3. Heat butter in a large non-stick skillet until lightly browned. Add crabmeat and toss gently. Add bread mixture and mix thoroughly.

4. Pour crabmeat mixture into a greased 1-quart casserole dish. Sprinkle with paprika. Bake at 350 degrees 10 to 15 minutes until hot, bubbly and lightly browned.

Yield: 4 servings

 Choose a medium-bodied California Chardonnay.

"Give me a laundry list and I'll set it to music."
~GIOACCHINO ROSSINI

Entrées ~ Fish & Seafood

CRAB LOAF WITH SHRIMP

The secret of this master chef's divine recipe is to use a shrimp forcemeat to bind the crab together. This dish can be made as individual crab cakes or as a loaf.

PARSLEY BUTTER SAUCE

3 teaspoons chopped shallots

2 tablespoons sherry or wine vinegar

¼ cup dry wine

½ cup fish broth or clam juice

½ cup heavy cream

3 tablespoons butter

Salt and pepper, to taste

1 tablespoon whole grain mustard

¼ cup finely chopped parsley

1. Combine shallots, vinegar, and wine in a saucepan. Bring to boil and cook until reduced by half. Add broth and cream. Bring to boil. Cook at a rolling boil about 45 seconds.

2. Swirl in butter. Stir in salt, pepper, mustard, and parsley. Keep warm.

CRAB LOAF

¾ pound uncooked shrimp, peeled and deveined

1 egg

¾ cup heavy cream

Salt and pepper, to taste

1 pound lump crabmeat, cartilage and shells removed

½ cup minced green onions

1 tablespoon Dijon mustard

1 teaspoon Worcestershire sauce

¼ teaspoon Tabasco sauce

½ cup vegetable oil

1. Purée shrimp, egg, cream, salt, and pepper in a food processor until smooth. Transfer to a bowl. Stir in crabmeat, onions, mustard, Worcestershire sauce, and Tabasco until thoroughly blended.

2. Preheat oven to 375 degrees. Shape mixture in a loaf and place in a buttered 9x5-inch loaf pan. Cover with a greased piece of foil. Place loaf pan in a 13x9x2-inch baking dish. Fill dish halfway with hot water.

3. Bake about 1 hour or until cake tester comes out clean. Serve in slices with Parsley Butter Sauce.

Yield: 4-6 servings, ¾ cup sauce

~ THE READING COUNTRY CLUB, READING, PENNSYLVANIA~
~JEAN-MAURICE JUGÉ, EXECUTIVE CHEF ~
~MITCH MARRON, GENERAL MANAGER~

♪ Variation: Shape mixture into 10 crab cakes. Heat 2 tablespoons olive oil in a non-stick skillet. Sauté several crab cakes 3 minutes per side until golden brown, adding oil as needed. Remove and keep warm. Repeat with remaining cakes. Serve with Parsley Butter Sauce.

CRAB MARYLAND

The crabmeat has a starring role in this rich, elegant, and simple to make dish. Your guests will swoon with pleasure.

1 pound jumbo lump or backfin crabmeat
2 tablespoons unsalted butter
¼-½ cup dry sherry wine
2 tablespoons all-purpose flour
2 cups cream

Salt and pepper, to taste
1¼ pounds fresh asparagus, cooked until tender but still firm and well drained
1 cup heavy cream, whipped
4 tablespoons freshly grated Parmesan cheese

1. Sauté crabmeat lightly in butter. Add sherry and simmer until reduced by one-half.

2. Add flour and cream and gently stir until thickened, taking care not to break up lumps.

3. Place asparagus in the bottom of a buttered 11x7x2-inch baking dish. Pour crabmeat mixture over asparagus. Spread whipped cream over crabmeat and sprinkle with cheese. Broil until topping is lightly browned.

Yield: 4-6 servings

~AN OLD MARYLAND RECIPE~

 Variation: Substitute 3 (10-ounce) bags of fresh spinach, wilted, for the asparagus.

 Pick a California full-bodied Chardonnay with no oak but lots of buttery notes.

CHUNKY MANGO-GINGER SAUCE

Colorful and tangy-sweet, this sauce will brighten the flavor of simple grilled fish such as sea bass, mahi-mahi, or grouper. It also partners well with grilled chicken breasts.

1 tablespoon extra virgin olive oil
2 cups chopped red onion
2 cups cubed, peeled ripe mango
1 cup chopped tomatoes
3 tablespoons minced gingerroot
1 tablespoon minced garlic, about 4 cloves

½ cup fresh lime juice
¼ cup orange juice
¼ cup dry sherry
3 tablespoons packed brown sugar
3 tablespoons white vinegar

1. Heat oil and sauté onion 5 minutes, stirring constantly. Add mango, tomatoes, ginger, and garlic. Cook 5 minutes.

2. Stir in lime juice, orange juice, sherry, brown sugar, and vinegar. Bring to boil. Reduce heat and simmer 20 minutes. Cool before serving.

Yield: 2½ cups

THAI SHRIMP IN COCONUT BROTH

This recipe shares the secret of the exotic Thai flavors that have become all the rage in today's trendy restaurants.

THAI COCONUT BROTH WITH NOODLES

2 (3-ounce) packages ramen noodle soup mix, any flavor
1 quart water
1 (14-ounce) can low sodium chicken broth
1 (14½-ounce) can unsweetened coconut milk
1 Thai chile or jalapeño pepper

1 tablespoon minced garlic
1 tablespoon minced gingerroot
1 tablespoon curry powder
1 tablespoon chopped fresh cilantro
1 tablespoon chopped shallot

1. Remove seasoning packet from soup for another use. Bring water to boil. Add noodles and cook 2 minutes. Drain and rinse with cold water.

2. Combine broth, milk, chile pepper, garlic, ginger, curry, cilantro, and shallots in a saucepan. Bring to boil. Reduce heat and simmer 10 minutes.

3. Remove chile pepper. Stir in noodles. Let stand 10 to 15 minutes while noodles absorb broth. Set aside.

SHRIMP

1½ pounds medium-size shrimp, peeled and deveined
2 teaspoons sesame oil
2 teaspoons minced garlic
2 teaspoons minced gingerroot
2 tablespoons chopped fresh cilantro
2 teaspoons chopped shallots
1 tablespoon lemon juice
1 teaspoon salt
½ teaspoon pepper

1. Sauté shrimp in oil 2 minutes until pink. Add garlic, ginger, cilantro, shallots, lemon juice, salt and pepper. Mix well.

2. Serve shrimp over Coconut Broth with Noodles.

Yield: 6 servings, 6 cups broth

 A not-too-sweet Johannesburg Riesling would be a perfect partner.

ORANGE-DILL SHRIMP IN SQUASH BOATS

This delicious dish and its most unusual and attractive presentation will make it a favorite choice for your next dinner party.

2 small acorn squash, split lengthwise, seeds and membranes removed
1 stick unsalted butter
1 tablespoon packed brown sugar
¼ teaspoon salt
⅔ cup thinly sliced red onion
1½ pounds uncooked large shrimp, peeled and deveined

3 tablespoons match-size strips orange peel
½ cup orange juice
½ cup dry white wine
2 teaspoons chopped garlic
2 tablespoons fresh dill or 2 teaspoons dried
Salt and pepper, to taste

1. Preheat oven to 350 degrees. Place squash cut side up in a 13x9x2-inch baking dish. Dot each with ½ tablespoon butter. Sprinkle with brown sugar and salt. Pour enough water into dish to reach depth of 1-inch.

2. Cover with foil and bake 40 minutes until tender. Loosen foil to tent squash. Keep warm.

3. Melt 2 tablespoons butter in a heavy skillet. Sauté onion 5 minutes, or until wilted. Add shrimp and orange peel. Sauté 1 to 2 minutes until shrimp are almost cooked through.

4. Add orange juice, wine, and garlic. Cook and stir 2 minutes until sauce is slightly thickened. Remove shrimp with a slotted spoon to a plate. Remove skillet from heat. Whisk in 4 tablespoons butter until melted. Add dill, salt and pepper.

5. Return shrimp to skillet. Toss to coat in sauce. Place one squash half on each of four serving plates. Divide shrimp mixture among squash and serve.

Yield: 4 servings

Tip: Squash may be cooked in the microwave. Pierce with a knife and cook on high 8 to 16 minutes, turning once. Let stand 5 minutes. Cut in half and remove membranes and seeds.

New Zealand Sauvignon Blanc is the perfect wine with this delicate dish.

"Who sent you to me? God?"
~GIACOMO PUCCINI
after hearing then-unknown Enrico Caruso sing
Recondita armonia for the first time.

RAGIN' CAJUN SHRIMP GUMBO

 Bring a taste of New Orleans to your table with this jazzy gumbo that combines the smokey taste of sausage with the sweetness of fresh shrimp.

1 (8-ounce) package smoked kielbasa or andouille sausage, cut into ¼-inch slices

1 small onion, diced

1 stalk celery, diced

1 (10-ounce) package frozen okra, thawed, or 1 pound fresh, washed and cut into slices

1 large bell pepper, cut into thin strips

2 garlic cloves, minced

1 (14½-ounce) can diced Italian tomatoes or ½ pound fresh, cut into ½-inch chunks

1 (14-ounce) can low sodium chicken broth

1¾ teaspoons gumbo filé or Cajun seasoning

⅓-½ teaspoon cayenne pepper

¾ cup uncooked long-grain rice

1 pound medium-size shrimp, peeled and deveined

1. Sauté sausage 3 to 4 minutes until browned. Add onion, celery, okra, pepper, and garlic and cook 2 to 3 minutes.

2. Stir in tomatoes, broth, filé, and cayenne. Bring to boil and stir in rice. Cover, reduce heat and simmer 15 to 20 minutes or until liquid is absorbed. Add more water if mixture becomes dry before rice is cooked.

3. Add shrimp and cook 3 to 5 minutes until shrimp turn pink. Serve immediately.

Yield: 6-8 servings

 Pop a brew or uncork a bottle of Zinfandel.

"New Orleans food is as delicious as the less criminal forms of sin."
~MARK TWAIN, 1884

LEMON CHIVE BEURRE BLANC

This rich, buttery lemon sauce is a perfect complement to raw oysters, poached lobster meat or sautéed soft-shell crabs.

⅓ cup white wine

⅓ cup red wine vinegar

3 shallots, finely chopped

3 sticks unsalted butter

1 tablespoon plus 1 teaspoon lemon zest

1 tablespoon plus 1 teaspoon chopped chives

1. Combine wine, vinegar, and shallots in a saucepan. Bring to simmer and reduce to 2 tablespoons liquid.

2. Reduce heat and add butter, one tablespoon at a time, whisking until each piece melts.

3. Add zest and chives. Remove from heat and keep warm.

Yield: ¾ cup, enough for 32 oysters or meat of four lobsters

~OLD MARYLAND RECIPE~

♪ Variation: SOFT-SHELL CRABS: lightly flour cleaned soft-shell crabs and sauté in foaming butter until golden and crisp. Place on a warmed platter and drizzle with sauce. Serve immediately allowing 1 to 2 crabs per person, depending on size.

Poultry & Game

CURRIED, SWEET, AND SPICY

ON THE GRILL

IN THE OVEN

WITH AN ITALIAN FLAVOR

ALL THE REST

BLACK PEPPER CHICKEN

♫ *Take the time to assemble the ingredients necessary to make this exotic and delicious authentic Indian dish. It is simply wonderful!*

2 medium onions, chopped into large pieces
2 tablespoons plain yogurt
1 teaspoon lemon juice
2 tablespoons ground cashews
1 tablespoon ground almonds
1 teaspoon crushed garlic
½ teaspoon grated gingerroot
1 teaspoon chopped green chilies
1 teaspoon ground coriander
½ teaspoon ground turmeric

½ teaspoon red chili powder
1 teaspoon pepper
1 teaspoon salt
12 chicken pieces, preferably skinless thighs
3 tablespoons vegetable oil
1 teaspoon mustard seeds
½ teaspoon cumin seeds
2 bay leaves
2 cups buttermilk
1 tablespoon chopped cilantro

1. Combine onions, yogurt, lemon juice, cashews, almonds, garlic, ginger, green chilies, coriander, turmeric, chili powder, pepper and salt. Mix well. Place chicken in marinade 15 to 20 minutes.

2. Heat oil in a deep stockpot. Sauté mustard seeds, cumin seeds, and bay leaves until seeds change color.

3. Add chicken and marinade. Cook and stir 5 to 10 minutes until spices become golden brown. Add buttermilk and cilantro.

4. Cook on low heat, partially covered, until chicken is done. Remove bay leaves before serving.

Yield: 4-6 servings

Tip: This recipe may be made in advance and frozen or refrigerated.

Pick a spicy California Zinfandel with a little age.

PON PON CHICKEN

 This is a famous Szechwan dish. It is served cold and can be prepared ahead of time as an appetizer or main dish.

1½ pounds boneless, skinless chicken breast halves
3 tablespoons creamy peanut butter
2 tablespoons sesame oil
2 teaspoons soy sauce
1 tablespoon red wine vinegar
2 tablespoons peanut oil
2 tablespoons crushed red pepper flakes
2 teaspoons minced fresh gingerroot

1 tablespoon chopped green onions
1 tablespoon chopped garlic
1 tablespoon dry sherry or sake
½ teaspoon cayenne pepper
1 tablespoon toasted and ground Szechwan
  peppercorns
Salted peanuts for garnish

1. Poach chicken, covered in water, over low heat 10 to 12 minutes or until done. Cool and slice into thin strips.

2. Combine peanut butter and sesame oil. Stir in soy sauce and vinegar until well blended. Add peanut oil, red pepper, ginger, green onions, garlic, sherry, cayenne, and ground peppercorns. Mix well.

3. Mix chicken strips and sauce. Top with peanuts and serve at room temperature.

Yield: 4-8 servings

 Why not try a glass of sake? Serve hot or cold.

ORANGE BOURBON CHICKEN

 You will enjoy the unusual flavor combination of the ingredients in this recipe. It is so quick and easy!

2 large boneless, skinless chicken breast halves
3 tablespoons unsalted butter
1 (6-ounce) can frozen orange juice concentrate,
  thawed and undiluted

Salt and pepper, to taste
3 tablespoons bourbon
¼ cup sliced almonds
Watercress for garnish (optional)

1. Brown chicken in butter for about 10 minutes. Reduce to low heat. Add orange juice, salt, and pepper. Cover and simmer 20 minutes.

2. Remove chicken and keep warm. Increase heat and stir until sauce thickens. Remove from heat and add bourbon.

3. Pour over chicken and top with almonds. Garnish with watercress.

Yield: 4 servings

 Pick a soft Chardonnay with a slightly oaky overtone.

GRILLED CHICKEN WITH BERRY SALSA

 Yummy and healthy! A new flavor combination for chicken.

BERRY SALSA

2½ cups ripe strawberries, hulled and diced

½ cup blackberries, halved if large

2 tablespoons sugar

⅓ cup diced sweet red pepper

3 tablespoons diced red onion

1 tablespoon balsamic vinegar

¼ teaspoon pepper

⅛ teaspoon crushed red pepper flakes

Dash of salt

1. Combine strawberries and blackberries in a glass bowl. Gently mix in sugar and let stand 5 minutes.
2. Add red peppers, onions, vinegar, pepper, red pepper, and salt. Mix well. Let stand 20 minutes to blend flavors.

CHICKEN

¼ teaspoon salt

¼ teaspoon pepper

¼ teaspoon crushed red pepper flakes

4 (4-ounce) boneless, skinless chicken breast halves

1 teaspoon olive oil

Cooked basmati rice

1. Preheat grill. Combine salt, pepper, and red pepper. Rub into both sides of chicken. Drizzle with oil.
2. Grill 5 to 7 minutes per side until done. Slice chicken on a diagonal and arrange on a bed of salsa. Serve with a fragrant rice such as jasmine or basmati (see Golden Bombay Rice recipe, page 167).

Yield: 4 servings

 Pick a New Zealand Sauvignon Blanc with fruity overtones.

YUMMY GRILLED CHICKEN

 The title tells the story of this great chicken barbeque recipe.

¼ cup cider vinegar

3 tablespoons Dijon coarse ground mustard

3 cloves garlic, peeled and minced

Juice of one lime

Juice of one-half lemon

½ cup brown sugar

Salt and pepper, to taste

6 tablespoons olive oil

6 boneless, skinless chicken breasts or thighs

1. Mix vinegar, mustard, garlic, lime juice, lemon juice, brown sugar, and salt. Whisk in oil and pepper.
2. Place chicken in a large zip-top bag, pour in marinade and refrigerate 8 hours or overnight.
3. Preheat grill and lightly oil the grate. Place chicken on grill, baste occasionally, and cook until juices run clear, about 10 minutes per side. Discard remaining marinade.

Yield: 6 servings

How about a chilled Mexican beer to marry with the flavors of the citrus-y sweet marinade?

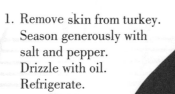

CRANBERRY GLAZED TURKEY BREAST WITH CORNBREAD STUFFING

Celebrate Thanksgiving in the 21st century with a dish that uses the same ingredients as the Pilgrams and native Americans did in 1621.

CRANBERRY GLAZE

1 (16-ounce) can whole cranberry sauce
¼ cup finely chopped yellow onion
¾ cup orange juice
¼ teaspoon cinnamon
¼ teaspoon ground ginger

1. Combine cranberry sauce, onion, orange juice, cinnamon, and ginger in a saucepan. Simmer 15 minutes. Keep warm for brushing on turkey.

TURKEY WITH CORNBREAD STUFFING

3 pounds boneless turkey breast or
    1 (4½- to 5-pound) bone in turkey breast
Salt and pepper, to taste
Vegetable oil
1 (12-ounce) package country style sausage
1 (16-ounce) package cornbread stuffing
1 stick unsalted butter, melted
3 stalks celery, diced
1 medium onion, diced
1 teaspoon chopped garlic
1 teaspoon dried thyme

1 teaspoon ground sage
¼ cup chopped parsley
2½ cups low sodium chicken or turkey broth
1 (6-ounce) package dried cranberries
1 cup pecan pieces or cooked chestnuts, chopped
Salt and pepper, to taste
Parsley, watercress, endive, or variegated kale for
    green garnish
Oranges, kumquats, stuffed mini pumpkins or
    grapes for fruit garnish

1. Remove skin from turkey. Season generously with salt and pepper. Drizzle with oil. Refrigerate.

2. Brown sausage in skillet breaking it into even-sized crumbs. Strain fat and return to skillet. Combine sausage with cornbread stuffing. Set aside.

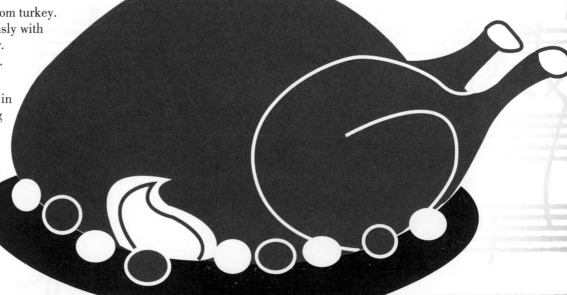

3. Add butter to skillet. Sauté celery, onion, and garlic until tender. Add thyme, sage, and parsley. Cook briefly. Stir in stuffing mixture until coated.

4. Add broth, cranberries, and nuts. Gently mix and season with salt and pepper. Spoon mixture into a baking dish only large enough so that the breast covers the surface of the stuffing. Place turkey breast on top. Roast turkey at 350 degrees 2 hours or until thermometer reaches 160 degrees. Brush glaze on turkey after first 30 minutes and then every 30 minutes during roasting. Do not overcook turkey; test with a thermometer to gauge doneness. Let rest, covered, 30 minutes before carving.

5. Arrange stuffing on center of a heated platter. Slice turkey on a diagonal, leaving glaze intact. Fan slices over stuffing and top with garnish of choice. Serve remaining warm glaze on the side.

Yield: 4-6 servings

 Pinot Noir or Zinfandel would be good choices for this savory dish.

"Endlich fortissimo!" (Fortissimo at last!)
~GUSTAV MAHLER, *witnessing Niagara Falls*

PORTUGUESE CHICKEN AND CLAMS

Portuguese heritiage combines with local bounty to create this unusual dish.

1 pound boneless, skinless chicken breast halves, cut into 20 strips
All-purpose flour
2 tablespoons olive oil
1 (8-ounce) package garlic sausage, sliced into 12 pieces
24 littleneck clams, scrubbed well
1 sweet red pepper, cut into thin strips

½ cup sofrito (mixture of sweet peppers, onion, garlic, coriander and other spices found in jars in the Spanish & Latin American section of the supermarket)
1 teaspoon chopped garlic
½ cup low sodium chicken broth
½ cup white wine
2 tablespoons chopped parsley

1. Dust chicken in flour. Heat oil in a large skillet. Sauté chicken on all sides until golden brown.

2. Add sausage and cook until browned. Add clams, pepper, sofrito, garlic, broth, and wine. Simmer until clams open.

3. Sprinkle with parsley and serve in deep bowls.

Yield: 2 servings

 Select a nice blond European style beer.

CHICKEN QUIGLEY

 This is a great recipe for company, since the chicken must be marinated overnight. It can also be served cold for a picnic.

8 boneless, skinless, chicken breast halves

1 garlic clove, crushed

2 tablespoons dried oregano

Salt and pepper, to taste

½ cup red wine vinegar

¼ cup olive oil

½ cup pitted dried plums

¼ cup green olives with pimientos

¼ cup capers, rinsed and patted dry

3 bay leaves

½ cup packed dark brown sugar

½ cup white wine

2 tablespoons finely chopped parsley

1. Combine chicken, garlic, oregano, salt, pepper, vinegar, oil, plums, olives, capers, and bay leaves in a bowl. Cover and marinate overnight in the refrigerator.

2. Preheat oven to 350 degrees. Arrange chicken in a single layer in a shallow baking dish. Spoon marinade evenly over chicken. Sprinkle with brown sugar. Pour wine around chicken.

3. Bake, uncovered, 45 minutes to 1 hour, basting with pan juices every 15 minutes.

4. Transfer chicken, plums, olives and capers with a slotted spoon to a serving platter. Drizzle with ½ cup pan juices and top with parsley. Serve with remaining pan juices.

Yield: 8 servings

A New Zealand Sauvignon Blanc would be a perfect flavor match.

CHICKEN ZANZIBAR

This is a wonderful, spicy, sweet and easy recipe. The golden raisins make it special.

1 (16-ounce) can diced tomatoes

½ cup golden raisins

1 tablespoon chopped green chiles

1 teaspoon sugar

1 teaspoon cinnamon

½ teaspoon salt

½ teaspoon ground cumin

⅛ teaspoon crushed red pepper flakes

2 tablespoons olive oil

8 boneless, skinless chicken thighs

½ cup chopped onion

1. Combine tomatoes, raisins, chiles, sugar, cinnamon, salt, cumin, and red pepper. Set aside.

2. Heat oil in a large skillet. Brown chicken 10 minutes. Add onion and cook and stir 2 to 3 minutes.

3. Drain oil and add tomato mixture. Reduce to medium heat. Cover and simmer 15 minutes.

Yield: 4 servings

 Pinot Noir goes well with this dish.

CORNISH HENS GLAZED WITH CHERRY PRESERVES

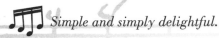 *Simple and simply delightful.*

2 Cornish game hens, split in half at purchase time
Salt and garlic powder
1-1½ cups cherry preserves

Hot cooked rice (see Fool-Proof Fluffy Rice recipe, page 168)

1. Preheat broiler to medium-high heat. Rinse hens and pat dry. Sprinkle generously with salt and garlic powder on both sides. Place hens skin side down on broiler pan.

2. Broil 6 minutes until charred. Turn skin side up and broil an additional 6 minutes until charred. Remove from oven. Spoon preserves onto skin side. Place more preserves in pan to make a sauce.

3. Reduce temperature to low and broil 2 minutes until preserves are heated and there is a glaze on hens. Meat should be fully cooked, moist and tender inside. Serve with rice.

Yield: 2 servings

"A painter paints pictures on canvas. But musicians paint their pictures on silence."
~LEOPOLD STOKOWSKI

CHICKEN AND CORN PIE

This traditional Pennsylvania Dutch dish is the ultimate recipe for comfort food.

2 tablespoons unsalted butter
½ pound small white onions, peeled
½ cup chopped celery
6 tablespoons all-purpose flour
1 teaspoon salt
¼ teaspoon pepper
¼ teaspoon dried thyme
1 cup low sodium chicken broth
1 cup light cream

1 (12-ounce) can whole kernel corn, drained or 1 package frozen corn, thawed
3 cups cooked chicken, cut into large pieces or a store-bought roasted chicken cut into large chunks
2 hard-cooked eggs, coarsely chopped
2¼ cups biscuit mix
¾ cup milk

1. Heat butter in a Dutch oven. Sauté, covered, onions and celery 10 minutes. Remove from heat. Stir in flour, salt, pepper, and thyme. Mix well.

2. Stir in broth, cream, corn, and chicken. Bring to boil, stirring constantly. Reduce heat and simmer 10 minutes, stirring occasionally.

3. Pour mixture into a 2½-quart casserole dish. Stir in eggs. Preheat oven to 400 degrees.

4. Mix together biscuit mix and milk with a fork. Drop batter by the spoonful on top of chicken mixture. Bake 30 minutes or until hot and biscuits are golden brown.

Yield: 6 servings

RABBIT "À LA CRÈME"

♫ *A French classic- need we say more?*

2-3 tablespoons olive oil
4 tablespoons unsalted butter
1 rabbit, cut into pieces

1 (7½-ounce) jar Dijon mustard
2 small or 1 medium onion, chopped
1 (16-ounce) package small whole white
  mushrooms
2 cups white wine
3 tablespoons sour cream
Salt and pepper, to taste
Hot cooked pasta, rice, or couscous

1. Heat oil and butter in a Dutch oven until sizzling. Cook rabbit pieces until golden brown on both sides. Remove to a plate. Brush with mustard on all sides.

2. Sauté onions in Dutch oven until tender. Add mushrooms, remaining mustard, wine, sour cream, salt, pepper, and rabbit.

3. Simmer, partially covered, 1 hour, 30 minutes, stirring occasionally. Serve with pasta, rice, or couscous.

Yield: 2-4 servings

Tip: For an enhanced flavor, prepare in advance, refrigerate, and reheat over low heat for 45 minutes. It also freezes well.

Splurge on Pouilly-Fuissé to complete the French flavor of this meal.

CHICKEN CACCIATORE

 Enjoy this timeless Italian classic.

12 chicken pieces, skinless, boneless breast halves
   or thighs
Salt and pepper, to taste
All-purpose flour
¼ cup vegetable oil
4 tablespoons olive oil, divided
1 small yellow onion, cubed

½ cup dry white wine
1 (28-ounce) can Italian plum tomatoes, crushed,
   cores removed, not drained
1 teaspoon dried oregano
1 (16-ounce) package sliced mushrooms
1 sweet red pepper, cut into ¼-inch strips
1 bell pepper, cut into ¼-inch strips

1. Season chicken pieces generously with salt and pepper on both sides. Dredge in flour, shaking off excess.

2. Heat vegetable and 2 tablespoons olive oil in a large skillet. Brown chicken on both sides in batches. Remove to a plate. Sauté onions 5 to 7 minutes in drippings.

3. Deglaze skillet with wine, scraping bottom bits and bring to boil. Cook 3 minutes until reduced by half. Add tomatoes and juice and oregano. Bring to boil. Tuck chicken under the sauce. Reduce heat, cover and cook, stirring occasionally, 20 minutes.

4. Heat remaining olive oil in a medium skillet. Sauté mushrooms and peppers 15 minutes until wilted. Season with salt. Add mixture to chicken. Cook, partially covered, 10 minutes until chicken is tender.

Yield: 4-6 servings

 Go for a Sangiovese or Chianti to keep with the Italian theme.

"The man that hath no music in himself
nor is not moved with concord of sweet sounds
is fit for treasons, stratagems, and spoils.
The motions of his spirit are dull as night,
and his affections dark as Erebus.
Let no such man be trusted."
~WILLIAM SHAKESPEARE, *The Merchant of Venice*

Entrées ~ Poultry & Game

FLORENTINE CHICKEN

Rich and creamy, these chicken breasts are an easy, make-ahead sensation.

8 boneless, skinless chicken breast halves
Salt and pepper, to taste
2 tablespoons unsalted butter, softened
1 (3-ounce) package cream cheese, softened
1 teaspoon oregano
½ teaspoon lemon juice

1 (8- to 9-ounce) package of fresh, baby spinach, cooked, drained and chopped
½ cup shredded Swiss cheese
4 tablespoons unsalted butter, sliced
½ cup freshly grated Parmesan cheese
2 tablespoons unsalted butter, sliced
½ cup water

1. Preheat oven to 400 degrees. Pound chicken with a mallet until thin. Season with salt and pepper. Set aside.

2. Cream butter, cream cheese, oregano, and lemon juice. Mix in spinach.

3. Spread ¼ cup spinach mixture over each flattened breast. Sprinkle with Swiss cheese. Roll up chicken and place seam side down in a 13x9x2-inch baking dish. Dot ½ tablespoon butter over each breast.

4. Sprinkle with Parmesan cheese and add water to dish. Bake 30 to 40 minutes until browned.

Yield: 6-8 servings

Variation: May substitute 1 (10-ounce) package frozen chopped spinach, thawed and squeezed dry for fresh spinach.

Why not try a Viognier or other crisp white to complement the richness of this dish?

"After silence, that which comes nearest
to expressing the inexpressible is music."
~ALDOUS HUXLEY

"What I do and what I dream include
thee—as the wine must taste of its own grapes."
~ELIZABETH BARRETT BROWNING

BEER-BASTED ROAST DUCKLING

The beer keeps the ducks moist and succulent. Changing the pans halfway through the roasting eliminates the fat.

2 (4- to 5-pound) ducks	½ teaspoon pepper
2 garlic cloves, minced	1 (12-ounce) bottle beer
2 teaspoons salt	¼ cup packed brown sugar
2 tablespoons curry powder	

1. Preheat oven to 350 degrees.

2. Remove giblets from ducks. Discard or save for gravy. Mix garlic, salt, curry, and pepper. Rub mixture inside and outside of ducks. Truss the duck. Place breast side up on a rack in a foil-lined roasting pan.

3. Roast 1 hour or until most of the fat has cooked off the duck.

4. Line a second shallow pan with foil. After 1 hour, lift rack and ducks to second pan. Whisk beer and brown sugar until sugar dissolves. Brush ducks with sauce in second pan. Return to oven.

5. Roast an additional 1 hour to 1 hour, 15 minutes, basting with sauce, until meat is tender and a deep crisp brown color. Remove to a carving board. Cut duck into quarters. Serve each guest a quarter.

Yield: 6-8 servings

Tip: To make giblet gravy, cover with water and simmer chopped giblets, chopped onions, 1 teaspoon salt, ½ teaspoon pepper and celery leaves for 2 hours to 2 hours, 30 minutes.

Just keep going with the beer.

"Wagner's music is better than it sounds."
~MARK TWAIN

GOOSE WITH DRIED PLUM AND APPLE STUFFING

Choose this recipe for the centerpiece of an old-fashioned Dickens' inspired holiday meal. Goose hunting has been an Eastern Shore tradition since colonial times.

1 cup pitted dried plums

Juice of one-half lemon

3 tablespoons sugar, divided

⅓ cup whole blanched almonds

6 tablespoons unsalted butter, divided

½ medium onion, finely sliced

1 teaspoon dried rosemary

1 teaspoon ground cloves

2 teaspoons crushed caraway seeds

1 tablespoon white wine vinegar

2 cups red wine

⅓ cup packed brown sugar

Salt and pepper, to taste

3 Granny Smith apples, peeled, and cut into
⅓-inch slices

1 teaspoon ground cloves

1 teaspoon crushed caraway seeds

⅓-½ cup fresh breadcrumbs

2 teaspoons lemon zest

5 tablespoons prune juice

1 (5-pound) goose, wings removed and
inside dried out

1. Cook plums, lemon juice, and 1 tablespoon sugar in a saucepan 5 minutes. Allow to cool. Stuff each plum with two almonds. Set aside.

2. Melt 2 tablespoons butter in a saucepan. Sauté onion until tender. Add rosemary, cloves, caraway seeds, vinegar, wine, and brown sugar. Season with salt and pepper. Bring to boil. Reduce heat and simmer 5 minutes. Cool basting sauce.

3. Melt remaining butter in a separate saucepan. Add apples and 2 tablespoons sugar. Stir in cloves and caraway seeds. Cook and stir 2 minutes.

4. Place breadcrumbs in a bowl. Add apple mixture, lemon zest, prune juice and season with salt and pepper. Mix thoroughly.

5. Preheat oven to 450 degrees.

6. Pierce goose with a sharp fork. Season with salt and pepper. Place four stuffed plums in the cavity. Add a handful of breadcrumb mixture. Alternate adding plums and breadcrumbs until goose is completely full. Close opening with poultry pins.

7. Roast at 450 degrees 30 minutes, basting with sauce. Reduce to 300 degrees and roast, basting occasionally, 2 hours, 45 minutes or until desired degree of doneness.

8. Allow goose to rest 10 minutes before carving. Separate pan juices from fat and serve with the goose.

Yield: 6 servings

 Select a red wine with a presence of tannin to cut the fruity flavors. A Cabernet would be ideal!

Meats

BEEF

VEAL

LAMB

PORK

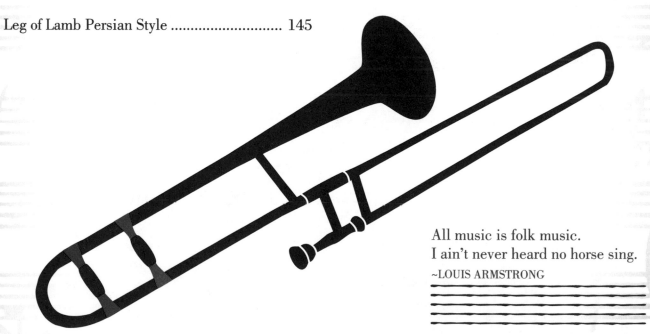

All music is folk music.
I ain't never heard no horse sing.
~LOUIS ARMSTRONG

LUSCIOUS PARTY STEAKS

This is a great gourmet presentation for a dinner party. All the work is done the day before.

2 garlic cloves, crushed into a paste
½ teaspoon seasoned salt
¼ teaspoon seasoned pepper
8 (6- to 8-ounce) filet mignon steaks
½ pound mushrooms, sliced
3 tablespoons brandy
5 tablespoons unsalted butter, divided
¼ cup all-purpose flour

1 tablespoon tomato paste
½ teaspoon crushed garlic
¾-1 cup dry red wine
1 cup low sodium chicken broth
½ cup low sodium beef broth
¼ teaspoon Worcestershire sauce
2½ tablespoons currant jelly

1. Combine garlic, salt and pepper. Rub paste on both sides of steaks. Heat 1 tablespoon butter in a heavy skillet. Brown steaks on both sides over high heat, but still raw in center. If butter begins to brown, reduce heat. Place steaks in casserole dish, leaving space between each steak.

2. Sauté mushrooms in same skillet until golden. Remove and set aside. Add brandy. Cook, stirring constantly, scraping bottom of skillet. Add 4 tablespoons butter. When foamy, whisk in flour. Reduce heat. Cook and stir until sauce is golden.

3. Add tomato paste and garlic and mix well. Remove from heat. Whisk in wine, chicken and beef broth. Bring to boil. Reduce heat and simmer, stirring occasionally, 10 minutes until sauce is reduced by one-third.

4. Stir in Worcestershire sauce and jelly. When jelly melts, add reserved mushrooms. If sauce is too thick, add more wine. Cool completely. Pour over steaks. Cover and refrigerate overnight.

5. Bring to room temperature. Bake at 400 degrees 15 to 20 minutes for medium-rare or 20 to 25 minutes for medium to medium-well. To serve, spoon sauce from dish to top steaks.

Yield: 8 servings

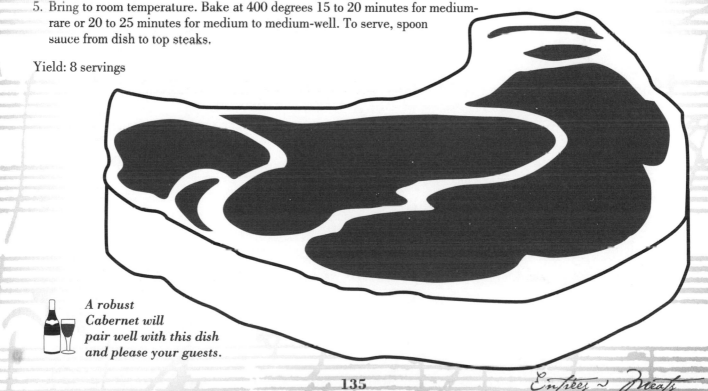

A robust Cabernet will pair well with this dish and please your guests.

Entrées ~ Meats

FILET OF BOEUF BOURGUIGNONNE

 Here is an elegant dinner dish using a filet of beef. It is always special and delicious!

3 pounds beef filet, trimmed and cut into 1½-inch steaks
Salt and pepper, to taste
3-4 tablespoons olive oil
4-6 slices bacon
2 garlic cloves, minced
1½ cups dry red wine
2 cups low sodium beef broth
1 tablespoon tomato paste
1 sprig fresh thyme
1 teaspoon salt
½ teaspoon pepper
½ pound pearl onions, blanched and peeled
8-10 carrots, cut diagonally into 1-inch slices
½ pound mushrooms, sliced ¼-inch thick
4 tablespoons unsalted butter, softened
2 tablespoons all-purpose flour

> "Great music is that which penetrates the ear with facility and leaves the memory with difficulty. Magical music never leaves the memory."
> ~SIR THOMAS BEECHAM

1. Season meat with salt and pepper on both sides. Heat 2 to 3 tablespoons oil in a large heavy skillet. Brown meat 5 to 8 minutes. Meat should be rare to medium rare on inside. Remove to a platter.

2. Sauté bacon 5 minutes until crisp. Remove to platter. Drain drippings, except for 2 tablespoons. Add garlic to skillet and cook 30 seconds. Deglaze pan with wine, cooking 1 minute and scraping bottom of pan.

3. Add broth, tomato paste, thyme, salt, and pepper. Bring to boil. Reduce to medium heat and cook, uncovered, 10 minutes.

4. Add onions and carrots. Simmer, partially covered, 20 to 30 minutes until sauce is reduced and vegetables are tender.

5. Sauté mushrooms in 1 tablespoon butter and 1 tablespoon oil in a separate skillet 15 minutes until browned and tender.

6. Combine 3 tablespoons butter and flour to make a roux. Whisk into sauce until thickened. Add mushrooms, meat, and crumbled bacon to sauce and vegetables. Cover and reheat gently until meat is desired degree of doneness, 10 minutes for medium.

Yield: 6-8 servings

 A Cabernet or French Burgundy, of course. Pour yourself a glass first!

FILETS WITH WILD MUSHROOMS FUMÉ

The intense mushroom sauce and elegant presentation complement these delicious steaks. Today Pennsylvania mushroom growers provide a wonderful selection to choose from.

1 cup dry sherry
1 cup port
1 cup red wine
3 cups beef broth
1 cup mirepoix vegetables
    (diced celery, onion, leeks and carrots)
4 bay leaves

1 bunch thyme sprigs
1 cup dried wild mushrooms
1 stick unsalted butter, cubed and chilled
4 (6-ounce) filet mignon steaks
4 medium-size portobello mushrooms, stems
    removed

1. Combine sherry, port, red wine, broth, vegetables, bay leaves, and thyme in a stockpot. Bring to boil. Reduce heat and simmer 1 hour.

2. Strain the sauce and return to pot. Add wild mushrooms. Cook over medium heat 40 minutes. Strain sauce through a fine sieve, return to pot and bring to boil. Add butter cubes, one at a time, stirring until a syrupy consistency is reached. Discard mushrooms.

3. Sauté steaks in a hot pan with butter 4 minutes per side for medium rare. Cook to desired degree of doneness. Remove from pan. Add portobello mushrooms to pan and sauté until browned. Drain on paper towels.

4. Arrange portobello mushrooms in the center of four dinner plates. Top with steaks. Pour small amount of mushroom sauce around steaks. Do not use too much sauce, as it is quite rich.

Yield: 4 servings

"The only real stumbling block is fear of failure. In cooking you've got to have a what-the-hell attitude."
~JULIA CHILD

Entrées ~ Meats

FABULOUS FILET OF BEEF

♫ *This James Beard recipe features one of the most delicious and unusual ways to serve a roast filet. It can be the centerpiece for a dinner party or for a holiday celebration.*

6-8 medium onions, thinly sliced
2 tablespoons butter
8-10 anchovies, coarsely chopped
12-15 black olives, pitted, and coarsely chopped
3-4 tablespoons diced ham
1 teaspoon dried thyme

1 tablespoon chopped parsley
Pepper, to taste
2 egg yolks, beaten
5-6 pound beef filet, trimmed
1 cup Madeira

1. Sauté onions in 2 tablespoons butter until translucent. Add anchovies, olives, ham, thyme, parsley, and pepper. Remove from heat and cool. Stir in egg yolks.

2. Cut "steak-sized" slices, about 1½-2 inches thick, not quite through the filet. Rub with remaining butter. Place 1 tablespoon onion mixture between each slice, "stuffing" the filet. Tie end to end if desired.

3. Roast at 350 degrees 50 minutes for rare. Use meat thermometer to measure desired degree of doneness.

4. Remove roast from pan and keep warm. Skim off fat. Pour drippings into a saucepan and add Madeira. Cook and stir until reduced.

5. Slice through steaks and serve each beef slice with a portion of onion mixture and Madeira gravy.

Yield: 6-8 servings

This rich dish deserves a well-aged Cabernet or open that wine in your cellar that you have been saving for a special meal.

"The secret of good cooking is, first, having a love of it…If you're convinced that cooking is drudgery, you're never going to be good at it, and you might as well warm up something frozen."
~JAMES BEARD

Entrées ~ Meats

BOURBON ROAST

 Unusual ingredients combine with an unusual cooking technique to make this roast a standout.

2½ pounds eye of round roast, scored on both sides
Garlic salt and pepper for coating
1 stick unsalted butter, melted

¼ cup Worcestershire sauce
¼ cup steak sauce
¾ cup bourbon
Juice of one-half lemon

1. Place meat in a Dutch oven. Sprinkle generously with garlic salt until meat is white. Sprinkle generously with pepper until meat is black. Pour butter over roast.

2. Whisk together Worcestershire sauce and steak sauce. Pour over roast. Drizzle bourbon and then lemon juice over roast.

3. Bring to boil 2 minutes until alcohol is burned off. Remove from heat. Marinate in Dutch oven in refrigerator at least 4 hours, basting occasionally.

4. Bring to room temperature. Grill roast over medium-high heat 20 to 30 minutes for rare or longer to reach desired doneness. Baste with marinade while grilling. To roast in the oven, preheat oven to 500 degrees. Put roast in oven and reduce heat to 350 degrees. Roast 18 to 20 minutes per pound or until desired degree of doneness is reached. Test with meat thermometer. Baste with marinade while roasting.

Yield: 6 servings

 Select your favorite red wine. It will marry well with this dish.

CONNECTICUT YANKEE POT ROAST

One of the great culinary lessons from New England cooks is their ability to transform an unpretentious cut of meat into a hardy, tender dish through slow cooking and a judicious addition of herbs and vegetables. Serve this delicious roast with buttered noodles and a vegetable casserole.

1 tablespoon vegetable oil
1 (4-pound) chuck roast
2 onions, sliced
¼ teaspoon ground cloves

¼ cup honey
¼ cup sugar
Juice of two lemons
Salt, to taste

1. Heat oil in a heavy braising pan with tight-fitting lid over medium-high heat. Add roast and onions. Brown, turning frequently.

2. Add cloves, honey, sugar, lemon juice, and salt. Cover and simmer 3 hours to 3 hours, 30 minutes until meat is tender. Turn meat every 45 minutes and uncover for last 15 minutes to reduce juices.

Yield: 4-6 servings

 Pick a light bodied red wine to enjoy with this dish.

Entrées ~ Meats

BEEF SHORT RIBS BRAISED IN RED WINE

Short ribs, accompanied by Irish Horseradish-Garlic Mashed Potatoes (see recipe page 153) make a hearty meal, and are reminiscent of the fare the colonists would prepare to ward off the chill of the New England winter. It also suited their parsimonious nature, as short ribs were ususlly a most economical cut of meat.

1 (750-ml) bottle dry red wine	¼ cup minced pancetta (non-smoked Italian bacon)
3-4 cups hot low sodium chicken broth	1½ cups grated carrots
½ cup dried porcini mushrooms	2 sprigs rosemary
6 pounds beef short ribs, cut into 5-6 ounce pieces	4 bay leaves
Salt and pepper, to taste	6 whole cloves
¼ cup vegetable oil	⅓ cup tomato paste
2 large onions, chopped	2 cups crushed plum tomatoes with juice

1. Bring wine to boil in a saucepan. Reduce heat and cook until reduced to 1 cup. Set aside.

2. Pour 1 cup hot broth over mushrooms in a heatproof bowl. Let stand 20 minutes to soften. Drain mushrooms, strain liquid and reserve. Rinse mushrooms and coarsely chop. Set aside.

3. Season ribs generously with salt and pepper. Heat oil in a Dutch oven. Brown ribs in batches on all sides. Transfer to a platter.

4. Pour off all except 2 tablespoons drippings from pan. Sauté onions and pancetta 6 minutes until lightly browned. Stir in carrots, rosemary, bay leaves, and cloves. Cook 3 minutes until carrots are tender. Add reserved mushrooms.

5. Stir and coat vegetables with tomato paste. Cook 2 to 3 minutes until paste darkens. Pour in reduced wine and tomatoes with juice. Tuck ribs under sauce in pan.

6. Pour reserved mushroom liquid and enough chicken broth in to barely cover ribs. Bring to boil. Reduce heat. Cook, covered, 2 hours, 30 minutes to 3 hours until ribs are tender and meat falls off the bone.

7. To serve, remove ribs and strain liquid through cheesecloth. Discard solids and add sauce to ribs. Serve or refrigerate up to 3 days. Bring back to a simmer until heated thoroughly.

Yield: 6 servings

Nothing less than a robust Cabernet will do.

AN EXAMPLE OF THE YANKEE PERSONALITY:

A lawyer's dog took a piece of beef from the butcher's cutting block.

The butcher went to the lawyer and asked, "If a dog should steal a piece of meat from my case, could I collect from the owner of the dog?"

"Why yes," said the lawyer. "you should go to the owner and tell him and I am sure he will compensate you for the loss of the meat."

"All right," said the butcher, "you owe me seven dollars. It was your dog."

"Well," said the lawyer, "my legal advice to is worth ten dollars, so you owe me three."

HONEY-CITRUS BRISKET

♫ *Read the ingredient list and you will certainly be tempted to make this interesting variation on brisket.*

1 (4-pound) beef brisket
2 onions, diced
1 (15-ounce) box dried plums
4 sweet potatoes, peeled and halved
8 medium to large red bliss or Yukon gold
    potatoes, peeled and halved

1 cup orange juice
Juice of one-half lime
Juice of one lemon
Salt and pepper, to taste
2 tablespoons honey

1. Sear meat and onions in a Dutch oven. Add dried plums, sweet potatoes, potatoes, orange juice, lime juice, lemon juice, salt and pepper. Cover and simmer 2 hours until meat is tender.

2. Drizzle with honey and cook 10 more minutes.

Yield: 8-10 servings

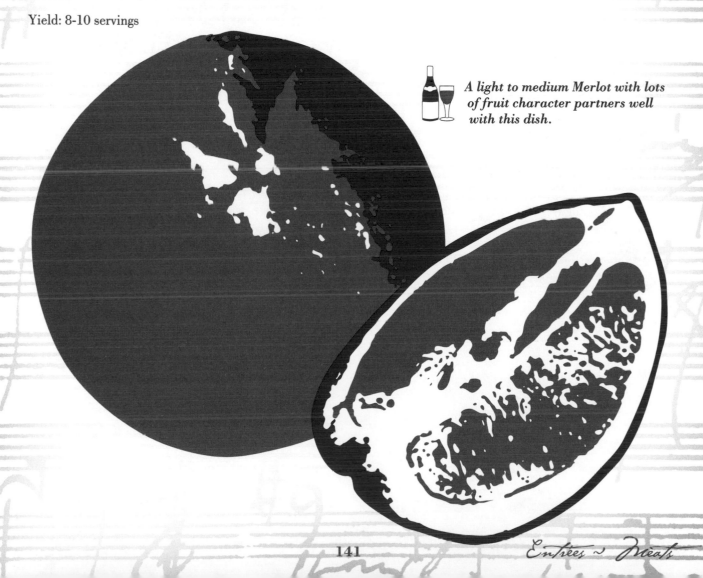

A light to medium Merlot with lots of fruit character partners well with this dish.

Entrées ~ Meats

BOBOTIE

 This dish hails from South Africa and features chopped beef in a fruity curried sauce with a custard topping.

MEAT

2 pounds ground beef or turkey

2 medium onions, finely chopped

2 small garlic cloves, finely chopped

2 slices white bread, crumbled, soaked in
    2 tablespoons milk and squeezed dry

2 tablespoons sugar

2 tablespoons white vinegar

2 tablespoons butter, melted

1 tablespoon strained apricot preserves

2 eggs, slightly beaten

2 teaspoons curry powder

1 teaspoon salt or to taste

¼ teaspoon ground ginger

⅔ cup raisins

2 teaspoons lemon juice

2 tablespoons butter, sliced

1 cup milk

1 egg

1. Preheat oven to 325 degrees.

2. Combine beef, onions, garlic, breadcrumbs, sugar, vinegar, butter, preserves, eggs, curry, salt, and ginger in a bowl. Mix well. Stir in raisins and juice. Pour mixture into a 1½-quart casserole dish, pressing mixture down.

3. Dot with butter slices. Bake 35 minutes.

4. Whisk together milk and egg. Pour over meat mixture. Bake an additional 15 minutes or until custard is set. Serve with yellow rice.

YELLOW RICE

1 cup long-grain wild rice, rinsed

¾ cup raisins

2 tablespoons sugar

2 teaspoons turmeric

1 teaspoon salt

1 cinnamon stick

2¼ cups water

1. Combine rice, raisins, sugar, turmeric, salt, cinnamon stick and water in a heavy saucepan. Bring to boil. Reduce heat, cover and simmer 20 minutes or until water is absorbed and rice is tender, stirring once or twice.

2. Discard cinnamon stick and keep warm.

Yield: 8 servings

 A fruity red Shiraz would be a good wine choice.

"Music is the shorthand of emotion."

~LEO TOLSTOY

CRANBERRY MEATLOAF

The cranberry-brown sugar "upside down cake" topping adds an interesting change to an old standard.

¼ cup packed brown sugar	2 eggs
½ cup cranberry sauce	1½ teaspoons salt or to taste
1½ pounds ground beef	⅛ teaspoon pepper
½ pound ground smoked ham	2 tablespoons diced onion
¾ cup milk	3 bay leaves
¾ cup cracker crumbs	Whole cranberries for garnish (optional)

1. Preheat oven to 350 degrees.

2. Spread brown sugar over bottom of greased 9x5x2-inch loaf pan. Mash cranberry sauce and spread over sugar.

3. Combine beef, ham, milk, cracker crumbs, eggs, salt, pepper, and onion. Shape into a loaf. Place on top of cranberry sauce.

4. Arrange bay leaves on top. Bake 1 hour. Remove bay leaves before serving. Turn loaf out onto serving platter along with any sauce left in pan.

Yield: 8-10 servings

~OCEAN SPRAY VISITOR'S CENTER, PLYMOUTH, MASSACHUSETTS~

VEAL WITH GORGONZOLA SAUCE

 Are you looking for a recipe that is a wow? Here it is!

1 cup low sodium beef broth	1 cup heavy cream
1 cup low sodium chicken broth	1 (28-ounce) can crushed tomatoes
1 pound veal scalloppine	4 tablespoons chopped basil
All-purpose flour	1 tablespoon tomato paste
Salt and pepper, to taste	⅔ cup crumbled Gorgonzola cheese, divided
3 tablespoons olive oil	2 tablespoons chopped basil

1. Boil beef and chicken broth 10 minutes until reduced to 1 cup. Remove from heat.

2. Sprinkle veal with salt and pepper. Dredge in flour to coat, shaking off excess.

3. Heat 1 tablespoon oil in heavy skillet. Working in batches, sauté veal 2 minutes per side until cooked through. Transfer to platter. Tent with foil to keep warm. Repeat with remaining veal, adding more oil to skillet.

4. Add reduced broth, cream, tomatoes, basil, and tomato paste to skillet. Simmer 10 minutes.

5. Add ⅓ cup cheese and stir until cheese melts. Pour sauce over veal. Sprinkle with remaining basil and cheese.

Yield: 4 servings

Entrées ~ Meats

VITELLO TONNATO

 This lovely classic summer dish from Northern Italy pairs cold veal with a creamy tuna fish sauce. Unlikely, yes, but try it! It is heavenly.

TUNA FISH SAUCE

3 cups mayonnaise

1 (12-ounce) can white tuna, drained, rinsed and patted dry

4-5 anchovy filets

4-5 tablespoons lemon juice

3-4 tablespoons capers, rinsed and patted dry

½-¾ cup olive oil

1. Combine mayonnaise, tuna, anchovies, lemon juice, and capers in a food processor. Blend until smooth.

2. Add enough oil and blend until creamy and sauce will pour. Set aside.

VEAL

2-3 pounds boneless veal roast, shoulder or top round, firmly tied

2 tablespoons olive oil

1 medium carrot, chopped

1 stalk celery, chopped

½ onion, chopped

½ cup white wine

1½ cups chicken broth

Cherry tomatoes and capers for garnish

1. Sear meat in oil in a Dutch oven. Add carrot, celery, onion, wine, and broth. Bring to boil. Reduce heat and simmer 1 hour, turning several times and adding water if necessary. Cool in broth. Refrigerate until very cold.

2. Slice chilled veal as thinly as possible. Spread a thin layer of sauce on a serving platter. Arrange slices in sauce in an almost single layer, overlapping slightly. Cover with sauce. Repeat meat layers and sauce, covering completely.

3. Refrigerate several hours. Garnish with tomatoes and capers.

Yield: 8-10 servings

 A fine California Fumé Blanc, well chilled, is a good choice for this summer dish, but Prosecco (an Italian sparkling white wine) would be even better.

"There are two means of refuge from the miseries of life: music and cats."
~ALBERT SCHWEITZER

LEG OF LAMB PERSIAN STYLE

The wonderful aroma of the lamb roasting fills the house and whets the appetite!

1 (6- to 7-pound) leg of lamb
2 garlic cloves, thinly sliced
1 cup plain yogurt
¼ cup olive oil

½ cup minced onion
Salt and pepper, to taste
1 tablespoon chopped rosemary

1. Trim lamb and score with deep slits. Insert garlic into slits. Combine yogurt, oil, onion, salt and pepper in a large zip-top plastic bag. Place lamb in bag and seal tightly. Distribute marinade all over meat. Refrigerate overnight, turning bag occasionally.

2. Preheat oven to 500 degrees. Place leg, bottom side up, on a rack in a large roasting pan that has a tight lid. Pour half of the marinade over lamb.

3. Bake, uncovered, 30 to 40 minutes until very browned on top. Add water to pan to prevent sticking. There should be ⅛- to ¼-inch liquid in bottom of pan at all times.

4. Turn lamb over; add rest of marinade and bake an additional 15 minutes.

5. Add rosemary. Cover tightly and reduce heat to 375 degrees. Bake 1 hour to 1 hour, 30 minutes until fork tender. Skim fat from pan juices. Serve juices and mint jelly with lamb.

Yield: 8-12 servings

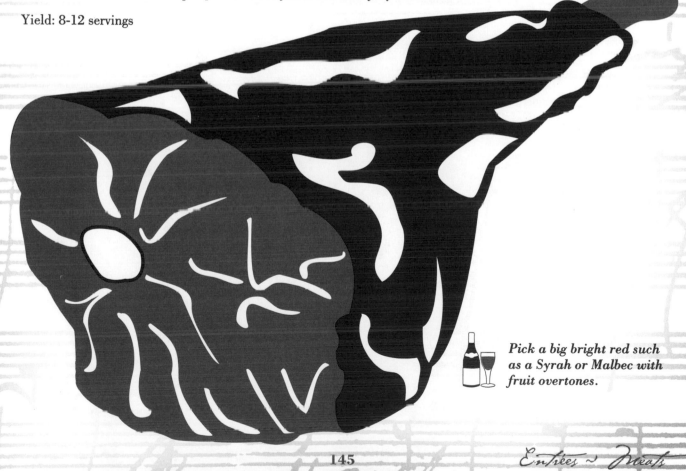

Pick a big bright red such as a Syrah or Malbec with fruit overtones.

Entrées ~ Meats

GRILLED PORK CHOPS
IN MUSTARD-TARRAGON CREAM

This classic combination of mustard and tarragon works with chicken breasts as well as with pork. If a grill is unavailable, the pork or chicken may be pan-seared.

MUSTARD-TARRAGON SAUCE

1½ cups heavy cream

1 teaspoon chopped fresh tarragon

2 tablespoons mustard, Polish or Dijon

½ teaspoon salt

¼ teaspoon pepper

1. Cook cream on high heat until it begins to boil. Add tarragon, mustard, salt and pepper.

2. Boil sauce, whisking occasionally, 3 minutes until it thickens and is reduced by half. Keep warm.

PORK CHOPS

4 (8-ounce) pork chops, trimmed

1 tablespoon olive oil

Salt and pepper, to taste

1. Brush pork chops with oil. Season with salt and pepper.

2. Grill over medium-high heat, turning once, 12 to 15 minutes. Serve chops with Mustard-Tarragon Sauce.

Yield: 4 servings

~DANS RESTAURANT, READING, PENNSYLVANIA~
~DAN GALLAGHER AND DAN SMITH, OWNERS~

 If you prefer white wine, a French Pouilly-Fuissé would go well with this entrée. For a red, we suggest a Pinot Noir from Oregon or the Russian River Valley of California.

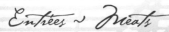

PORK CHOPS WITH APPLES AND STUFFING

Apples are a bountiful crop in the orchards along the Atlantic Coast, especially in Pennsylvania, Connecticut and Rhode Island and they appear in many recipes both savory and sweet. In this recipe they are paired with pork in an easy preparation with delicious results.

6 boneless pork loin chops, 1-inch thick
1 tablespoon vegetable oil

1 (6-ounce) package prepared stuffing mix
1 (10-ounce) package frozen scalloped apples, thawed

1. Prheat oven to 350 degrees. Brown chops in oil in a skillet. Remove from heat.

2. Crush stuffing and prepare according to package directions.

3. Spread apples in the bottom of a 13x9x2-inch baking dish. Place chops on apples. Spoon stuffing over chops. Cover and bake 35 minutes.

4. Uncover and bake an additional 10 minutes.

Yield: 6 servings

If you want to be adventurous, try a crisp, oaky Chardonnay to balance the sweet pork chops in this recipe.

"All music is important if it comes from the heart."
~CARLOS SANTANA

PORK BARBEQUE

This very interesting cooking technique will reward you with a great barbeque dish!

1 stalk celery, finely chopped
2 medium onions, chopped
1 bell pepper, chopped
1 (24-ounce) bottle ketchup
2 tablespoons chili powder
2 tablespoons barbeque sauce

2 teaspoons salt or to taste
1 teaspoon pepper
1⅓ cups water
4 pound boneless pork roast
1 (12-ounce) jar apricot preserves

1. Preheat oven to 350 degrees. Combine celery, onions, pepper, ketchup, chili powder, barbeque sauce, salt, pepper, and water. Mix thoroughly.

2. Place roast in pan and pour barbeque mixture over it. Cover and bake 6 hours. Check periodically to add more water to pan.

3. Pull pork apart with a fork. Pour preserves over pork just before serving.

Yield: 15 servings

Tip: This recipe can be doubled.

Entrées ~ Meats

APRICOT AND WALNUT STUFFED PORK TENDERLOIN

Definitely a company dish with a wonderful marriage of flavors.

½ cup bourbon

½ cup finely chopped dried California apricots

½ cup boiling water

6 tablespoons dried currants

¾ cup fresh white breadcrumbs

½ cup chopped walnuts

2 tablespoons minced parsley

½ teaspoon dried rosemary, crumbled

½ teaspoon salt

¼ teaspoon dried sage, crumbled

1 egg, beaten

2 (12- to 14-ounce) pork tenderloins, trimmed

Salt and pepper, to taste

1 tablespoon unsalted butter

1 tablespoon vegetable oil

2 cups low sodium chicken broth

1 cup dry white wine

½ cup apricot preserves, strained

1 tablespoon cornstarch dissolved in ¼ cup cold water

Rosemary sprigs

1. Pour bourbon over apricots in a small bowl. Let stand 20 minutes. Pour water over currants in another bowl. Let stand 10 minutes. Drain apricots, reserving ¼ cup liquid. Drain currants.

2. Combine apricots, currants, breadcrumbs, walnuts, parsley, rosemary, salt, and sage in a large bowl. Mix in egg.

3. To butterfly pork, slice each tenderloin lengthwise down center, cutting ⅔ of the way through. To flatten, cut ⅓-inch deep slit lengthwise down center on each half of tenderloin. Pound meat between sheets of waxed paper to ½-inch thickness. Distribute stuffing evenly between two tenderloins.

4. Roll up jelly-roll fashion, starting at one long side. Secure with string. Pat meat dry. Sprinkle with salt and pepper.

5. Melt butter and oil in Dutch oven. Brown meat on all sides. Remove meat and place on a rack in a roasting pan.

6. Combine reserved apricot liquid and broth. Pour over pork. Roast at 350 degrees 45 minutes, basting with pan juices.

7. Transfer meat to a platter and cover with foil to keep warm. Pour pan juices into a bowl. Skim off fat. Add enough broth to juices to equal 1 cup. Pour wine into pan and cook over medium-high heat, scraping browned bits. Add pan juices. Boil 3 minutes until reduced by one-third.

8. Stir in preserves. Add cornstarch mixture and boil, stirring constantly, 1 minute until thickened. Strain sauce. Season with salt.

9. Cut pork into half inch slices. Pour sauce over pork and top with rosemary. Serve with remaining sauce.

Yield: 6 servings

Choose a light red such as a Pinot Noir, or if you prefer white, a Viogner would be an excellent match.

Tip: For the most intense fruit flavor, be sure to purchase the California apricots.

"Too many pieces finish long after the end."
~IGOR STRAVINSKY

CARIBBEAN PORK TENDERLOIN

Let your palate sail away to a tropical paradise with this tasty entrée.

SALSA

½ mango, small dice

½ papaya, small dice

½ pineapple, small dice

1 scallion, cut into thin strips

¼ red pepper, diced

2 tablespoons brown sugar

¼ cup apple cider vinegar

2 tablespoons Myers dark rum

1. Combine all ingredients.

2. Set aside for 1 hour at room temperature

TENDERLOIN

8 ounces cleaned pork tenderloin

2 tablespoons Caribbean Jerk seasoning

1 tablespoon vegetable oil

1 tablespoon Myers dark rum

1. Marinate pork tenderloin in Jerk seasoning, oil and rum for 1 hour.

2. Preheat grill.

3. Grill to desired doness or until still moist in the center.

SWEET POTATOES

2 sweet potatoes, peeled and chopped

1 orange

2 tablespoons brown sugar

2 tablespoons honey

Salt and pepper

Leeks, julienned and quickly fried as garnish

"Goodness is a decision for the mouth to make."
~ANONYMOUS

1. Chop sweet potatoes, place in large stockpot and cover with water. Cut orange in half and add to pot. Boil until potatoes are tender. Drain well and remove orange.

2. Mash potatoes with brown sugar and honey. Salt and pepper, to taste.

3. Place sweet potatoes on center of plate. Slice pork on the bias and place on top of sweet potato mound. Top with salsa and julienned fried leeks.

~JIMMIE KRAMER'S THE PEANUT BAR RESTAURANT, READING, PENNSYLVANIA~
~MICHAEL AND HAROLD LEIFER, OWNERS~

Entrées ~ Meats

PORK TENDERLOIN WITH BALSAMIC-CRANBERRY SAUCE

The tangy-sweet prepared cranberry sauce makes a colorful and tasty glaze for this easy pork roast.

2½ tablespoons unsalted butter, divided
4 (8 to 10-ounce) pork tenderloins
Salt and pepper, to taste
½ cup chopped onion
⅓ cup chopped shallots

1 tablespoon chopped fresh rosemary leaves
1 (14-ounce) can low sodium chicken broth
1 (16-ounce) can whole berry cranberry sauce
1½ tablespoons balsamic vinegar

1. Preheat oven to 450 degrees. Melt 1 tablespoon butter in heavy large ovenproof skillet over medium-high heat. Sprinkle pork with salt and pepper. Sear pork on all sides, about 4 to 5 minutes. Place skillet with pork in oven. Roast pork until thermometer inserted into center registers 160 degrees (or until desired doneness) about 20 to 25 minutes.

2. Meanwhile, melt remaining 1½ tablespoons butter in another heavy medium skillet over medium-high heat. Add onion, shallots and rosemary; sauté until onion softens, about 3 to 5 minutes. Add broth, cranberries and vinegar and whisk until cranberry sauce melts, about 2 minutes.

3. Transfer pork to a platter and keep warm. Scrape any juices from the pork skillet into the cranberry mixture skillet. Boil until sauce has reduced enough to coat spoon thickly, about 6 minutes. Season with salt and pepper. Slice pork and serve with sauce.

Yield: 6-8 servings

A medium bodied Merlot or Sangiovese would complement this dish.

"Music is the universal language of mankind."
~HENRY WADSWORTH LONGFELLOW

HAM LOAF

This homey recipe appears on many Pennsylvania Dutch tables.

⅔ pound ground ham
1⅓ pounds ground pork
1 cup dry breadcrumbs
¼ teaspoon pepper
2 eggs, beaten

1 cup milk
1 tablespoon dry mustard
¼ cup vinegar
⅓ cup packed brown sugar

1. Preheat oven to 350 degrees. Combine ham, pork, breadcrumbs, pepper, eggs, and milk. Mix thoroughly. Shape into a loaf and place in a 9x5-inch loaf pan.

2. Mix together mustard, vinegar, and brown sugar. Spread over loaf.

3. Bake 1 hour, basting frequently.

Yield: 1 loaf

A Fumé Blanc is the perfect match for this family favorite.

Pasta,
Potatoes
Rice & Grains

POTATOES

STUFFING

PASTA

MISCELLANEOUS

IRISH HORSERADISH-GARLIC MASHED POTATOES

When Irish immigration began in the early 1700's, potatoes were tucked away on their ships and quickly flourished as an important crop in the rich soil of the Northeast. These tasty tubers provided a hearty and reliable diet staple and their inclusion in a variety of recipes formed the basis of many food traditions. Being Irish is not, however, a prerequisite for indulging in these incredible mashed potatoes.

2¾ pounds Red Bliss or Yukon Gold potatoes, peeled and cut into 1-inch pieces

6 garlic cloves

½ teaspoon salt

½ cup heavy cream, warmed

4 tablespoons butter, unsalted

4 tablespoons prepared horseradish, or to taste

1½ teaspoons salt

¾ teaspoon pepper

¼ cup chopped green onions

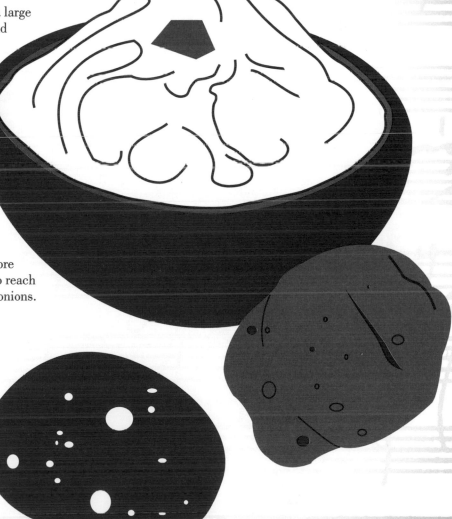

1. Bring 2 inches of water to boil in a large saucepan. Add potatoes, garlic, and salt. Return to boil and reduce heat. Cover and cook 12 minutes or until potatoes are tender. Drain well and return to saucepan.

2. Cook, stirring constantly, 1 minute to evaporate moisture. Remove from heat.

3. Beat potatoes and garlic with an electric mixer or potato masher until smooth. Add cream, butter, horseradish, salt, and pepper. Stir until blended. Add more cream, one tablespoon at a time, to reach desired consistency. Stir in green onions.

Yield: 4-6 servings

"Laughter is brightest where food is best."
--IRISH PROVERB

BASIC MASHED POTATOES

8-10 red or white potatoes, peeled and cut in half   **Warm milk, unsalted butter, and salt, to taste**

1. Boil potatoes until tender and soft. Drain well. Return to pot. Cook, over low heat, 1 to 2 minutes to evaporate moisture.

2. Mash with a potato masher. Add milk, butter, and salt to reach desired consistency.

Yield: 4 cups or 4 servings

~LENORE PELOSO~

Tip: Do not use a food processor when making mashed potatoes. It will cause them to become glue-like instead of fluffy.

"True music must repeat the thoughts and inspirations of the people and the times. My people are Americans and my time is today."
~GEORGE GERSHWIN

MAKE AHEAD MASHED POTATOES

2 (3-ounce) packages cream cheese, softened   **Salt, pepper, and butter to taste**
1 cup sour cream   **4 cups basic mashed potatoes**
2 teaspoons onion salt

1. Combine cream cheese, sour cream, onion salt, salt, pepper, and butter with hot mashed potatoes. Mix well.

2. Spoon mixture into a greased 2-quart casserole dish and refrigerate. When ready to serve, bake at 350 degrees 30 minutes.

Yield: 8 servings

POTATO SOUFFLÉ

6 cups basic mashed potatoes   **2 eggs, beaten**
1 (8-ounce) container whipped cream cheese with **¼ cup sour cream**
**   chives, softened**   **Salt and unsalted butter, to taste**

1. Preheat oven to 400 degrees. Combine mashed potatoes, cream cheese, eggs, sour cream, salt, and butter. Mix thoroughly.

2. Pour mixture into a 1½-quart soufflé dish. Bake 45 minutes.

Yield: 6 servings

MASHED POTATOES WITH TURNIPS

2 pounds russet potatoes
1 pound small white turnips, peeled and coarsely
   chopped
¼ cup milk

½ cup plain yogurt
2 tablespoons unsalted butter
Salt and pepper, to taste
Paprika for garnish

1. Bake potatoes at 400 degrees until tender. Cut in half and scoop out flesh into a bowl and mash. Reserve skins.
2. Cook turnips in boiling water 10 to 12 minutes. Drain. Purée turnips with milk in a food processor or blender until smooth. Set aside.
3. Beat mashed potatoes and yogurt until light and fluffy. Stir in butter, salt, and pepper. Beat in turnip purée.
4. Spoon mixture into potato skins. Dust with paprika. Reheat if necessary.

Yield: 4-6 servings, allowing ½ potato per person.

"What I say is that, if a man really likes potatoes,
he must be a pretty decent sort of fellow."
~A.A. MILNE

SMOKEY MASHED POTATOES

8-10 red or white potatoes, peeled and cut in half
2 tablespoons ground hickory, apple or cherry
   wood chips, for stovetop smokers

Warm milk, unsalted butter, salt, and pepper to
   taste

1. Cook potatoes until tender. Drain well. Do not mash.
2. Scatter ground wood chips in a 16x11x2-inch roasting pan with a rack so that it spans two stovetop burners. Cover the rack with a double layer of foil, crimping borders for a secure fit.
3. Arrange potatoes in a single layer over foil-covered rack. Cover pan with a double layer of foil. Place pan on stove top with two burners on medium-low heat.
4. Smoke potatoes 15 minutes. Transfer to a bowl and mash. Stir in milk, butter, salt, and pepper. Can also be done on an outdoor grill.

Yield: 4 servings

LEEK AND WILD MUSHROOM MASHED POTATOES

These fabulous mashed potatoes are not only sophisticated in taste, but also feature one of Pennsylvania's most noted food products: mushrooms.

2 medium leeks (white and pale green parts only), quartered lengthwise, finely chopped, rinsed and drained
½ teaspoon salt, divided
2 teaspoons unsalted butter, divided
1½ pounds yellow-fleshed potatoes such as Yukon Gold

½ pound each of portobello and shiitake caps chopped fine
⅓ cup low-sodium fat-free chicken broth
⅔ cup milk, heated
½ teaspoon black pepper

1. Cook leeks with ¼ teaspoon salt in 1 teaspoon butter in a 10-inch nonstick skillet over moderately low heat, stirring occasionally, until soft and beginning to brown, 6 to 8 minutes, then transfer to a bowl. Reserve skillet.

2. Peel and quarter potatoes. Place in saucepan, cover with salted cold water by 1-inch and simmer until tender, 20 to 25 minutes.

3. Cook chopped mushrooms with remaining ¼ teaspoon salt in remaining butter in skillet over moderate heat, stirring occasionally, until softened, about 5 minutes. Add broth and simmer, 3 minutes.

4. Drain potatoes and force through ricer or food mill back into saucepan. Stir in milk, leeks, mushrooms, and pepper.

Yield: 4 servings

~ THE READING COUNTRY CLUB, READING, PENNSYLVANIA~
~JEAN-MAURICE JUGÉ, EXECUTIVE CHEF ~
~MITCH MARRON, GENERAL MANAGER~

HOT POTATO SALAD

Tangy and colorful. Try this dish at a picnic or barbeque.

8 potatoes, peeled and cubed
1 (8-ounce) package processed cheese, cubed
1 cup mayonnaise

½ cup sliced green olives
8-10 slices bacon, cooked and crumbled

1. Preheat oven to 325 degrees.

2. Cook potatoes until tender. Drain well. Mix potatoes with cheese, mayonnaise, green olives, and bacon. Spoon mixture into a casserole dish.

3. Bake 1 hour. Stir mixture after 30 minutes baking.

Yield: 6-8 servings

ORANGE AND BROWN SUGAR–GLAZED SWEET POTATOES AND CHESTNUTS

These tender sweet potatoes sparkle with a sheer glaze made from brown sugar, orange juice, maple syrup, and spices.

2 tablespoons unsalted butter

4 pounds sweet potatoes, baked until barely soft and peeled

1½ cups roasted chestnuts, peeled or 1 (1 pound) jar prepared

⅓ cup fresh orange juice

1 stick unsalted butter

½ cup packed light brown sugar

3 tablespoons maple syrup

¾ teaspoon cinnamon

¼ teaspoon ground nutmeg

3 tablespoons chopped walnuts

"Music, the greatest good that mortals know, and all of heaven we have below."

~JOSEPH ADDISON

1. Preheat oven to 400 degrees. Spread butter on the inside of a 13x9x2-inch baking dish. Cut potatoes into thick slices. Place in an overlapping single layer in dish. Bury chestnuts between potatoes.

2. Combine orange juice, butter, brown sugar, maple syrup, cinnamon, and nutmeg in a saucepan. Cook, stirring constantly, over low heat until sugar melts. Bring to boil. Boil 2 minutes. Pour sauce over potatoes.

3. Bake 25 to 30 minutes, basting with sauce.

4. Top with walnuts during last 5 minutes or until nuts are lightly browned.

Yield: 8-10 servings

~ADAPTED FROM THE INN AT MITCHELL HOUSE~
~CHESTERTOWN, MARYLAND~

Tip: May microwave sweet potatoes until barely soft. This may be done a day in advance.

THAI SWEET POTATO WEDGES

The creamy sweet potatoes are the perfect foil for the exotic, spicy sauce with a hint of Thai.

1½ pounds sweet potatoes, cut lengthwise into thick wedges

2 tablespoons olive oil

1 tablespoon sesame oil

1 tablespoon toasted sesame seeds

Sea salt, to taste

2 tablespoons creamy peanut butter

1 tablespoon lime juice

½ red serrano chile pepper, seeded and diced

1 tablespoon soy sauce

1 tablespoon ketchup

¼ cup warm water

Pepper, to taste

Chopped cilantro for garnish

1. Preheat oven to 400 degrees. Arrange potato wedges in a single layer on a baking sheet. Drizzle with olive and sesame oils. Sprinkle with sesame seeds and salt.

2. Roast 35 minutes or until tender.

3. Purée peanut butter, lime juice, chile pepper, soy sauce, ketchup, and water in a food processor until smooth. Season with salt and pepper. Transfer to a saucepan and warm over low heat.

4. Sprinkle potato wedges with cilantro and serve with sauce.

Yield: 6-8 servings

PENNSYLVANIA DUTCH POTATO FILLING

If one had to pick a single recipe that typifies Pennsylvania Dutch cooking, it would be a hard choice between shoofly pie and potato filling. Unique to the region, every family looks forward to a casserole of potato filling on their holiday table. Interestingly, each recipe is quite similar in content and procedure. The recipe we feature in this book came to us from two authentic Berks County sources.

5 pounds potatoes, peeled and cubed

⅓-½ cup milk, or more to reach desired consistency

1 medium onion, finely chopped

1 cup finely chopped celery

8 tablespoons unsalted butter

3 cups cubed baguette bread, dried out overnight

½-¾ teaspoon salt

2 teaspoons sugar

3 tablespoons chopped parsley

2 eggs, beaten

1. Cover potatoes in cold water in a stockpot. Bring to boil. Reduce heat and simmer 30 minutes or until tender. Drain well and mash potatoes. Add milk to reach a smooth consistency.

2. Sauté onion and celery in 2 tablespoons butter until soft. Remove from pan and set aside.

3. Brown 6 tablespoons butter in skillet. Add bread cubes and toss until coated. Add onion, celery, and bread cubes to potatoes. Add more milk if necessary to achieve desired consistency.

4. Add salt, sugar, and parsley. Stir in eggs. Pour mixture into a greased 13x9x2-inch baking dish. Bake at 325 degrees 45 minutes.

Yield: 8-12 servings

RICE STUFFING FOR LAMB OR CHICKEN

This unique dish can do double duty as a stuffing for lamb or chicken or as an aromatic side dish.

1½ pounds lamb, finely chopped

4 tablespoons unsalted butter

2 cups rice

Salt, to taste

½ teaspoon pepper

½ teaspoon ground allspice

½ teaspoon cinnamon

½ teaspoon ground nutmeg

3½ cups low sodium chicken broth, hot

1 cup toasted pine nuts or blanched almonds

1. Brown meat lightly in butter. Add rice, salt, pepper, allspice, cinnamon, and nutmeg. Cook and stir 2 minutes.

2. Pour in broth. Bring to boil. Cover and simmer 25 minutes.

3. Add pine nuts and mix well. Use to stuff a boned leg of lamb or a chicken; or to serve as a side dish, simmer 5 more minutes until rice is tender.

Yield: 6-8 servings

PASTA STUFFED WITH FIVE CHEESES

An easy, make-ahead dish that will wow your guests with the creamy rich flavors and attractive presentation.

1 (16-ounce) package jumbo pasta shells

1 (8-ounce) package cream cheese, softened

1 cup mascarpone cheese

1 cup shredded mozzarella cheese

¼ cup freshly grated Parmesan cheese

¼ cup grated Romano or Asiago cheese

1 egg

2 tablespoons chopped parsley

2 teaspoons dried basil

½ teaspoon dried oregano

½ teaspoon dried thyme

Dash of nutmeg

¼ teaspoon lemon zest

Tomato sauce, purchased or from your favorite recipe

Parmesan cheese for garnish

1. Cook shells according to package directions. Drain and place open side down on towels until dry.

2. Combine cream cheese, mascarpone, mozzarella, Parmesan, and Romano cheeses in a large bowl. Stir in egg, parsley, basil, oregano, thyme, nutmeg, and zest. Mix thoroughly.

3. Stuff shells with cheese filling. Arrange in a lightly greased 13x9x2-inch baking dish. Cover with foil and bake at 350 degrees 25 minutes or until heated.

4. Heat tomato sauce and spoon a pool of sauce onto individual dinner plates. Arrange 2-3 shells on sauce. Sprinkle with Parmesan cheese.

Yield: 6 servings

LINGUINE WITH FRESH TUNA, OLIVES, AND CAPERS

Charter a fishing boat from one of New Jersey's busy Atlantic seaports and know that when you haul in a prizewinning tuna, you can impress your guests, not only with an amazing "fish tale" but also by serving this special dish that will please every palate.

1 pound sushi quality tuna, about ¾-inch thick slices
Salt and pepper, to taste
8 tablespoons extra virgin olive oil, divided
2 medium red onions, thinly sliced
3 tablespoons finely grated lemon zest
2 tablespoons very finely chopped garlic

¼ cup lemon juice
12 kalamata olives, pitted and coarsely chopped
2 tablespoons capers, rinsed, drained and patted dry
1 pound linguine, cooked al dente
2 tablespoons chopped flat-leaf parsley

1. Season tuna with salt and pepper. Heat 2 tablespoons oil in a large skillet. Cook tuna over medium-high heat, turning once, about 6 minutes until browned on both sides but pink in the center. Tuna may also be grilled.

   Transfer to a plate. Cool and cut into 1-inch pieces.

2. Heat remaining 6 tablespoons oil in a deep skillet. Cook onions, covered, 8 minutes until softened. Add zest and garlic. Cook and stir 3 minutes.

3. Stir in lemon juice, olives, capers, and tuna about 2 minutes until heated through. Add linguine and toss until well combined. Season with salt and pepper. Sprinkle with parsley.

   Yield: 4 servings

"Everything you see I owe to spaghetti."
~SOPHIA LOREN

FETTUCCINI WITH LEMON CREAM SAUCE

Forget counting calories! The lemony, creamy taste of this elegant pasta, straight from the Isle of Capri, is worth every bite.

6 tablespoons unsalted butter
6 tablespoons fresh lemon juice
1 packed tablespoon lemon zest
1 cup heavy cream

¾ cup freshly grated Parmesan cheese, divided
12 ounces fettuccini, cooked al dente
½ cup finely chopped parsley
Salt and pepper, to taste

1. Melt butter in large skillet. Stir in juice and zest and simmer 5 minutes. Whisk in cream and ½ cup Parmesan cheese. Bring to simmer. Remove from heat.

2. Add fettuccini and parsley to sauce. Return to heat and toss to coat. Season with salt and pepper.

3. Transfer to a serving bowl. Sprinkle with remaining Parmesan cheese and serve immediately.

Yield: 4 servings

"Hell is full of musical amateurs."
~GEORGE BERNARD SHAW

PENNE WITH VODKA SAUCE

Although the alcohol cooks off, the vodka flavor lingers in this rosy, delicious pasta dish.

1 tablespoon extra-virgin olive oil
1 tablespoon unsalted butter
2 garlic cloves, minced
2 small shallots, minced, or 1 large
1 cup vodka
1 cup low sodium chicken broth
1 (28-ounce) can plum tomatoes, crushed

Kosher salt and pepper, to taste
½ cup heavy cream
1 pound penne rigate, cooked al dente and drained
10 fresh basil leaves, stems removed and leaves
  cut, shredded or torn
Freshly grated Parmesan cheese

1. Heat a large skillet over medium heat. Add oil, butter, garlic, and shallots. Sauté 3 minutes.

2. Remove from heat. Pour in vodka. Return to medium heat. Cook and stir 5 to 7 minutes until reduced by half.

3. Add broth and tomatoes with their juice and bring to boil. Reduce heat and season with salt and pepper. Simmer 20 to 25 minutes.

4. Whisk in cream and bring to gentle boil. Remove from heat. Toss with pasta and basil. Serve with Parmesan cheese.

Yield: 4 servings

♪ Variation: Try substituting pepper vodka for the regular vodka for a more intense flavor.

SUMMER FRESH TOMATO AND BASIL LINGUINE

This recipe is just waiting for those perfect New Jersey tomatoes that are juicy, meaty, and intensely flavored. Accept no substitutes!

4 ripe large tomatoes, cut into ½-inch cubes
1 pound Brie cheese, rind removed and cut into
    irregular pieces
1 cup basil leaves, cut into strips
3 garlic cloves, minced
1 cup olive oil

½ teaspoon salt
½ teaspoon pepper
2 teaspoons salt
1½ pounds linguine
Freshly grated Parmesan cheese

1. Combine tomatoes, Brie, basil, garlic, oil, salt, and pepper in a large serving bowl. Prepare at least 2 hours before serving. Cover and set aside at room temperature.

2. Bring 6 quarts water to boil. Add salt, stir in linguine and cook 8 to 10 minutes until tender but firm. Drain well and immediately toss with tomato sauce. Serve with Parmesan cheese.

Yield: 4-6 servings

> "The most important thing I look for in a musician is whether he knows how to listen."
> ~DUKE ELLINGTON

RISOTTO WITH SCAMPI

Made the traditional way, this creamy, delicate dish is a winner every time.

1 tablespoon unsalted butter
1 tablespoon extra virgin olive oil
1 large onion, finely chopped
1½ cups rice, Vialone Nano or Carneroli variety
2 tablespoons brandy

1 tablespoon tomato paste
5 cups low sodium chicken broth, hot
1 pound medium shrimp, peeled, deveined and cut
    in half lengthwise
½ cup heavy cream, warmed

1. Heat butter and oil over medium heat. Sauté onion, stirring frequently, 5 minutes until tender. Add rice and cook 2 to 3 minutes. Pour in brandy and stir until absorbed.

2. Blend tomato paste with ½ cup broth. Pour into rice and cook briefly.

3. Add 1 cup broth and stir until absorbed. Repeat with remaining broth, adding 1 cup at a time and allowing broth to be absorbed before adding more. Cook and stir 20 minutes or until rice is al dente.

4. Add shrimp and cream and cook until shrimp turn pink. Do not overcook.

Yield: 4 servings

Tip: Italians know that the best rice for making risotto is either Vialone Nano or Carneroli. Try to find it for the very best results with this recipe.

SHOW STOPPING SPAGHETTI
WITH RAGÚ BOLOGNESE AND WHIPPED CREAM

 This spectacular pasta dish features a rich, classic ragú sauce, served at the table with a topping of whipped cream and Parmesan cheese. Almost a spaghetti sundae. Traditionally made with homemade pasta, the commercially available fresh pasta works well to create this unusual, sinfully rich dish.

RAGÚ

2 tablespoons chopped yellow onion

3 tablespoons olive oil

3 tablespoons unsalted butter

2 tablespoons finely chopped celery

2 tablespoons finely chopped carrot

¾ pound ground lean beef

¼ pound chicken livers, chopped

Salt, to taste

½ cup milk

1 cup dry white wine

⅛ teaspoon ground nutmeg

2 cups canned Italian tomatoes, coarsely chopped with their juice

1. Combine onion, oil, and butter in a deep cast-iron stockpot. Sauté over medium heat until translucent. Add celery and carrot and cook 2 minutes.

2. Add beef, crumbling it with a fork. Stir in livers and salt. Cook and stir until meat is browned. Pour in milk and increase heat. Cook, stirring occasionally, until milk evaporates.

3. Reduce heat to medium and add wine and nutmeg. Cook until wine evaporates, stirring frequently. Add tomatoes and bring to low boil. Reduce heat and simmer, uncovered, 3½ to 4 hours, stirring occasionally.

PASTA

1½ pounds homemade spaghetti or fresh pasta from the supermarket

Extra virgin olive oil

Unsalted butter

1 cup heavy cream, stiffly beaten

Freshly grated Parmesan cheese

1. Warm six rimmed soup plates. When ready to serve, reheat ragú and pour into a warm serving bowl.

2. Cook pasta until al dente. Drain well and place into a second heated serving bowl. Toss lightly with enough oil and butter to moisten.

3. Place whipped cream in a chilled serving bowl. To serve at the table, quickly place a portion of pasta into a warmed soup plate. Top with a generous spoonful of ragú and a generous dollop of whipped cream. Sprinkle with lots of Parmesan cheese. Serve immediately.

Yield: 6 servings

 Tip: Ragú may be refrigerated for up to 5 days or frozen. Reheat until it simmers for 15 minutes before serving.

MUSHROOM ORZO, RISOTTO STYLE

Chef Gable shares one of his specialties and by all means, find the truffle oil.

2 tablespoons unsalted butter
1 cup assorted wild mushrooms (shiitake, oyster,
  black trumpet, or morels), sliced
½ cup orzo pasta, cooked al dente

⅓ cup heavy cream
2 tablespoons freshly grated Parmesan cheese
Truffle oil, to taste (optional)
Salt and pepper, to taste

1. Melt butter in a saucepan. Add mushrooms. Cover and sauté until tender.

2. Add orzo, cream, and Parmesan cheese. Cook and stir until sauce is reduced and thickened. When sauce sticks to pasta, add truffle oil. Season with salt and pepper.

3. Spoon mixture into a ring mold or pasta bowl.

Yield: 2 servings

~THE RESTAURANT AT DONECKERS, EPHRATA, PENNSYLVANIA~
~GREGORY GABLE, EXECUTIVE CHEF~

"The history of a people is found in its songs."
~GEORGE JELLINEK

SEVEN-MINUTE RISOTTO

A pressure cooker to make risotto? Spend the time with your family or guests instead of in the kitchen stirring a pot. The results are outstanding. To determine portions, calculate about ⅓-½ cup dry rice per person and a generous double amount of broth. Adjust other ingredients accordingly.

¾ cup finely chopped onion
4 tablespoons unsalted butter
2 cups rice, Vialone Nano or Carneroli variety
¾ cup dry white wine
5 cups low sodium chicken broth, warmed
Salt and pepper, to taste
Unsalted butter, to taste
Freshly grated Parmesan cheese

"Music is the eye of the ear."
~THOMAS DRAXE

1. Sauté onion in butter over medium heat in a pressure cooker until tender. Add rice and toss to coat in butter. Pour in wine and raise the heat. Stir until wine is absorbed.

2. Add all of the broth. Season with salt and pepper. Stir and seal lid. Cook 7 minutes after pressure is built up.

3. Serve risotto with a swirl of butter and generous portion of Parmesan cheese.

Yield: 6 servings

Variation #1: Risotto alla Milanese—Add a generous pinch of saffron to the broth. Stir to dissolve. Broth will be golden.

Variation #2: Risotto with Mushrooms—Pour boiling water over 1-2 ounces dried mushrooms. Let stand at least 30 minutes. Gently remove mushrooms, leaving grit in bottom of bowl. Add mushrooms to rice. May use some strained mushroom liquid to replace broth.

Variation #3: Risotto with Vegetables—Add 1½-2 cups asparagus, cut into 1-inch pieces or 1½-2 cups diced small zucchini.

Variation #4: Rosy Risotto—Sauté 1 large head (or 2 small) radicchio, thinly sliced and ⅓ cup chopped shallots in 1 tablespoon olive oil. Substitute red for white wine. Proceed as in basic recipe.

Tip: Contrary to popular belief, Arborio is not the best rice for risotto! Search out an Italian grocer and ask for "Vialone Nano" or "Carneroli" variety and you will be rewarded with a superior dish.

"A good composer does not imitate; he steals."
~IGOR STRAVINSKY

SWEET CORN RISOTTO

This dish can be served as a warm, comforting meal for dinner, by itself with a green salad, or as a special side dish. Prepare before guests arrive and serve with grilled meat or fish.

2 medium-sized ears of corn, 8-inches long, husked and cleaned
2 cups finely chopped mild sweet onion, divided
1 tablespoon unsalted butter
1 cup rice, Vialone Nano or Carneroli variety (see tip page 162)
4 cups vegetable or low sodium chicken broth, warmed
2-3 tablespoons lime juice
1-2 tablespoons thinly sliced green onion tops or chives
¼ cup finely shaved Parmesan cheese
Salt, pepper, and lime juice, to taste

1. Cut corn kernels from cobs. With blunt end of knife, scrape juice from cobs. Reserve juice and kernels.

2. Combine 1 cup onion, butter, and 2 tablespoons water. Cook over medium heat, stirring often, 5 minutes until liquid is absorbed and onion is tender.

3. Add rice and cook 3 minutes until rice turns opaque.

4. Pour in 3 cups broth and lime juice. Cook and stir 10 minutes until liquid is absorbed. Add the other cup of broth, corn kernels with juice, and remaining onion. Cook 7 minutes or until rice is tender and mixture is creamy.

5. Spoon risotto into warm, wide rimmed soup bowls. Sprinkle with green onions and top with Parmesan cheese slivers. Season with salt, pepper, and lime juice.

Yield: 2-4 servings

~GLORIA BALLAMY~

PINE NUT AND ORANGE RICE

Here are cranberries appearing again to liven up this versatile dish. Fruity and crunchy, you will use this recipe on many occasions.

5 cups water
1 cup wild rice
1 cup brown rice
1 cup dried cranberries
½ cup toasted pine nuts
4 tablespoons chopped flat-leaf parsley

2 tablespoons orange zest
¼ cup olive oil
2 tablespoons fresh orange juice
Salt and pepper, to taste
Freshly grated Parmesan cheese
¼ cup toasted pine nuts

1. Bring 3 cups water to boil. Add wild rice and bring to boil. Stir, cover and simmer 15 to 20 minutes until tender. Rinse with cold water and drain. Transfer to a bowl.

2. Bring 2 cups water to boil in a separate saucepan. Add brown rice. Stir, cover and simmer 12 to 15 minutes. Rinse with cold water and drain. Transfer to bowl with wild rice.

3. Combine cranberries, pine nuts, parsley, zest, oil, orange juice, salt, and pepper. Add to rice and toss to coat. If preparing in advance, cover but do not refrigerate.

4. Spoon mixture into a casserole dish. Cover with foil. Bake at 350 degrees 20 minutes until heated through. Sprinkle with cheese and pine nuts just before serving.

Yield: 6-8 servings

Variation: To serve as a SALAD: omit cheese and serve at room temperature.

> "There is no sincerer love than the love of food."
> ~GEORGE BERNARD SHAW

GOLDEN BOMBAY RICE

 Pair this perfumed rice with grilled lamb. Perfection!

1 tablespoon olive oil
1 onion, diced
2 garlic cloves, minced
2 cups basmati rice
4 whole cloves
4 cardamom pods

1 bay leaf
Salt, to taste
3 cups chicken broth, warmed
Few threads of saffron
½ cup toasted almonds
½ cup raisins

1. Heat oil in a saucepan. Sauté onion and garlic until tender. Add rice and stir to coat.

2. Add cloves, cardamom, bay leaf, salt, broth, and saffron. Cover and simmer 15 minutes until liquid is absorbed.

3. Remove from heat. Remove cloves, cardamom pods, and bay leaf. Top with almonds and raisins. Serve immediately.

Yield: 8 servings

FOOL-PROOF FLUFFY RICE

 Every cook needs a recipe or two that never fails. Here is a dandy one for rice.

1 cup long-grain rice

1. Bring 1½ quarts water to boil in a deep stockpot. Stir in rice. Bring to boil again. Cook 8 minutes until slightly firm but more than half cooked. Remove from heat.
2. Rinse in a colander with hot water. Drain well. Sprinkle rice back into pot. Cover and return to low heat or place in 300 degree oven. Steam rice 20 to 35 minutes until tender. The bottom layer will stick to the pot, but remainder of rice will be very light and fluffy.

Yield: 1 cup dry rice makes 3 cups cooked rice or about 3 to 4 servings

BRIE AND PARMESAN POLENTA

 Homey, yet elegant, polenta pleases every palate.

Coarse-ground or regular white or yellow cornmeal
Water
1 teaspoon salt
1 garlic clove, crushed

5 ounces chilled Brie, rind removed and cut into ½-inch pieces
1⅓ cups freshly grated Parmesan cheese, divided
Cayenne pepper, ground white pepper, ground nutmeg, to taste

1. Follow directions on the package of cornmeal for preparing 6 servings. Add in crushed garlic and cook until smooth and creamy.
2. Stir in Brie and ⅔ cup Parmesan cheese. Season with cayenne, white pepper, and nutmeg. Whisk 2 minutes until polenta thickens.
3. Transfer to a large bowl. Sprinkle with remaining Parmesan cheese and serve.

Yield: 6 servings

♪Variation: May substitute Saint André, a French triple cream cheese, for Brie.

Tip: May be prepared 2 hours in advance. Cover and let stand at room temperature. Reheat at 450 degrees for 10 minutes, thinning with water if needed.

Vegetables & Side Dishes

VEGETABLES AND SIDE DISHES

"What's best in music is not to
be found in the notes."
~GUSTAV MAHLER

APRICOT GLAZED CARROTS

Sweet and fruity, this is a beautiful dish to serve.

**2 pounds carrots, peeled and cut on the
     diagonal**
3 tablespoons unsalted butter
⅓ cup apricot preserves
¼ teaspoon ground nutmeg
¼ teaspoon salt
**2 tablespoons fresh lemon or
     orange juice**
½-1 teaspoon orange zest
Parsley sprigs for garnish

1. Steam carrots in salted boiling water
   just until tender. Drain.

2. Melt butter in a saucepan. Stir in preserves and cook until
   melted.

3. Add nutmeg, salt, orange juice and zest. Pour over carrots
   and toss until well coated.

4. Garnish with parsley and serve immediately.

Yield: 8 servings

"We do not sing because we are happy;
we are happy because we sing."
~ANONYMOUS

Vegetables & Sides Dishes

ACORN SQUASH WITH PEAR STUFFING

Perhaps the early settlers in New England were wise enough to create this delicious combination. A very different and delicious version of an old favorite.

2 acorn squash, cut in half lengthwise, seeds and membranes removed
2 tablespoons unsalted butter
1 small onion, chopped
2 medium-sized ripe pears, peeled and chopped
2 tablespoons packed light brown sugar

2 tablespoons bourbon
1 teaspoon salt or to taste
½ teaspoon ground ginger
½ teaspoon ground nutmeg
1½ cups orange juice
¼ cup sugar

1. Preheat oven to 400 degrees.

2. Place squash halves, cut side down, in a 13x9x2-inch baking dish. Add water to depth of 1-inch. Bake, covered, 45 minutes. (Or microwave at 10 to 15 minute intervals until tender.) Drain. Return squash to dish, cut side up. Set aside.

3. Melt butter in a skillet. Cook onion, stirring occasionally, 20 minutes. Add pears, brown sugar, bourbon, salt, ginger, and nutmeg. Cook and stir 5 minutes. Spoon mixture into squash halves.

4. Bake at 350 degrees 15 to 20 minutes. Boil orange juice in a saucepan. Add sugar and cook 10 minutes. Pour over squash and serve.

Yield: 4 servings

SUGAR RUN CRUNCH CELERY

*Celery has a starring role in this unusual crunchy dish that has been adapted from a recipe from Longfellow's Wayside Inn in Sudbury, Massachusetts. Recognized as the oldest inn in America, it was originally called the Red Horse Tavern. It was given its present name after Henry Wadsworth Longfellow published **Tales of a Wayside Inn.***

4 cups sliced celery, 1-inch pieces
1 (8-ounce) can sliced water chestnuts, rinsed and drained
½ teaspoon dried basil

1 (10¾-ounce) can cream of celery soup, low sodium, if available
½ cup soft breadcrumbs
⅓ cup toasted slivered almonds
2 tablespoons unsalted butter, melted

1. Preheat oven to 350 degrees. Steam celery 8 minutes. Drain well. Combine celery, water chestnuts, basil, and soup. Mix thoroughly.

2. Pour mixture into a 2-quart casserole dish. Combine breadcrumbs, almonds, and butter. Sprinkle over celery.

3. Bake 35 minutes.

Yield: 4-6 servings

BRUSSELS SPROUTS SOUFFLÉ

 Brussels sprouts are elevated to new heights in this imaginative presentation. Keep the main ingredient a secret until everyone has swooned over the delicious flavor.

1 tablespoon unsalted butter, softened	4 egg yolks
2 tablespoons freshly grated Parmesan cheese	⅔ cup freshly grated Parmesan cheese
1 (8-ounce) package Brussels sprouts, trimmed, cooked and rinsed in cold water	5 egg whites
	¼ teaspoon cream of tartar
3 tablespoons unsalted butter	¼ teaspoon salt
⅓ cup minced onion	¼ teaspoon pepper
1 cup milk	¼ teaspoon ground nutmeg
3 tablespoons all-purpose flour	

1. Preheat oven to 425 degrees. Butter a 1½-quart soufflé dish and sprinkle with 2 tablespoons Parmesan cheese. Purée cooked sprouts in a food processor. Set aside.

2. Melt butter in a saucepan. Sauté onion until tender. Bring milk to boil in a separate saucepan. Remove from heat. Sprinkle flour over onions and cook an additional 5 minutes, stirring constantly. Add hot milk, stirring until smooth and thickened. Remove from heat.

3. Stir in egg yolks, one at a time. Add all but 1 tablespoon Parmesan cheese. Whisk in sprout purée.

4. Beat egg whites until foamy. Add cream of tartar and beat until stiff but not dry. Add one-third of egg whites to sprouts mixture and mix well. Fold in remaining egg whites. Pour mixture into prepared dish. Sprinkle with remaining 1 tablespoon cheese.

5. Set in center of oven and reduce heat to 375 degrees. Bake 25 to 30 minutes.

Yield: 4-6 servings

"Opera is where a guy gets stabbed in the back, and instead of dying, he sings."
~ROBERT BENCHLEY

Vegetables & Sides Dishes

HOT FRUIT COMPOTE

A marvelous accompaniment to grilled chicken or fish.

1 (15-ounce) can pear halves, drained and coarsely chopped

1 (15-ounce) can peach halves, drained and coarsely chopped

1 (10-ounce) can pineapple tidbits, drained

1 (11-ounce) can Mandarin oranges, drained

1 stick unsalted butter

¾ cup packed brown sugar

1½ tablespoons cornstarch

1 teaspoon curry powder or to taste

1. Preheat oven to 325 degrees.

2. Combine pears, peaches, pineapple, and oranges in a greased 11x7x2-inch baking dish.

3. Melt butter in a saucepan. Add brown sugar, cornstarch, and curry. Cook until sugar melts and mixture is blended but do not boil. Pour mixture over fruit. Bake 1 hour.

Yield: 6-8 servings

~ADAPTED FROM THE QUEEN VICTORIA~
~CAPE MAY, NEW JERSEY~

"Diets are mainly food for thought."
~N. WYLIE JONES

CORN BREAD PUDDING

A wonderful side-dish with ham, pork, barbeque, burgers or hot dogs. This is an easy variation of an old New England favorite.

4 eggs, beaten

2 (8½-ounce) packages Jiffy cornbread mix

1 (15-ounce) can cream-style corn

1 (15-ounce) can whole kernel corn, drained

2 cups sour cream

2 sticks unsalted butter, melted

1. Preheat oven to 325 degrees.

2. Combine eggs, cornbread mix, cream-style corn, whole corn, sour cream, and butter. Mix well.

3. Pour into ungreased 9x13-inch glass rectangular baking dish.

4. Bake 40 to 50 minutes or until set and golden brown.

BUTTERNUT SQUASH PUFF

Here are those wonderful squash again, with another New England flavor—maple syrup—added into the dish.

1 medium butternut squash, cut in half lengthwise, remove seeds and membranes

3 eggs, separated

1¼ cups heavy cream

4 tablespoons unsalted butter, melted

¼ cup maple syrup

3 tablespoons cornstarch

2 tablespoons packed brown sugar

1 teaspoon salt

3 tablespoons slivered almonds

1. Preheat oven to 375 degrees.

2. Place squash halves, cut side down, in a 13x9x2-inch baking dish. Add water to depth of 1-inch. Bake, covered, 30 to 40 minutes. Drain and cool. Scoop out pulp and mash.

3. Beat pulp with egg yolks, cream, butter, syrup, cornstarch, brown sugar, and salt with an electric mixer until blended. Set aside.

4. Beat egg whites until stiff peaks form. Gently fold into squash mixture. Spoon mixture into a lightly greased 2-quart soufflé dish. Sprinkle with almonds.

5. Bake at 350 degrees 55 minutes or until puffed and golden brown. Serve immediately.

Yield: 4-6 servings

Tip: To shorten prep time, peel squash, cut into chunks and microwave 13 to 15 minutes on high or until tender.

Tip: When choosing a squash, pick one with a long neck and small bulb. It will yield the most flesh and the fewest seeds.

Vegetables & Sides Dishes

CORN "OYSTERS"

We can only guess that this recipe with the deceiving name was developed to partially satisfy the longing for oysters during the months that they were unavailable in the Chesapeake.

2 eggs, separated
1 cup cut fresh corn or frozen corn, thawed, lightly
    puréed in food processor
1 teaspoon sugar
¼ teaspoon salt
Dash of pepper
1 tablespoon butter, melted

"Music is the wine that fills
the cup of silence."
~ROBERT FRIPP

1. Combine egg yolks, corn, sugar, salt, pepper and butter. Fold in stiffly beaten egg whites.

2. Drop small teaspoonsful of batter into a medium-hot, buttered skillet. Cook, turing once, until lightly browned.

Yield: 2 servings

BRAISED MUSHROOMS

Rich, earthy flavors dominate this delicious dish which would make a perfect side to a simple filet.

4-6 large shallots, broken into cloves
1 teaspoon olive oil
1 carrot, peeled and diced
1 stalk celery, diced
1½ tablespoons olive oil
1 pound assorted mushrooms, rinsed, dried, and
    sliced

Salt and pepper, to taste
Juice of one-half lemon
1 cup low sodium chicken broth
½ cup heavy cream
2 teaspoons butter (optional)

1. Preheat oven to 375 degrees. Toss shallots with oil and roast 30 minutes or until browned and softened. Set aside to cool.

2. Sauté carrots and celery 3 minutes in oil. Add mushrooms and sauté until browned.

3. Add salt, pepper, lemon juice, broth, and cream. Bring to boil. Reduce heat and simmer 20 minutes until reduced to ¼ cup liquid.

4. Squeeze flesh from shallots. Mash and chop. Add to mushrooms and heat thoroughly. Add butter if desired.

Yield: 4 servings

~FROM BERKS COUNTY, PENNSYLVANIA~
~MUSHROOM CAPITOL OF THE USA~

PINEAPPLE CASSEROLE

This yummy, fruity, bread casserole partners well with ham and roast pork.

5-6 slices premium quality white bread

3 eggs

½ cup sugar

1 (20-ounce) can crushed pineapple, slightly drained

1 stick unsalted butter, melted

1. Preheat oven to 350 degrees.

2. Remove crust from bread and tear slices into medium pieces.

3. Combine eggs, sugar, and pineapple with some of its juice and pour over bread. Toss with butter and put into a greased 11x7x2-inch baking dish. Refrigerate overnight.

4. Place dish in a larger baking dish and fill outer dish with small amount of water. Bake 40 minutes.

Yield: 8 servings

"Music alone with sudden charms can bind the wand'ring sense, and calm the troubled mind."
~WILLIAM CONGREVE

YOU WON'T BELIEVE IT'S SAUERKRAUT

You have to try this recipe to know how really good sauerkraut can taste.

2 pounds sauerkraut, rinsed and drained

1 (15-ounce) can diced tomatoes, undrained

1¼ cups firmly packed dark brown sugar

4 slices lean bacon, halved crosswise

1. Preheat oven to 300 degrees.

2. Spread sauerkraut in a buttered 13x9x2-inch baking dish. Top with tomatoes and juice.

3. Sprinkle with brown sugar. Arrange bacon on top.

4. Bake 2 hours. Remove from oven. Cut bacon into pieces and stir into sauerkraut mixture.

5. Cover loosely and bake an additional 1 hour. Add water to dish if necessary to prevent mixture from drying out.

Yield: 8 servings

~A PENNSYLVANIA DUTCH FAVORITE~

Vegetables & Sides Dishes

MARBLEIZED ROOT VEGETABLE PURÉE

Root vegetables became a mainstay of the New England diet. The crops grew well during the summer and could be stored in barrels of sand or in root cellars to keep through the long winter. This spectacular casserole has potatoes, parsnips, turnips, and carrots and is sweetened with just a hint of pear. The puréed vegetables are swirled together in the baking dish to create a pretty marbled effect. It is a wonderful addition to a holiday meal.

2 pounds russet potatoes, peeled, cut into 2-inch pieces
½ pound turnips, peeled, cut into 2-inch pieces
½ pound parsnips, peeled, cut into 1-inch pieces
1 medium pear, peeled, cut into 1-inch pieces
½ cup heavy cream, warmed
5 tablespoons unsalted butter

Salt and pepper, to taste
1½ pounds carrots, peeled, cut into 1-inch pieces
1 large sweet potato
2 tablespoons unsalted butter
⅛ teaspoon ground nutmeg
1 tablespoon butter, melted

1. Cook potatoes, turnips, parsnips, and pear in salted boiling water 20 minutes or until tender. Drain well. Return to pot.

2. Stir 1 minute over low heat to remove excess moisture. Add cream and butter. Mash until smooth. Season with salt and pepper. Set aside.

3. Cook carrots 15 minutes or until tender. Drain well. Microwave sweet potato until tender. Remove flesh. Combine carrots and sweet potato in food processor. Add butter and nutmeg. Purée until smooth. Season with salt and pepper.

4. Spoon ½ cupsful of potato and carrot purée in alternating fashion in a buttered 2-quart shallow casserole dish. Swirl through purées with a knife to create a marbleized effect.

5. Drizzle with butter. Sprinkle with additional nutmeg if desired. Cover with foil. Bake at 350 degrees 35 minutes.

Yield: 10 servings

Tip: May be made in advance without baking. Refrigerate and, when ready to serve, bake at 350 degrees 45 minutes.

"Music should go right through you, leave something inside you, and take some of you with it when it leaves."
~HENRY THREADGILL

SPINACH GRATIN

 Cheese, spinach and cream combine in this rich and delicious gratin. It would make Popeye smile.

3 tablespoons unsalted butter
5 (9-ounce) packages fresh baby spinach
4 tablespoons unsalted butter
1¼ pounds onions, chopped
¼ cup all-purpose flour
½ teaspoon ground nutmeg
1½ cups whole milk

1 cup heavy cream
½ cup freshly grated Parmesan cheese
Salt, to taste
½ teaspoon ground pepper
½ cup freshly grated Parmesan cheese
½ cup bleu cheese, crumbled

1. Preheat oven to 425 degrees.

2. Melt 3 tablespoons butter in a large heavy stock pot. Add two packages of spinach. Cook 1 minute. Add the remaining packages of spinach. Tossing until lightly wilted but still bright green. Transfer to a colander and drain.

3. Melt 4 tablespoons butter in same pot. Sauté onions until tender. Whisk in flour and nutmeg. Cook 2 minutes but do not brown.

4. Whisk in milk and cream. Cook, stirring often, 5 minutes until thickened and boils. Add cheese, salt, pepper, and sautéed spinach. Mix well. Transfer to a buttered 13x9x2-inch baking dish. Sprinkle with remaining Parmesan cheese and bleu cheese. Bake 20 to 25 minutes.

Yield: 8-10 servings

Variation: ½ cup grated Gruyère cheese can be substituted for the bleu cheese.

Tip: May be prepared up to six hours in advance, covered, and refrigerated. Bake at 350 degrees until it bubbles around the edges, about 25 minutes, before serving.

"Without music, life would be a mistake."
~FRIEDRICH NIETZSCHE

CATALAN SPINACH

♫ Spinach is the perfect foil for the sweet, crunchy and savory ingredients in this tasty, quick dish.

6 tablespoons olive oil

2 medium Golden Delicious apples, peeled and cut into ½-inch cubes

1 cup pine nuts

3 shallots, finely chopped

1 cup raisins

3 (9-ounce) packages fresh baby spinach

1. Heat 2 tablespoons oil in a large heavy saucepan over high heat. Sauté apples 3 minutes until golden brown around edges. Remove to a plate.

2. Sauté pine nuts 3 minutes in the same pan until lightly toasted. Remove to a plate.

3. Heat remaining oil. Add shallots, raisins, and spinach, stirring to combine. Cover and cook 2 minutes, stirring occasionally, until spinach is just wilted.

4. Return apples and nuts and toss. Season with salt and pepper. Transfer to a serving bowl.

Yield: 8 servings

TOMATO FRITTERS

Try serving a batch of each of these veggie pancakes for a light supper. A hearty green salad and crusty bread would complete the meal.

1 cup all-purpose flour

1 teaspoon baking powder

1 teaspoon sugar

¼ teaspoon salt

2 tablespoons minced basil or ¼ teaspoon dried

2 pounds ripe tomatoes, peeled, seeded, cut into ½-inch pieces and drained on paper towels

1 tablespoon finely minced onion, lightly sautéed in 1 to 2 teaspoons of butter

1 tablespoon finely minced parsley

½ teaspoon Worcestershire sauce

1 egg, beaten

½ cup vegetable oil

1. Combine flour, baking powder, sugar, salt, and basil in a large bowl. Add tomatoes, onion, parsley and Worcestershire sauce. Do not mix.

2. Add egg and blend lightly with a fork.

3. Heat oil in a deep skillet. Drop ¼ cup of batter into skillet, patting down into the oil. Fry a few batches at a time until golden brown. Turn to cook other side. Keep warm in the oven while cooking remaining batter.

Yield: 26 fritters

~AN OLD PENNSYLVANIA DUTCH RECIPE~

TOMATOES PROVENÇAL

If food and place were ever linked together, tomatoes and New Jersey would certainly be popular partners. From the daring first bite, taken in New Jersey in the early 1800's, tomatoes have been grown in New Jersey's rich, loamy soil for the past century and a half. Most of this cultivation takes place on small "truck" farms"—so named because the farmers "trucked" their produce to the local markets or roadside stand. Dozens of varieties are available today, each with distinctive characteristics and the importance of this single vegetable (did you know it really is a fruit?) as a key ingredient in many cuisines world-wide is immeasurable.

6 ripe tomatoes, cored, halved, seeds removed and drained
1½ cups soft breadcrumbs
¼ cup minced green onions
¼ cup minced basil leaves
2 tablespoons minced flat-leaf parsley
2 garlic cloves, minced
½ teaspoon minced fresh thyme leaves
1 teaspoon kosher salt
Salt and pepper, to taste
½ cup grated Gruyère cheese
Olive oil

1. Preheat oven to 400 degrees. Place prepared tomato halves in a baking dish. Combine breadcrumbs, onions, basil, parsley, garlic, thyme, and salt. Mix well.

2. Sprinkle tomato halves with salt and pepper. Fill tomatoes with breadcrumb mixture. May refrigerate at this point and bake before dinner.

3. Bake 15 minutes or until tender. Sprinkle with cheese and drizzle with oil. Bake an additional 4 to 5 minutes until cheese melts. Serve warm or room temperature.

Yield: 6-8 servings

Vegetables & Sides Dishes

SUMMER TOMATO PIE

Stop at a country roadside stand for meaty, solid tomatoes which will guarantee the success of this simple dish. Shredded fresh basil leaves can be layered in as well.

1 cup Italian seasoned breadcrumbs
3-4 large ripe tomatoes, sliced
1 medium onion, thinly sliced
1 tablespoon olive oil
½ teaspoon salt
¼ teaspoon pepper

1 cup shredded Swiss cheese
3 large eggs, slightly beaten
½ cup light cream
¼ teaspoon grated nutmeg
4-5 slices bacon, diced

1. Spread half of breadcrumbs in bottom of a buttered 9-inch pie dish. Arrange half the tomatoes in an overlapping fashion.

2. Sauté onion in oil 10 minutes until caramelized and spread half over the tomato layer. Season with salt, and pepper. Sprinkle with half the cheese. Repeat all ingredients except breadcrumbs to make a second layer.

3. Combine eggs and cream. Pour over layers. Top with remaining breadcrumbs. Sprinkle with nutmeg and bacon pieces.

4. Bake at 325 degrees 40 to 50 minutes until bacon is crisp.

Yield: 6-8 servings

Kitchen Science Factoid: Onions must be cooked to the desired degree of doneness prior to incorporation with tomatoes as the acid in the tomatoes will prevent the onions from cooking.

WINTER VEGETABLES BRAISED IN VERMOUTH

An unusual paring of ingredients gives this dish an intriguing flavor.

1 small bulb fennel with leaves, rinsed and outer layer removed
4 tablespoons unsalted butter
1 bunch carrots, peeled and cut into ½-inch slices
⅔ cup dry vermouth

1 (8-ounce) package mushrooms, cleaned and cut into ¼-inch slices
½ cup heavy cream
Salt and pepper, to taste

1. Cut fennel in half, and then slice into ½-inch across and 3-inch long pieces. Finely chop leaves and set aside.

2. Melt butter in a large skillet. Add in fennel and carrots and toss until coated. Add vermouth. Cover partially and simmer 5 minutes.

3. Add mushrooms and simmer, partially covered, an additional 5 minutes. Remove cover. Stir in cream and reserved fennel leaves. Cook until liquid thickens and vegetables are tender. Season with salt and pepper. Serve hot.

Yield: 4-6 servings

GINGERY VEGETABLES

The ginger perks up the taste buds in this attractive dish.

GARLIC-GINGER BUTTER SAUCE

5⅓ tablespoons unsalted butter

1 tablespoon packed brown sugar

1 tablespoon grated fresh ginger

¼ teaspoon orange zest

1 garlic clove, minced

1. Combine butter, brown sugar, ginger, zest, and garlic in a saucepan.

2. Cook, stirring constantly, over medium heat until sugar melts. Keep warm.

VEGETABLES

3 carrots, peeled and cut into thin strips

3 small red potatoes, sliced

1 pound small asparagus, ends trimmed

Chopped parsley and orange zest for garnish

1. Steam carrots and potatoes 5 minutes, covered, in a steamer basket. Add asparagus. Cover and steam an additional 5 minutes until crisp-tender (or cook individually in microwave).

2. Arrange vegetables on serving plate. Drizzle with Garlic-Ginger Butter Sauce. Sprinkle with parsley and zest.

Yield: 4 servings, ¾ cup sauce

CURRIED VEGETABLES

This curry dish can be made with almost any combination of fresh vegetables. Cabbage, cauliflower, eggplant or string beans work well. For a hotter curry, add the ¼ teaspoon cayenne pepper.

1 medium onion, quartered

1 garlic clove, chopped

2 tablespoons vegetable oil

1 teaspoon ground cumin

¾ teaspoon ground coriander

½ teaspoon ground ginger

½ teaspoon turmeric

⅛-¼ teaspoon cayenne pepper or to taste

1 potato, sliced and parboiled

1 head cabbage, shredded or 1 cauliflower, cut in small florets

1 cup fresh peas or 1 (10-ounce) package frozen, thawed

Salt, to taste

1. Sauté onion and garlic in oil until tender. Add cumin, coriander, ginger, turmeric, and cayenne.

2. Add potato and cook 15 minutes. Add cabbage and peas.

3. Cover and cook 20 minutes. Season with salt.

Yield: 6-8 servings

Vegetables & Sides Dishes

VEGETABLE GRATIN WITH CRÊPES

This wonderful dish is great for a luncheon main course or an elegant first course of a company dinner. Make the crêpes and sauté the vegetables in advance, and assemble it early in the day.

VEGETABLES

4 tablespoons unsalted butter
2 stalks celery, sliced
2 medium leeks, rinsed and sliced, white part only
2 carrots, peeled and sliced into rounds
1 yellow pepper, sliced into thin strips
1 (8-ounce) package sliced mushrooms
2 zucchini, sliced into ¼-inch rounds

1 package George Washington bouillon powder
2 dashes of pepper
2 cups heavy cream
2 grates of fresh nutmeg
1 batch of crêpes (see recipe below)
1-2 cups freshly grated Parmesan cheese

1. Preheat oven to 375 degrees. Melt butter in a large, deep skillet. Sauté celery, leeks, carrots, yellow pepper, and mushrooms 15 minutes until tender. Add zucchini and cook 1 minute.

2. Add bouillon powder and pepper. Stir in cream and nutmeg. Cook until thickened. Cool.

3. Butter a 13x9x2-inch baking dish. To assemble, place a layer of crêpes in dish. Spread a thin layer of vegetable mixture. Sprinkle a generous amount of cheese. Continue with 4 to 5 layers, ending with vegetable mixture. Top with cheese.

4. Bake 15 minutes or until cheese melts and is bubbly. Let sit 10 minutes before serving.

Yield: 6-8 servings

Tip: The secret to this dish is to assemble it like a lasagna, using thin layers of vegetable mixture between the crêpes.

BASIC CRÊPES

Batter for crêpes may be stored in refrigerator. Crêpes may be made ahead and stored in plastic wrap in refrigerator or freezer.

3 eggs
Dash of salt
1½ cups milk

1 cup all-purpose flour
2 tablespoons butter

1. Blend eggs and salt in a blender on low speed 5 seconds. Slowly add milk while running on low speed. Funnel in flour, using a paper towel or waxed paper, running on low speed. Let rest 1 hour.

2. Melt butter in crêpe pan. Slowly pour in 2 tablespoons batter. Tilt pan immediately so batter will completely spread over entire bottom of pan.

3. Cook quickly over medium heat until both sides are browned. Carefully stack crêpes with second browned side up. After baking each crêpe, wipe pan with a lightly buttered cheesecloth or pastry brush.

4. Cover with plastic wrap and refrigerate.

Yield: 30-34 crêpes

ZUCCHINI AND YELLOW SQUASH GRATIN

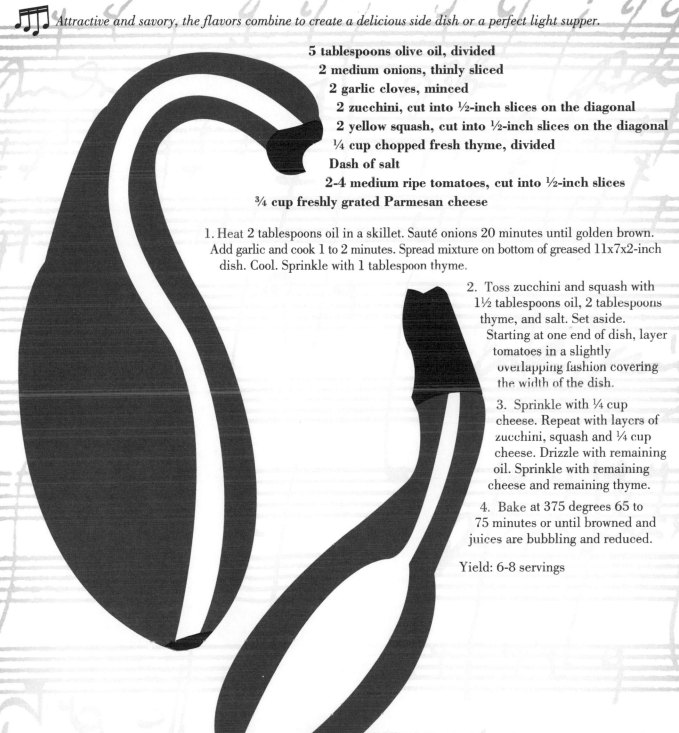

Attractive and savory, the flavors combine to create a delicious side dish or a perfect light supper.

5 tablespoons olive oil, divided
2 medium onions, thinly sliced
2 garlic cloves, minced
2 zucchini, cut into ½-inch slices on the diagonal
2 yellow squash, cut into ½-inch slices on the diagonal
¼ cup chopped fresh thyme, divided
Dash of salt
2-4 medium ripe tomatoes, cut into ½-inch slices
¾ cup freshly grated Parmesan cheese

1. Heat 2 tablespoons oil in a skillet. Sauté onions 20 minutes until golden brown. Add garlic and cook 1 to 2 minutes. Spread mixture on bottom of greased 11x7x2-inch dish. Cool. Sprinkle with 1 tablespoon thyme.

2. Toss zucchini and squash with 1½ tablespoons oil, 2 tablespoons thyme, and salt. Set aside. Starting at one end of dish, layer tomatoes in a slightly overlapping fashion covering the width of the dish.

3. Sprinkle with ¼ cup cheese. Repeat with layers of zucchini, squash and ¼ cup cheese. Drizzle with remaining oil. Sprinkle with remaining cheese and remaining thyme.

4. Bake at 375 degrees 65 to 75 minutes or until browned and juices are bubbling and reduced.

Yield: 6-8 servings

GRILLED ZUCCHINI BOATS WITH STIR-FRY VEGETABLES AND WILD MUSHROOMS

A beautiful presentation of a delicious dish makes this recipe a sure winner.

3 medium zucchini, split lengthwise
2 tablespoons olive oil
1 teaspoon chopped garlic
Kosher salt, to taste
White pepper, to taste
1 tablespoon unsalted butter
1 small carrot, peeled and julienned
1 small sweet red pepper, julienned
1 small yellow pepper, julienned
10 snow peas, julienned

1 ounce dried morel mushrooms
1 cup water
1 tablespoon butter
2 tablespoons minced shallots
½ cup sliced mushrooms
½ cup sliced shiitake mushrooms
1 small tomato, seeded and diced
¾ cup heavy cream or ½ cup chicken broth
Chopped fresh herbs

1. Hollow out a small amount of zucchini center. Brush with oil. Sprinkle with garlic, salt, and pepper. Grill briefly. Keep warm.

2. Melt remaining oil and butter in a skillet. Stir-fry carrot, peppers, and peas 1 minute or less. Divide vegetables over six zucchini boats. Place extra mixture on side of plates.

3. Combine morel mushrooms and water. Simmer 10 minutes. Strain liquid over a bowl through several layers of cheesecloth to remove any grit that might be present. Chop mushrooms. Cook liquid until reduced by three-fourths and reserve.

4. Melt butter and sauté shallots, and all mushrooms until browned. Add tomato, cream, and reserved mushroom liquid. Cook and stir over high heat until slightly thickened.

5. Spoon sauce over zucchini boats and sprinkle with herbs.

Yield: 6 servings

~GREEN HILLS INN, READING, PENNSYLVANIA~
~JAY SCHAEFFER, OWNER~

"Chamber music—a conversation between friends."
~CATHERINE DRINKER BOWEN

Desserts

CAKES

CHEESECAKES

PIES

BAR COOKIES

COOKIES

SWEETS

DOMI-CON CHOCOLATE CAKE

The origin of the name of this cake is lost, but it was handed down from a housemother at Cornell University in the 1930's. It is the darkest, moistest, most densely chocolate cake you will ever taste, with pudding filling and topped with an unusual double icing.

CAKE

4 ounces bittersweet chocolate
1 stick unsalted butter
1 cup boiling water
2 cups all-purpose flour
2 cups sugar

1½ teaspoons baking soda
½ cup sour milk (made by adding 1 teaspoon white vinegar to milk and let sit)
2 eggs, lightly beaten
1 teaspoon vanilla

1. Preheat oven to 350 degrees. Melt chocolate and butter with water in top of a double boiler. Beat in flour and sugar.

2. Add baking soda to sour milk. Stir into batter. Add eggs and vanilla.

3. Pour batter into two greased and floured 9-inch round cake pans. Bake 22 to 25 minutes.

4. Remove from pans. When cool, wrap in plastic wrap and freeze.

FILLING

2 ounces semi-sweet chocolate
2 tablespoons unsalted butter
½ cup milk
1 egg yolk, lightly beaten

½ cup sugar
2 tablespoons cornstarch
1 teaspoon vanilla

1. Melt chocolate and butter with milk in a saucepan. Stir in egg yolk. Combine sugar and cornstarch. Whisk into chocolate mixture.

2. Bring to boil and cook until thickened. Remove from heat. Cool slightly. Stir in vanilla and refrigerate.

ICING

1½ sticks unsalted butter, softened
3 cups powdered sugar
1 teaspoon vanilla

2 egg yolks, beaten or 3 tablespoons heavy cream
¾ cup semi-sweet chocolate morsels, melted

1. Beat butter, sugar, and vanilla until creamy. Add egg yolks and beat until well blended.

TO ASSEMBLE

1. Remove cake layers from freezer, spread filling between layers. Spread butter icing over entire cake. Don't worry if crumbs show through. The next step will cover them.

2. Drizzle melted chocolate all over top and sides of cake in a criss-cross random fashion. Refrigerate until 30 minutes before serving.

Yield: 8-10 servings

"Youth and beauty are fleeting, but the ability to bake a good chocolate cake lasts forever."
~CHRIS BROWNE, *Hagar the Horrible*

Desserts

CREAM CHEESE POUND CAKE

Put your other pound cake recipes to the back of the box. This one has the finest texture and the most perfect balance of flavors we have ever encountered.

1 (8-ounce) package cream cheese, softened	3 cups all-purpose flour
3 sticks unsalted butter, softened	1 teaspoon vanilla
3 cups sugar	1 teaspoon lemon zest
6 eggs	Powdered sugar for garnish

1. Preheat oven to 325 degrees. Beat cream cheese and butter with an electric mixer until fluffy. Add sugar and beat until creamy.
2. Add eggs and flour alternately, beating well after each addition, ending with flour. Add vanilla and zest.
3. Pour batter into a buttered Bundt pan. Bake 1 hour, 30 minutes. Do not open oven door while baking. Cool 15 to 20 minutes in pan. Invert onto a platter and cool completely. Dust with powdered sugar.

Yield: 12-15 servings

Variation: 1 tablespoon orange zest may be substituted for the lemon zest.

"The most dangerous food is wedding cake."
~AMERICAN PROVERB

MOLTEN CHOCOLATE CAKE

1 stick unsalted butter, plus additional for molds	2 large eggs
2 teaspoons all-purpose flour, plus additional for molds	2 large eggs, separated
4 ounces bittersweet chocolate, preferable Valrhona	¼ cup sugar

1. Preheat oven to 450 degrees
2. Butter and lightly flour 4 (4-ounce) molds, ramekins, or custard cups. Tap out excess flour; butter and flour them again. Set aside.
3. Melt butter and chocolate in the top of a double boiler or heat-proof bowl set over simmering water.
4. Beat eggs, yolks and sugar until light and fluffy. Add melted chocolate, beat to combine; quickly fold in 2 teaspoons flour.
5. Whip the egg whites until soft peaks form and fold them into the chocolate mixture. Divide the batter evenly among the molds.
6. Place filled molds on a baking sheet and bake until the sides have set, but the centers remain shiny and soft, about 6 to 7 minutes. Invert each mold onto a serving plate and let rest 10 seconds. Unmold by lifting up the side of a mold; serve immediately.

Yield: 4 servings

~ THE READING COUNTRY CLUB, READING, PENNSYLVANIA~
~JEAN-MAURICE JUGÉ, EXECUTIVE CHEF ~
~MITCH MARRON, GENERAL MANAGER~

ALMOND APRICOT POUND CAKE

 Just reading the list of ingredients in this recipe should excite the palate-and the taste is fabulous! Use a decorative Bundt pan for a beautiful presentation.

1½ cups blanched almonds, lightly toasted
3 tablespoons sugar
2 sticks unsalted butter, softened
3 cups sugar
4 ounces almond paste, softened
6 large eggs, room temperature
2 teaspoons almond extract
1½ teaspoons vanilla
¼ cup amaretto

¼ cup apricot brandy
2¼ cups all-purpose flour
½ cup cake flour, sifted
¾ teaspoon salt
½ teaspoon baking soda
1 cup full fat sour cream
1 cup chopped dried California apricots, tossed
   with ¼ cup flour

1. Preheat oven to 325 degrees. Grease and flour a 10-inch tube or decorative Bundt pan, tapping out excess. If using a decorative pan, there may be an excess of batter.

2. Process almonds and sugar in a food processor until finely ground. Set aside.

3. Cream butter and sugar with electric mixer 3 to 4 minutes until fluffy. Add almond paste and blend well.

4. Add eggs, one at a time, beating well after each addition. Beat in almond extract, vanilla, amaretto, and brandy.

5. Sift together flours, salt, and baking soda. Add flour mixture, alternately with sour cream, to creamed batter in three batches, beginning and ending with dry ingredients.

6. Fold in apricots and reserved ground nuts. Pour batter into prepared pan, smoothing top. Bake 1 hour, 30 minutes to 1 hour, 45 minutes or until cake tester comes out with moist crumbs attached.

7. Cool 15 minutes in pan. Run a knife around outside and center tube. Invert onto a wire rack. Cool completely before serving.

Yield: 16-20 servings

 Tip: If a recipe calls for cake flour, sift regular flour several times and use 2 tablespoons less per cup required.

 Tip: A quick and easy way to fill a tube pan without worring about batter dropping through the tube is to prepare the pan and then cover the tube opening with a small paper cup.

"Here will we sit, and let the sounds of music
creep in our ears. Soft stillness and the night
become the touches of sweet harmony."
~WILLIAM SHAKESPEARE, *The Merchant of Venice*

Desserts

AUSTRIAN 6-LAYER TORTE

This cake employs an unusual technique. The cake and the meringue layers are baked together! This easy to make cake makes a fabulous visual impression, is delicious to eat, and light enough to follow any holiday meal.

1 stick unsalted butter, softened

1½ cups sugar

4 eggs, separated

1 cup all-purpose flour

1 tablespoon baking powder

5 tablespoons milk

1 teaspoon vanilla

½ cup heavy cream, whipped

1 cup fresh strawberries or raspberries or 1 cup cooked, sweetened puréed dried apricots

1. Preheat oven to 350 degrees. Cream butter and ½ cup sugar. Add egg yolks, flour, baking powder, milk and vanilla. Mix thoroughly.

2. Pour batter into two greased 9-inch round cake pans with parchment paper on the bottom.

3. Beat egg whites until foamy. Gradually add remaining sugar. Beat until glossy. Divide meringue and spread over the top of batter.

4. Bake 15 minutes. Reduce heat to 300 degrees and bake an additional 15 minutes. Cool 15 minutes in pans. Carefully remove from pans and cool completely, meringue side up, on wire rack.

5. Place first cake layer on a cake plate, meringue side down. Top with whipped cream and fresh fruit. (If using apricot mixture, spread it on cake layer first and then top with whipped cream.) Place second layer on top with meringue side up.

Yield: 12-15 servings

 Tip: Recipes that call for beating egg whites until stiff are best prepared on dry days. Humidity can drastically affect the stiffness of the whites and their ability to "dry out" as in meringue type of recipes.

BLUEBERRY KUCHEN

The blueberries burst in your mouth in this recipe. The unusual technique is that fresh blueberries are combined with cooked berries for maximum flavor.

1 cup sifted all-purpose flour

Dash of salt

¾ cup sugar, divided

1 stick unsalted butter, chilled and cut into pieces

1 tablespoon white vinegar

2 tablespoons sifted all-purpose flour

½ teaspoon cinnamon

3 cups fresh blueberries, divided

Powdered sugar

1. Preheat oven to 400 degrees. Process 1 cup flour, salt, and 2 tablespoons sugar in a food processor. Add butter pieces. Pulse several times. Add vinegar and pulse until coarse crumbs form.

2. Press mixture into bottom and up sides of a 9-inch springform pan.

3. Combine remaining sugar, 2 tablespoons flour, cinnamon, and 2 cups blueberries. Spoon mixture into crust.

4. Bake 50 minutes to 1 hour. Remove from oven and sprinkle remaining blueberries on top.

5. Cool completely. Dust with powdered sugar and serve.

Yield: 10-12 servings

Desserts

GERMAN APPLE CAKE

We are not sure exactly how this cake got its "German" name, but surmise that it is because variations of this delicious dessert appear all across southeastern Pennsylvania where the Germans arrived in the early 1700's and where the apple crop is abundant.

CAKE

1 cup sugar
1 cup all-purpose flour
4 tablespoons unsalted butter, cut into 4 pieces
1 teaspoon baking powder

1 teaspoon vanilla
1 large egg
4 large crisp, tart-sweet apples, peeled and thinly
    sliced

1. Preheat oven to 350 degrees. Process sugar, flour, butter, egg, baking powder, and vanilla in food processor until mixture resembles cornmeal. Press into the bottom of a 9-inch springform pan.

2. Arrange apple slices in layers over crumb mixture. Bake 45 minutes.

TOPPING

3 tablespoons sugar
3 tablespoons unsalted butter, melted

1 teaspoon cinnamon
1 large egg

1. Process sugar, butter, cinnamon, and egg in food processor until smooth and sugar dissolves. Spoon mixture over apples and bake 25 to 30 minutes until top is firm.

Yield: 15 servings

"Already too loud!"
~BRUNO WALTER, *at his first rehearsal with an American orchestra, on seeing the musicians reach for their instruments.*

Desserts

APPLE CAKE

Hidden under the apple topping is a surprise cream cheese center, making this apple tart a standout. Pick a crunchy New England apple to feature in this tasty cake.

CRUST

1 stick unsalted butter, softened

⅓ cup sugar

¼ teaspoon vanilla

1 cup all-purpose flour

1. Cream butter, sugar, and vanilla. Blend in flour. Press crumbs into bottom of a 9-inch springform pan.

FILLING

1 (8-ounce) package cream cheese, softened

¼ cup sugar

1 egg

½ teaspoon vanilla

1. Beat cream cheese and sugar until smooth. Stir in egg and vanilla. Mix thoroughly.

2. Pour filling over crust.

TOPPING

⅓ cup sugar

½ teaspoon cinnamon

4 cups peeled and thinly sliced firm, tart-sweet apples

¼ cup sliced almonds

1. Preheat oven to 450 degrees. Combine sugar, cinnamon, and apples. Spoon over filling. Sprinkle with almonds.

2. Bake 10 minutes. Reduce heat to 400 degrees and bake an additional 25 minutes. Cool completely before removing sides of pan.

Yield: 8-10 servings

I may not be healthy or wealthy or wise;
I may not have dreamy, mysterious eyes;
I may not wear clothes from a French fashion book;
But I'm never lonely, for boy, can I cook!

~ANONYMOUS

You be the judge of which of these next four flourless, sinfully rich, silky cakes you prefer. We defy you to pick a favorite. They are each unique and so extraordinary, the committee could not decide so we have included them all.

CHOCOLATE MOUSSE CAKE WITH RASPBERRIES

Firm on the outside, fudge-y and gooey on the inside, complemented by raspberries—sheer bliss!

1 cup sugar

4 sticks unsalted butter

1 cup water

1 teaspoon instant espresso powder (optional)

2 (8-ounce) packages semi-sweet chocolate

8 eggs, slightly beaten

½ cup chilled heavy cream

1 tablespoon powdered sugar

Raspberries for garnish

1. Preheat oven to 350 degrees. Combine sugar, butter, water, espresso, and chocolate in a 3-quart saucepan. Cook, stirring constantly, over low heat until smooth.

2. Remove from heat and quickly stir in eggs. Pour batter into a greased 9-inch springform pan.

3. Bake 45 to 50 minutes or until cake tester comes out clean. Cool completely. Remove sides of pan and place on serving platter. Cover and refrigerate at least 4 hours but no longer than 24 hours.

4. Beat cream and powdered sugar just before serving. Decorate cake with whipped cream and raspberries.

Yield: 12-15 servings

Desserts

PALFY TORTE

 Mousse and soufflé in a single pan, this torte of Austrian origin, is light as air and uses the same batter to create both layers. Quite a trick!

7 ounces semi-sweet chocolate
1 stick unsalted butter
¾ cup sugar

7 eggs, separated
¼ cup sugar
Whipped topping and chocolate shavings

1. Preheat oven to 325 degrees. Melt chocolate and butter over low heat. Add sugar and egg yolks. Beat 3 minutes. Remove from heat.

2. Beat egg whites with sugar until stiff. Fold into chocolate mixture.

3. Pour three-fourths batter into an ungreased 9-inch springform pan. Bake 35 minutes. Let torte cool and fall.

4. Remove sides of pan and pour remaining batter over top. Refrigerate. Garnish with whipped topping and chocolate shavings.

Yield: 12-15 servings

"Music…the favorite passion of my soul."
~THOMAS JEFFERSON

PILAR'S MIDNIGHT MAGIC

Our source in Spain has never shared the secret of this ultimate flourless cake that is as black as night and tastes like chocolate nirvana.

4 ounces prepared espresso or other strong coffee
1 cup sugar
7 ounces European bittersweet chocolate
1½ sticks unsalted butter

4 eggs, slightly beaten
1 tablespoon all-purpose flour
1½ teaspoons vanilla
Whipped topping for garnish

1. Preheat oven to 375 degrees. Heat coffee, sugar, and chocolate over low heat, stirring constantly, until chocolate melts.

2. Remove from heat. Whisk in butter, one tablespoon at a time, until well blended. Add eggs, flour, and vanilla. Mix thoroughly.

3. Butter an 8-inch springform pan. Line the pan by placing two aluminum strips, 12-inches wide and 16-inches long, criss-crossing the bottom and up the sides of pan.

4. Pour batter into prepared pan. Place inside larger baking dish and fill with water to 1-inch depth. Bake 45 minutes.

5. Remove cake pan from water bath and return to oven for an additional 25 to 30 minutes. The cake will rise quite a bit.

6. Place cake under broiler until small blisters form on top. Watch cake closely. Remove from oven and cool completely. The cake will fall and be quite flat. To serve, invert cake, remove foil, and re-invert on a serving plate. Can be made a day ahead of time. Garnish with whipped topping.

Yield: 12-15 servings

BITTERSWEET APRICOT-WALNUT TORTE

 If you love the combination of chocolate and apricots, this dense, rich cake flavored with Grand Marnier is for you. A chocolate glaze adds a glorious finishing touch.

1 cup finely chopped dried California apricots	1 cup finely chopped toasted walnuts
¼ cup Grand Marnier or other orange flavored liqueur	4 tablespoons butter
	6 ounces bittersweet or semi-sweet chocolate
1 stick unsalted butter	1 tablespoon light corn syrup
8 ounces bittersweet or semi-sweet chocolate	6 dried apricot halves for garnish
3 eggs	6 walnut halves for garnish
¾ cup sugar	½ cup finely chopped toasted walnuts

1. Combine apricots and liqueur in a bowl. Set aside 15 minutes. Grease an 8-inch springform pan. Line bottom with parchment paper. Butter parchment. Dust with flour, tapping our excess.

2. Combine butter and chocolate in a glass bowl. Microwave on high 1½ to 2 minutes, stirring once or twice, until melted and smooth. Set aside.

3. Beat eggs and sugar with an electric mixer 5 minutes until light and thickened. Add chocolate mixture and beat 2 minutes. Stir in walnuts and apricot mixture.

4. Pour batter into prepared pan. Bake at 350 degrees 35 minutes or until cake tester comes out clean. Cool cake in pan.

5. Combine butter and chocolate in a glass bowl. Microwave on high 1 to 1½ minutes until smooth when stirred. Stir in corn syrup. Cool 15 minutes.

6. Run a knife around edge of pan. Remove sides of pan. Invert onto a serving platter. Peel off parchment paper. Spread glaze over top and sides of cake. Decorate edges with apricot and walnut halves. Sprinkle chopped walnuts in the center.

7. Cover and refrigerate until 1 hour before serving.

Yield: 12-15 servings

RASPBERRY SWIRL CHEESECAKE

Easy, delicious and pastry shop pretty, this recipe will quickly become an old stand-by when you are in a hurry and want to impress your guests.

1 (8-ounce) package cream cheese, softened	1 (9-inch) unbaked regular or graham cracker pie crust (see Basic Pie Crust recipe, page 200)
1 (14-ounce) can sweetened condensed milk	
1 egg	½ cup raspberry preserves
3 tablespoons lemon juice	1 teaspoon lemon juice

1. Preheat oven to 300 degrees. Beat cream cheese until fluffy. Gradually beat in milk until smooth.

2. Add egg and lemon juice. Beat until well blended.

3. Pour batter into pie shell. Combine preserves and juice. Drizzle over cheese mixture in 4-5 parallel stripes. Use a knife to swirl, making a decorative pattern.

4. Bake 55 minutes. Cool and refrigerate before serving.

Yield: 6-8 servings

Desserts

PUMPKIN CHEESECAKE

The aroma of this variation on a holiday favorite will make you swoon with anticipation.

CRUST

1½ cups graham cracker crumbs

⅓ cup ground almonds

½ teaspoon ground ginger

½ teaspoon cinnamon

5⅓ tablespoons unsalted butter, melted

1. Preheat oven to 425 degrees.

2. Mix together cracker crumbs, almonds, ginger, cinnamon, and butter. Press into the bottom of a 10-inch springform pan.

3. Bake 10 minutes. Cool slightly.

FILLING

3 (8-ounce) packages cream cheese, softened

1¼ cups sugar

4 eggs

1 cup canned pumpkin

1 teaspoon ground ginger

1 teaspoon cinnamon

¼ teaspoon ground cloves

3 tablespoons brandy

3 tablespoons maple syrup

¼ cup heavy cream

1. Lower oven to 325 degrees.

2. Beat cream cheese and sugar until fluffy. Add eggs, one at a time, beating well after each addition. Add pumpkin.

3. Stir in ginger, cinnamon, and cloves. Add brandy, syrup, and cream. Mix thoroughly.

4. Pour mixture over crust. Bake 45 minutes or until cake tester comes out clean.

TOPPING

2 cups full-fat sour cream

¼ cup sugar

1 tablespoon maple syrup

1 tablespoon brandy

1 egg, beaten

2 tablespoons butter, melted

½ cup slivered almonds

1. Raise oven to 425 degrees.

2. Combine sour cream, sugar, maple syrup, brandy, and egg. Mix until well blended. Pour over cheesecake.

3. Bake 10 minutes. Cool completely.

4. Combine butter and almonds. Toast in oven until lightly browned. Spoon around edge of cake.

Yield: 10-12 servings

~OLEY VALLEY INN, OLEY, PENNSYLVANIA~

~STEVEN YEANISH, OWNER AND EXECUTIVE CHEF~

Tip: If you can't find the cake tester, you can improvise one with a strand of spaghetti.

CHOCOLATE ESPRESSO CHEESECAKE

 The combination of chocolate and coffee is a culinary marriage made in heaven. Prepare the cheesecake a day before serving so the flavors have time to blend.

CHOCOLATE CRUST
24 chocolate wafers, finely crushed
4 tablespoons unsalted butter, softened
¼ teaspoon cinnamon

1. Combine chocolate crumbs, butter, and cinnamon.

2. Press into an ungreased 9-inch springform pan. Set aside.

"There's only two ways to sum up music: either it's good or it's bad. If it's good, you don't mess with it, you just enjoy it."
~LOUIS ARMSTRONG

FILLING
4 tablespoons ground espresso coffee
⅔ cup boiling water
3 (8-ounce) packages cream cheese, softened
1 cup sugar
2 eggs

1 cup full-fat sour cream
8 ounces semi-sweet chocolate, melted
1 teaspoon vanilla
Chocolate curls for garnish

1. Preheat oven to 350 degrees. Brew a strong extract of espresso with water in a coffeemaker or place espresso in a cheesecloth-lined strainer over a bowl. Moisten with boiling water and squeeze to extract the concentrate. Measure ½ cup extract and set aside to cool.

2. Beat cream cheese, sugar, and eggs until smooth. Mix in sour cream, chocolate, espresso concentrate, and vanilla.

3. Pour mixture over crust. Bake 45 minutes, or until almost set. Center will appear soft. Cool and refrigerate until center is firm.

4. Remove sides of pan. Top with chocolate curls.

Yield: 10-12 servings

After playing the violin for the world famous cellist Gregor Piatigorsky, Albert Einstein asked, "Did I play well?" "You played relatively well" replied Piatigorsky.

Desserts

BASIC PIE CRUST

 Use for savory or sweet filling. You will swear off prepared crusts forever, once you have tried this speedy recipe. And all you have to clean up is a fork, a spoon and a measuring cup.

1½ cups all-purpose flour
2 teaspoons sugar (eliminate for savory fillings)
2 tablespoons milk

Dash of salt
½ cup vegetable oil

1. Combine flour, sugar, milk, salt, and oil a 9-inch pie plate. Mix thoroughly with a fork until dough comes together.

2. Pat into the bottom and up sides of the plate. Flute edges for a decorative design.

Yield: 1 (9-inch) pie crust

"The popular song is America's greatest ambassador."
~SAMMY CAHN

PERFECT PUMPKIN PIE

One of the most glorious sights on a late October day, especially in Connecticut or Pennsylvania, is to drive by a field of fully ripe pumpkins. The bright orange globes against the backdrop of fall foliage are truly one of nature's most colorful displays. While these "jack-o-lanterns in waiting" are a visual feast and delight youngsters who carve them into Halloween centerpieces, sadly they are not good candidates for pie making as their flesh is watery and stringy. In colonial times, settlers would prepare pumpkins by slicing off the tops, filling the hollow with milk and honey and then burying it in a bed of hot ashes to bake. Today several varieties are cultivated for their creamy and dense flesh and are perfect as the prime ingredient for inclusion in pies, other desserts and soups.

1 (¼-ounce) envelope unflavored gelatin
¼ cup cold water
3 eggs, separated
¾ cup packed brown sugar
1½ cups canned pumpkin
½ cup milk or half-and-half or ¼ cup milk and
    ¼ cup rum

¼ teaspoon salt
1 teaspoon cinnamon
½ teaspoon nutmeg
¼ cup sugar
1 (9-inch) pie crust, baked and cooled
    (see Basic Pie Crust recipe, page 200)
Whipped topping for garnish (optional)

1. Soak gelatin in cold water until softened. Combine egg yolks, brown sugar, pumpkin, milk, salt, cinnamon, and nutmeg in top of double boiler. Cook and stir until thickened.

2. Add gelatin and stir until dissolved. Cool 45 minutes until mixture drops from spoon.

3. Beat egg whites and sugar until stiff. Fold pumpkin mixture into egg whites. Pour filling into prepared pie crust. Chill until set and garnish with whipped topping.

Yield: 6-8 servings

Desserts

GEORGE WASHINGTON'S FAVORITE CHERRY PIE

George himself would surely approve of this unusual cherry pie. The lemon juice "clots" the condensed milk to make an easy, luscious no-bake dessert. Try the Lemon-Crunch version for a delicious and easy variation.

CRUST
1 Basic Pie Crust recipe from page 200
½ cup finely chopped almonds

1. Preheat oven to 400 degrees. Make crust according to directions, adding the almonds to the dough.

2. Bake 10 minutes, or until golden brown. Cool completely.

FILLING
1 (14 ounce) can sweetened condensed milk
Juice of three lemons
Zest of one lemon
½ teaspoon almond extract
½ cup heavy cream, whipped

1. Combine milk, lemon juice, zest, and almond extract, stirring constantly until thickened. Fold in whipped cream.

2. Pour mixture into prepared pie crust. Refrigerate for several hours.

CHERRY TOPPING
1 (14 ounce) can pitted sour pie cherries, drained, reserving juice
¼ cup sugar
1 tablespoon cornstarch
⅔ cup juice from the cherries
2 drops red food coloring

1. Combine sugar, cornstarch, and reserved juice in a saucepan. Cook over medium heat, stirring until thick and clear. Fold in cherries and food coloring. Cool to room temperature. Pour over filling and refrigerate until ready to serve.

Yield: 6-8 servings

Variation: To make LEMON CRUNCH PIE, make a pie crust by combining 1½ cups ground gingersnap cookies and 1 stick unsalted butter, melted, until crumbs form. Pat evenly into a 9-inch pie plate and bake for 10 minutes at 400 degrees. Cool and fill with the Filling Recipe above, omitting the almond extract. Chill until ready to serve.

Desserts

PEACHY PEACH PIE

The almond extract in the moist cake-like topping enhances the flavor of the peaches. New Jersey peaches will make this dish a delight.

6-8 peeled and sliced peaches
5⅓ tablespoons unsalted butter, melted
⅓ cup all-purpose flour
½ teaspoon baking powder
Dash of salt
¾ cup sugar

1 egg
1 teaspoon vanilla
2-3 drops almond extract
1 (9-inch) pie crust, unbaked
    (see Basic Pie Crust recipe, page 200)

1. Preheat oven to 400 degrees. Arrange peaches in pie crust. Combine butter, flour, baking powder, salt, sugar, egg, vanilla, and almond extract. Mix thoroughly. Pour over peaches.

2. Bake 15 minutes. Reduce heat to 300 degrees and bake an additional 45 minutes. Cover the crust if it browns too quickly.

Yield: 6-8 servings

"What is the musician's calling? Is it not to send light into the deep recesses of the human heart?."
~ROBERT SCHUMANN

BUTTERMILK COCONUT PIE

A cross between cream and custard, this is one recipe you will want to put in your repertoire of special desserts.

3 tablespoons unsalted butter, softened
1¼ cups sugar
3 eggs
1 tablespoon all-purpose flour
½ cup buttermilk

1 teaspoon vanilla
3 cups flaked coconut
1 prepared 9-inch pie crust
    (see Basic Pie Crust recipe, page 200)

1. Preheat oven to 300 degrees. Cream butter and sugar until light and fluffy. Stir in eggs, flour, buttermilk, vanilla, and coconut.

2. Pour mixture into pie crust. Bake 45 minutes or until knife comes out clean when inserted in center. Cool before serving.

Yield: 6-8 servings

BOSTON CREAM PIE

Originally called "Boston Pie" in the early nineteenth century, this confection consisted of a plain two layer sponge cake filled with a vanilla custard. In 1855, the German-born pastry chef of Boston's famous Parker House added a luscious chocolate glaze and the dessert now known as Boston Cream Pie was created. The fact that it is not a pie, but a cake, troubles not the folks of Boston, who brush off this observation with a "Who cares? It is delicious and that's all that matters."

CAKE

1 cup milk

3 tablespoons unsalted butter

4 eggs

1 teaspoon vanilla dash of salt

2 cups sugar

2 cups all-purpose flour

2 teaspoons baking powder

1. Preheat oven to 350 degrees. Scald milk and butter and set aside. Beat eggs with vanilla. Stir in salt, sugar, flour and baking powder.

2. Add milk mixture to creamed mixture. Pour into two greased and floured 9-inch round cake pans.

3. Bake for 22 to 25 minutes or until the sides begin to pull away from the pan. Turn cakes out onto cake racks to cool.

CUSTARD FILLING

½ cup light cream

½ cup milk

¼ cup sugar

Pinch of salt

4 teaspoons cornstarch

2 eggs, lightly beaten

½ teaspoon vanilla

1. Warm cream and ¼ cup milk in a heavy saucepan over moderate heat. When bubbles begin to form on the edge of the pan, add the sugar and pinch of salt, stirring until the sugar is dissolved.

2. Combine the remaining milk with the cornstarch, whisking until smooth. Add the eggs and, stirring constantly, pour in the warm cream-milk mixture in a slow, thin stream. Cook over low heat, stirring all the while until the custard thickens and is smooth. Remove from heat as over-cooking will cause it to become lumpy. Add the vanilla and cool.

CHOCOLATE GLAZE

3 (1-ounce) squares semi-sweet chocolate, cut into small bits

2 tablespoons unsalted butter

¼ cup light cream

½ cup confectioners' sugar

½ teaspoon vanilla

1. Melt chocolate and butter in a medium-sized, heavy saucepan, stirring until smooth. Remove from heat and continuing to stir, pour in the cream in a thin, steady stream.

2. Sift the confectioners' sugar over the top and beat vigorously for a minute or two. Add the vanilla.

ASSEMBLY

1. Place one layer of the cake, upside down on a serving plate, and with a spatula, spread the top evenly with the cooled custard.

2. Set the second layer, also upside down, over the custard. Use toothpicks temporarily to hold everything in place, if necessary.

3. Pour the glaze over the top, spreading it evenly and allowing it to dribble down the sides of the cake. Refrigerate. Remove 30 minutes before serving.

Yield: 8-10 servings

Desserts

BERRY BLUEBERRY CREAM PIE

New England or New Jersey blueberries are everyones favorite and this recipe treats them in a very special way.

¾ cup sugar

3 tablespoons cornstarch

Dash of salt

1 tablespoon lemon juice

4 cups blueberries, divided

1 tablespoon butter

1 cup heavy cream

2 teaspoons sugar

¼ teaspoon vanilla

1 (9-inch) pie crust, baked and cooled
   (see Basic Pie Crust recipe, page 200)

1. Combine sugar, cornstarch, salt, lemon juice, and 1½ cups blueberries in a saucepan. Cook and stir 4 to 5 minutes until thickened and a jam-like consistency.

2. Stir in butter and remaining blueberries. Pour into crust and refrigerate until set.

3. Beat cream with sugar and vanilla until stiff. Top pie when ready to serve.

Yield: 6-8 servings

SHOOFLY PIE

This cake-like pie, with a name that has much lore attached to it, may have its roots in the early bake-ovens of Pennsylvania. Dense cakes with heavy dough were put into the ovens following the weekly bread baking. This hybrid cake within a pie shell is the signature dish at every Amish farm table, with partisans for "wet" and "dry" bottom competing for top honors. Another variation, Montgomery Pie, adds a subtle mix of spices. We hope this version satisfies all camps.

1 cup all-purpose flour

⅔ cup packed light brown sugar

1 tablespoon vegetable shortening

1 egg, slightly beaten

1 cup light molasses or golden syrup

1 cup boiling water

1 teaspoon baking soda

1 (9-inch) pie crust, unbaked
   (see Basic Pie Crust recipe, 200)

1. Preheat oven to 425 degrees. Mix flour and sugar. Cut in shortening. Remove ½ cup crumbs and set aside.

2. Add egg and molasses to remaining crumbs. Stir in ¾ boiling cup water. Whisk ¼ cup water with baking soda. Add to crumb mixture.

3. Pour mixture into pie crust. Sprinkle reserved crumbs on top. Bake 15 minutes.

4. Reduce heat to 350 degrees and bake an additional 40 to 45 minutes.

Yield: 6-8 servings

♪ Variation: MONTGOMERY PIE: add ½ teaspoon cinnamon, ⅛ teaspoon each of ground nutmeg, ground ginger, and ground cloves to crumb mixture in step 1.

PAPER BAG APPLE PIE

Aren't you a bit curious about the title of this recipe? Check out the unique baking technique.

½ cup sugar

2 tablespoons all-purpose flour

½ teaspoon nutmeg

4 large New England variety or other juicy but tart and firm apples, peeled, and cut into chunks

1 (9-inch) pie crust, unbaked (see Basic Pie Crust recipe, page 200)

2 tablespoons lemon juice

½ cup sugar

½ cup all-purpose flour

2 sticks butter

1. Preheat oven to 425 degrees. Combine sugar, flour, and nutmeg. Add apples and toss to coat. Spoon into prepared pie crust. Sprinkle with lemon juice.

2. Mix together sugar and flour. Cut in butter using two knives until mixture resembles coarse cornmeal. Spoon evenly over apples.

3. Place pie in a large brown paper bag. Fold end and fasten with paper clips. Place bag on a baking sheet. Bake 1 hour.

Yield: 6-8 servings

"Apple pie without cheese is like a kiss without a squeeze."
~NEW ENGLAND SAYING

Desserts

ANDIE'S BROWNIES

You will never make box brownies again! These super easy, super chocolate-y brownies will become favorites after the first bite.

4 ounces unsweetened chocolate

2 sticks unsalted butter

1 cup all-purpose flour

2 cups sugar

2 teaspoons vanilla

4 eggs, beaten

1. Preheat oven to 325 degrees. Melt chocolate and butter in a double boiler or microwave. Stir in flour, sugar, vanilla, and eggs. Mix thoroughly.

2. Pour batter into a well greased 13x9x2-inch glass baking dish. Bake 30 minutes.

Yield: 15-20 servings

Tip: These brownies are extremely decadent, and therefore this recipe can serve a large number of guests. Serve with whipped topping, ice cream or fresh berries.

LAYERED CHOCOLATE BAR COOKIES

The Mainstay Inn and Cottage in Cape May, New Jersey was built as an exclusive gentlemen's gambling club in 1872. Sparing no expense, the elegant Victorian mansion featured towering fourteen-foot ceilings, sparkling crystal chandeliers, ornate walnut carvings, and flamboyant furnishings. Many of these relics of its former life remain and the original Victorian atmosphere is preserved today as the Mainstay flourishes as a splendid historic Inn. Guests who indulge in four o'clock tea are treated to many temptations, often including something delicious and sweet. This recipe, which has many variations, should satisfy anyone's sweet tooth.

1¾ cups all-purpose flour

1½ cups confectioners' sugar

½ cup cocoa

1 cup (two sticks) cold unsalted butter

1 (8-ounce) package cream cheese, softened

1 (14-ounce) can sweetened condensed milk

1 egg

2 teaspoons vanilla extract

½ cup semi-sweet chocolate morsels

½ cup chopped walnuts

1. Preheat oven to 350 degrees. Combine flour, sugar, cocoa in the bowl of the food processor. Cut the butter into chunks and put in the bowl. Pulse until crumbs form.

2. Set aside 2 cups and press the remaining mixture into the bottom of a greased 9x13x2-inch baking dish. Bake for 13 minutes.

3. Beat the cream cheese until fluffy, then add the milk, egg, and the vanilla. Fold in the chocolate morsels and pour over the baked crust.

4. Add the walnuts to the reserved crumbs and sprinkle over the batter. Bake for 20 minutes or until bubbly. Cool, cover and chill. Cut into bars and serve.

Yield: about 20 bars

Desserts

KEY LIME COCONUT BARS

 The toasted coconut adds a wonderful texture to these cool, creamy citrus-y delights.

1 cup shredded sweetened coconut, divided
1½ cups all-purpose flour
½ cup powdered sugar
10 tablespoons unsalted butter, cut into small
   pieces

6 large egg yolks
2 (14-ounce) cans sweetened condensed milk
4 teaspoons Key lime or regular lime zest
1 cup Key lime or regular lime juice
Powdered sugar and zest for garnish

1. Preheat oven to 350 degrees. Spread coconut in a rimmed baking sheet. Toast, tossing every 2 minutes, 6 to 8 minutes until golden brown. Transfer to a plate to cool.

2. Combine flour, sugar, and ½ cup toasted coconut. Cut in butter until mixture resembles coarse meal. Press mixture in the bottom of a 13x9x2-inch baking dish. Bake 20 to 25 minutes until golden brown. Cool slightly.

3. Whisk together egg yolks and milk until thickened. Add zest and lime juice. Pour over cooled crust. Sprinkle with remaining coconut.

4. Bake 6 to 8 minutes. Cool completely. Refrigerate until ready to serve. Cut into six 2⅓-inch rows. Cut rows on a diagonal to form diamonds. Dust with powdered sugar and additional zest.

Yield: 24 bars

"Through music we may wander where we will in time, and find friends in every century."
~HELEN THOMSON

MATRIMONIAL BLISS

 While we offer no guarantees, as the title implies, we have seen many a blissful smile following a bite of this delicious, super-sweet bar cookie.

1 cup all-purpose flour
2 tablespoons powdered sugar
1 stick unsalted butter
2 eggs, beaten
1¼ cups packed brown sugar
2 tablespoons all-purpose flour
1 cup chopped walnuts

½ teaspoon baking powder
1 teaspoon vanilla
5⅓ tablespoons unsalted butter, softened
3 cups sifted powdered sugar
3 tablespoons heavy cream or milk
1½ teaspoons vanilla

1. Preheat oven to 350 degrees. Combine flour and sugar in a bowl. Cut in butter with knives until mixture resembles coarse crumbs. Press into the bottom of a greased and floured 11x7x2-inch baking dish.

2. Whisk together eggs, brown sugar, flour, walnuts, baking powder, and vanilla. Pour over crust.

3. Bake 30 minutes. Cool completely.

4. Cream butter and powdered sugar until smooth. Blend in milk and vanilla. Spread frosting over bar cookie. Cut into small squares when ready to serve.

Yield: 12 servings

Desserts

TROPICAL PARADISE BARS

 Picture yourself on a sunny island, enjoying these sugary, lemony, chewy treats.

CRUST
2 sticks unsalted butter, softened
1 cup packed dark brown sugar
2 cups all-purpose flour

1. Preheat oven to 350 degrees. Cream butter and brown sugar. Stir in flour. Press into the bottom of a greased 13x9x2-inch baking dish.
2. Bake 10 to 15 minutes.

FILLING
2 eggs, slightly beaten
1½ cups packed light brown sugar
½ cup flaked coconut
¼ teaspoon salt

1 teaspoon vanilla
1 cup chopped pecans
2 tablespoons all-purpose flour
½ teaspoon baking powder

1. Whisk together eggs and brown sugar. Add coconut, salt, vanilla, pecans, flour, and baking powder. Mix well.
2. Spread over hot crust. Bake 20 to 25 minutes.

GLAZE
1¼ cups powdered sugar
Juice of one lemon

1. Whisk powdered sugar and juice. If glaze is too thick, thin with more juice to reach spreading consistency.
2. Spread over warm baked filling. Cut into squares when cool.

Yield: 24-36 squares

Tip: To soften brown sugar, place a cup or so in a glass pie plate or bowl, cover with a small piece of waxed paper and then top with a slice of bread. Loosely cover the plate with plastic wrap and microwave for 20 to 30 seconds or until soft.

"Seize the moment. Remember all those women on the 'Titanic' who waved off the dessert cart."
~ERMA BOMBECK

PISTACHIO AND CHOCOLATE BISCOTTI

 These twice-baked Italian delights are a traditional dipping cookie. Tuscans enjoy dipping in wine (vin Santo) and Sicilians with coffee (café latté). I like them as an ice cream accompaniment. Choose your passion.

1 stick unsalted butter, softened	2 teaspoons baking powder
½ cup sugar	¼ teaspoon salt
3 eggs, separated	½ cup plus 2 tablespoons sugar
1½ teaspoons vanilla	1¼ cups shelled whole pistachio nuts
2 teaspoons lemon zest	⅓-½ cup semi-sweet chocolate morsels
3 cups all-purpose flour	

1. Preheat oven to 325 degrees. Cream butter and sugar until light and fluffy. Beat in egg yolks, vanilla, and zest.

2. Combine flour, baking powder, and salt. Stir into creamed mixture until just crumbly.

3. Beat egg whites until soft peaks form. Add sugar and beat until stiff but not dry. Fold meringue into dough mixture. Fold in nuts and chocolate morsels.

4. Divide dough in half. Shape dough into two logs, 1-2-inches thick, 1½-inches wide and 16-inches long. Place on a greased and floured baking sheet 2-inches apart.

5. Bake 25 to 30 minutes or until golden brown and firm. Cool 5 minutes on a rack. Place on a cutting board. Slice diagonally with a serrated knife into ½-inch slices. Place slices upright on a baking sheet. Return to oven and bake at 300 degrees 10 to 15 minutes until slightly dry. Cool on a rack. (See tip below.)

Yield: 4 dozen

Tip: Traditionally, biscotti (the Italian word for "cooked twice") are baked in a log, then cut into slices and baked a second time. The slices must be flipped halfway through the second baking. Instead, bake the log as usual and cut into slices. Place the slices on a wire rack set on a cookie sheet and bake again. The elevation of the rack allows the air to circulate and dry all sides at once.

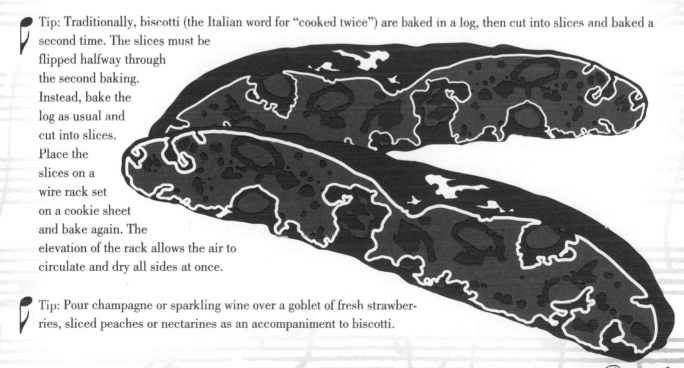

Tip: Pour champagne or sparkling wine over a goblet of fresh strawberries, sliced peaches or nectarines as an accompaniment to biscotti.

Desserts

POTATO CHIP COOKIES

Yes, you read correctly! These buttery shortbread cookies have a subtle crunch, due to the generous addition of crushed potato chips. From the heart of potato chip country, here is a recipe that uses them in a surprising, delicious way.

2 sticks unsalted butter, softened
1 cup vegetable shortening
1½ cups sugar
1 tablespoon vanilla

2 egg yolks
4 cups sifted all-purpose flour
2 cups coarsely crushed potato chips

1. Preheat oven to 350 degrees.

2. Cream butter, shortening, and sugar until smooth. Add vanilla and egg yolks. Mix well.

3. Add flour in batches, beating well after each addition. Blend in potato chips.

4. Drop dough by teaspoonfuls on a lightly greased baking sheet. Bake 12 to 15 minutes until lightly browned on the bottom. Remove and cool on racks.

Yield: 6-8 dozen cookies

Tip: Dough may also be refrigerated for up to several days and baked later. Roll chilled dough into small balls.

Tip: Use a small ice cream scoop to measure out cookie dough. Dip the scoop in cold water between scooping to ensure easy release.

SUSPIROS

From the early Portuguese colonists who settled in Rhode Island, these light-as-air "Sighs" (translation of Suspiro) are a delightful sweet to accompany fresh fruit, ice cream or afternoon tea.

1 tablespoon unsalted butter, softened
3 egg whites
¾ cup sugar
⅛ teaspoon vanilla extract

½ teaspoon lemon juice
1 teaspoon grated lemon rind
1 cup slivered blanched almonds

1. Preheat the oven to 250 degrees. Prepare two cookie sheets by lightly coating them with the softened butter.

2. Beat the egg whites in a large mixing bowl with the whisk attachment until they begin to froth. Gradually add the sugar and continue to beat until the whites form stiff peaks.

3. Fold in the lemon juice, zest and almonds using an over-and-under motion rather than stirring.

4. Drop the meringue by the teaspoonful onto the buttered sheet, leaving about 1 inch between each mound.

5. Bake in the center of the oven for 40 minutes, then transfer the cookies to wire racks to cool to room temperature.

Yield: about 4 dozen cookies

Tip: Recipes that call for beating egg whites until stiff are best prepared on dry days. Humidity can drastically effect the stiffness of the whites and their ability to "dry out" in meringue type recipes.

SARAH BERNHARDTS

We do not know how they got their glamorous name, but these extraordinary beauties, part truffle, and part macaroon, are worth the tiny extra effort they require.

MACAROONS

1 (8-ounce) can or tube of almond paste

½ cup sugar

2 large egg whites

¼ teaspoon almond extract

Dash of salt

1. Preheat oven to 350 degrees. Line three baking sheets with foil. Beat almond paste, sugar, egg whites, almond extract, and salt with an electric mixer until smooth. Increase speed to high for 2 minutes.

2. Spoon batter into a pastry bag fitted with a ½-inch plain tip. Pipe ¾-inch rounds onto prepared baking sheets. Bake 10 to 12 minutes until light golden. Cool on racks. Carefully peel cookies from foil. Set aside.

CHOCOLATE FILLING

¾ cup heavy cream

8 ounces semi-sweet chocolate

2 tablespoons unsalted butter

1 teaspoon dark rum

1. Heat cream until just boiling. Remove from heat. Add chocolate, butter, and rum. Cook and stir until smooth. Let stand 40 minutes, stirring occasionally, until mixture reaches a thick consistency.

2. Fit pastry bag with ½-inch plain tip. Spoon in filling and pipe a small mound on the flat side of each macaroon. Return to foil lined sheets and refrigerate 1 hour until firm.

CHOCOLATE GLAZE

8 ounces semi-sweet chocolate, chopped

1 tablespoon vegetable shortening

1. Melt chocolate and shortening in top of double boiler over hot, not boiling water, stirring until smooth. Keep warm.

2. Dip macaroon, filling side down, into chocolate. Place chocolate side up on foil lined sheets. Repeat with remaining cookies. Refrigerate until firm.

Yield: 8 dozen

~ADAPTED FROM THE ST. MORITZ BAKERY~
~GREENWICH, CONNECTICUT~

"There are four basic food groups:
milk chocolate, dark chocolate,
white chocolate, and chocolate truffles."
~ANONYMOUS

Desserts

BACI DI ANGELI (ANGEL'S KISSES)

 *Remember the sweetest kiss you ever had? Here is a heavenly recipe to recall that delicious memory.*

2 ounces semi-sweet chocolate, broken into small
    pieces
1 cup blanched almonds, toasted and very finely
    ground
1 cup shelled hazelnuts, toasted, skinned and very
    finely ground

1½ cups sugar
⅓ cup cocoa powder
2 tablespoons honey
2-3 drops vanilla
3 egg whites
5 ounces semi-sweet chocolate, broken into pieces

1. Preheat oven to 425 degrees. Line several baking sheets with nonstick parchment paper.

2. Melt chocolate in top of double boiler, stirring until smooth.

3. Combine melted chocolate, ground almonds, ground hazelnuts, sugar, cocoa powder, honey, and vanilla in a bowl. Mix well. Add the egg whites and stir until a smooth dough forms.

4. Place dough in a pastry bag fitted with a ¼-inch star or rosette tip. Pipe dough onto parchment paper, making a star or rosette shape about 1-1½ inches in diameter.

5. Bake in batches 8 to 10 minutes or until set and just beginning to brown. Transfer to wire racks to cool.

6. Melt chocolate in top of double boiler. Spread on a thin layer of chocolate to sandwich cookies together in pairs. Let stand until set.

Yield: 36 cookies

Variation: Chocolate may be melted in the microwave at about 30 to 40 seconds intervals, stirring each time. May also roll the dough into balls with your hands and forget the pastry bag!

Tip: These cookies should be stored in an airtight container. The longer they are kept, the chewier they will become.

Tip: When baking cookies on parchment-covered tins, spray the tin with a light coating of cooking spray to keep the sheets from slipping.

"Music is well said to be the speech of angels; in fact nothing among utterances allowed to man is felt to be so divine. It brings us near to the infinite."
~THOMAS CARLYLE

AMARETTI (PINE-NUT ALMOND MACAROONS)

If you have ever longed for those wonderful, chewy, pine nut topped almond cookies that you see only in Italian pastry shops, yearn no more. Here is the authentic and easy recipe.

1 (8-ounce) can almond paste, cut into small pieces
⅔ cup sugar
2 egg whites

1 teaspoon lemon zest
¾ cup pine nuts

1. Preheat oven to 350 degrees. Beat almond paste pieces, sugar, egg whites, and zest with an electric mixer until smooth.

2. Drop dough by teaspoonful 1-inch apart onto a parchment paper-lined baking sheet. Top with pine nuts, pressing lightly into dough.

3. Bake 15 to 20 minutes or until tops are firm and dry when softly touched. Do not overbake. Cookies will be light in color. Cool on the baking sheet on a wire rack.

4. Peel off parchment paper and store in an airtight container.

Yield: 2 dozen cookies

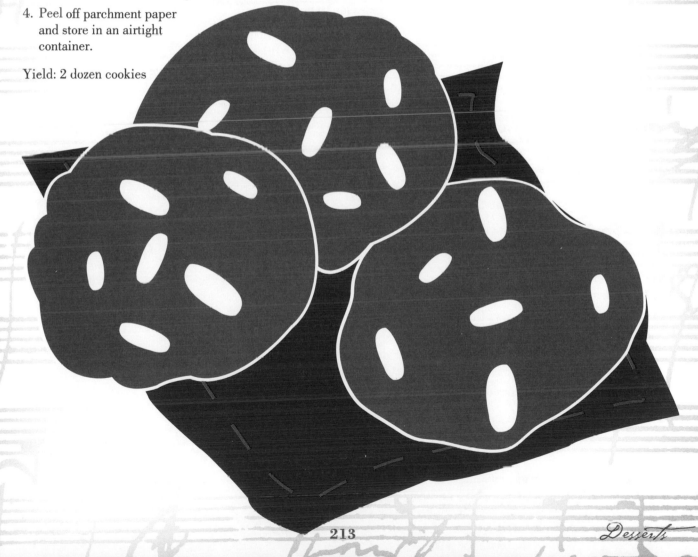

Desserts

SAND TARTS

This recipe for traditional Pennsylvania Dutch Christmas cookies comes to us from a champion cookie baker. For thirteen years, led by octogenarian Mary Norton, the ladies of the Olivet Presbyterian Church in Reading, PA had six-week pre-holiday baking marathons, making thousands of cookies to sell from a 525 pound batch of dough. Wow!

1½ sticks unsalted butter, softened
1 egg, slightly beaten
1½ cups all-purpose flour
1 cup plus 2 tablespoons sugar

3 tablespoons sugar
2 teaspoons cinnamon
2 egg whites, lightly beaten
Pecan halves

1. Cream butter until smooth; add egg. Stir in flour and 1 cup plus 2 tablespoons sugar, mixing until dough forms a ball. Wrap in plastic wrap and refrigerate overnight.

2. Mix 3 tablespoons sugar and cinnamon. Shape dough into small balls and flatten with the palm of your hand or a water glass dipped in sugar. Brush with egg white, dust with sugar-cinnamon mixture and place a pecan half on top.

3. Bake on lightly greased cookie sheets, at 350 degrees for 10 to 12 minutes.

Yield: 8 dozen cookies

> "All I really need is love, but a little chocolate now and then doesn't hurt."
> ~LUCY VAN PELT, "PEANUTS"

CHOCOLATE SALAMI

 Kids love to help make this funky dessert that is both creamy and crunchy. But the enjoyment of eating it is shared equally by young and old.

1½ sticks butter, softened
¾ cup plus 1 tablespoon sugar
2 eggs

7 tablespoons cocoa powder
1 (7-ounce) package Petit Beurre or Social Tea Biscuits, broken into ¾-inch pieces

1. Cream butter with an electric mixer. Add sugar one tablespoon at a time. Add eggs, one at a time, beating well after each addition.

2. Add cocoa one tablespoon at a time. Beat until mixture is smooth and sugar is dissolved. Stir in cookie pieces by hand, coating well.

3. Place dough on a sheet of waxed paper. Shape into a log that is 4-inches in diameter and 12-14 inches long. Make as compact as possible. Wrap salami in waxed paper and then in foil.

4. Freeze at least 6 hours. Remove 10 minutes before serving. Cut into 1-inch slices and serve.

Yield: 10-12 servings

♪ Irish Variation: Add 2-3 tablespoons golden raisins that have been soaked in Irish whiskey and drained.

♪ Variation: If you are uncomfortable using raw eggs, 4-ounces of cream cheese can be substituted. May also press dough into a plastic wrap-lined or foil-lined loaf pan.

CHOCOLATE CRANBERRY COOKIES

What a shame that the early settlers probably did not have chocolate morsels to go with their cranberries. It is such a great combination.

1 cup unsalted butter, softened
1 (3-ounce) package cream cheese, softened
1 cup sugar
1 large egg
2 ounces unsweetened chocolate, melted and
    cooled
2 tablespoons milk
1½ teaspoons vanilla
2 cups plus 2 tablespoons all-purpose flour
½ teaspoon baking powder
½ teaspoon salt
¼ cup cocoa
1 cup marshmallow cream
1 cup chopped pecans
1 (12-ounce) package semi-sweet chocolate morsels
½ cup sweetened dried cranberries

1. Preheat oven to 325 degrees.

2. Beat butter and cream cheese until smooth. Add sugar and beat well. Beat in egg.

3. Stir in chocolate, milk, and vanilla. Combine flour, baking powder, salt, and cocoa. Beat flour mixture into creamed mixture.

4. Add marshmallow cream, pecans, chocolate morsels and cranberries. Mix thoroughly.

5. Drop dough by heaping tablespoonsful onto a lightly greased baking sheet. Bake 15 minutes or until barely done. Cool 1 minute on baking sheet. Remove to rack to cool completely.

Yield: 2½-3 dozen medium cookies

"Brass bands are all very well in their place—outdoors and several miles away."
~SIR THOMAS BEECHAM

Desserts

CRÈME BRÛLÉE

Silky and elegant, now you can enjoy this popular dessert at home with a perfect recipe from Frank and Diannah's Arbor Inn.

1 quart heavy cream

6 tablespoons sugar

1 vanilla bean, halved and seeds scraped from pod
  or 1½ tablespoons vanilla

11 egg yolks

6 tablespoons sugar

Sugar for topping

1. Preheat oven to 300 degrees. Combine cream, sugar, and vanilla pod in a saucepan. Bring to boil.

2. Whisk together egg yolks and sugar. Add one-third hot cream mixture to egg yolk mixture. Whisk until well blended.

3. Stir egg mixture into remaining hot cream mixture until well blended. Cool in an ice bath.

4. Strain to remove vanilla pod. Divide evenly into 8-10 (6-ounce) shallow ramekins and place them in a baking dish. Place in oven and pour hot water to come halfway up on ramekins.

5. Bake 40 minutes or until firmly set. Refrigerate until completely cool.

6. Sprinkle an even layer of sugar over custard. Using a butane torch or placing under a broiler, melt sugar until it is an amber color. Serve immediately.

Yield: 8-10 servings

~ARBOR INN, READING, PENNSYLVANIA~

~FRANK AND DIANNAH PARADISO, CHEFS/OWNERS~

"In opera, there is always too much singing."
~CLAUDE DEBUSSY

INDIAN ICE CREAM (KULFI)

Ben and Jerry take note. This is an unusual, exotic ice cream!

1 (14-ounce) can evaporated milk, chilled
  overnight

1 egg white

1 cup powdered sugar

½ teaspoon cardamom

½ tablespoon rose water

¼ cup shelled pistachios, chopped

¼ cup golden raisins

¼ cup flaked coconut

1 tablespoon candied cherries, quartered

1. Beat milk with an electric mixer until doubled in volume. Beat egg white with clean beaters. Fold into milk.

2. Fold in powdered sugar, cardamom, rose water, pistachios, raisins, coconut, and cherries. Refrigerate in a sealed container 1 hour.

3. Process with an electric ice cream maker until frozen. Transfer to plastic freezer container and freeze for several hours before serving.

Yield: 1 quart

Desserts

PROSECCO AND SUMMER FRUIT PYRAMID OR BOMBÉ

Though I know you'd probably expect something more decadent from me, I fell in love with this recipe the first time I tried it and would find a way to include it in our line of desserts if it could be frozen. It is a visual feast for the eyes—colorful fruit displayed in a transparent amber sparkling gel. Dazzling!

2¾ teaspoons unflavored gelatin
   (two ¼-ounce envelopes)
2 cups Prosecco (Italian Sparkling White Wine)
½ cup sugar
2 teaspoons fresh lemon juice

4 cups mixed fresh fruits such as sliced strawberries, blackberries, and raspberries; peeled and thinly sliced peaches, halved seedless grapes, honey dew balls, kumquats
Diced candied ginger (optional)

1. Sprinkle gelatin over ¼ cup Prosecco in a small bowl and let stand several minutes to soften.

2. Bring 1 cup Prosecco and sugar to a boil, stirring until sugar is dissolved. Remove from heat and add gelatin mixture. Swirl until gelatin is dissolved.

3. Stir in remaining ¾ cup Prosecco and lemon juice. Transfer to a metal bowl set in a larger bowl of ice. Cool mixture to room temperature.

4. Cut fruit into attractive shapes and sliver kumquats, if including them. Spoon a portion of mixed fruit into 6 individual 8-ounce decorative molds. A pyramid or bombé shape is attractive.

5. Cover fruit with 3 tablespoons of gelatin and chill for an hour. Add another layer of fruit and 3 more tablespoons of gelatin. Refrigerate until firm, about 3 hours.

6. Unmold by dipping mold into a bowl of hot water for 3 to 5 seconds. Invert a serving plate over the mold and invert onto plate.

Yield: 6 servings

~SANDY SOLOMON, OWNER~
~SWEET STREET DESSERTS, READING, PENNSYLVANIA~

"The discovery of a new dish does more
for the happiness of the human race than
the discovery of a star."
~BRILLAT-SAVARIN

COLD LEMON SOUFFLÉ

Light, fluffy, and oh so lemony, this dessert is the perfect menu choice to conclude a rich meal.

1 (¼-ounce) envelope unflavored gelatin	**½ cup sugar**
¼ cup cold water	**1 tablespoon lemon zest**
¾ cup lemon juice	**¼ cup sugar**
4 eggs, separated	**1 cup heavy cream, whipped**
½ teaspoon salt	**1 tablespoon lemon zest**

1. Sprinkle gelatin over water to dissolve. Set aside. Whisk together lemon juice, egg yolks, salt, and sugar in top of double boiler. Cook, stirring constantly, until thick and custard-like.

2. Remove from heat and stir in gelatin and zest. Set aside to cool.

3. Beat egg whites until soft peaks form. Add sugar and beat until stiff. Fold together cooled lemon mixture, egg whites and whipped cream.

4. Pour into a 2-quart soufflé dish or individual dishes. Sprinkle with zest and refrigerate.

Yield: 6-8 servings

~ADAPTED
FROM THE
MAYFLOWER INN
AND RESTAURANT~
~WASHINGTON,
CONNECTICUT~

"The man who has music in his soul will be most in love with the loveliest."
~PLATO

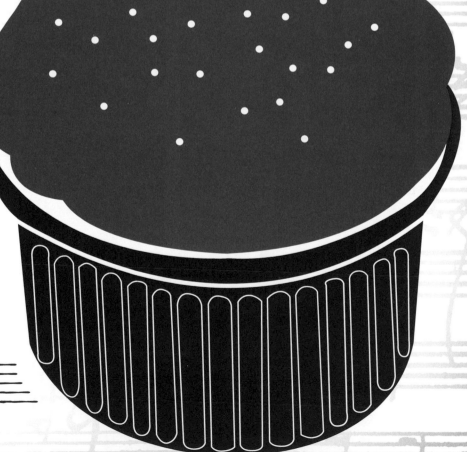

CHOCOLATE RASPBERRY CHAMBORD FUDGE SAUCE

 Use this sinfully rich sauce to top premium ice cream for an adult sundae. Or pour it over angel food or pound cake.

⅓ cup sugar

1 (12-ounce) package frozen raspberries, thawed

¼ cup water

½ cup sugar

½ cup heavy cream

½ cup cocoa

1 stick unsalted butter

6 ounces bittersweet chocolate

½ cup Chambord liqueur

½ teaspoon vanilla

1. Combine sugar, raspberries, and water in a saucepan. Cook and stir over medium heat 5 minutes until soft. Mash raspberries to a pulp. Simmer 10 minutes. Strain mixture to remove pulp, reserving ½ cup syrup.

2. Cook sugar, cream, and cocoa until sugar dissolves and is smooth. Add butter, simmer and stir until butter melts. Remove from heat. Add chocolate and stir until chocolate melts.

3. Cool sauce until able to touch side of pan with your hand. Whisk in Chambord, reserved raspberry syrup, and vanilla. Mix thoroughly. Pour into an airtight container and refrigerate.

Yield: 3 cups sauce

CHOCOLATE-DIPPED APRICOTS

 You can add a plate of these wonderful treats to almost any dessert table and watch the smiles appear when the secret pocket of flavor is revealed.

26 whole small dried apricots, about 6 ounces– "Mediterranean style"

3½ ounces almond paste

1 (6-ounce) package semi-sweet chocolate morsels

1. Cut the seam halfway around each of the apricots with a sharp knife. Make a small pocket and fill each slit with ½ teaspoon almond paste. Press the sides of the apricots together. The paste may not be completely enclosed.

2. Melt chocolate in the top of a double boiler, stirring until smooth. Dip the unfilled side of each apricot in chocolate. Place in a single layer on waxed paper-lined tray and refrigerate 1 hour.

3. Store apricots in an airtight container lined with waxed paper, separating each layer with paper. Keep in a cool, dry place. May keep for 2 weeks.

Yield: 26 apricots

Tip: The apricots may be filled using a pastry bag with a small round tip.

Desserts

ESPRESSO TO GO

Part candy, part miniature sweet, these coffee-chocolate morsels are a great way to finish the evening.

¾ cup heavy cream

3 tablespoons instant espresso powder

¼ cup sugar

4 tablespoons unsalted butter

12 ounces semi-sweet chocolate, chopped into
 ¼-inch pieces

4 ounces unsweetened chocolate, chopped into
 ¼-inch pieces

30 chocolate-covered espresso beans

30 miniature foil candy/dessert cups

1. Heat cream, espresso powder, sugar, and butter in a 1½-quart saucepan over medium-high heat. When hot, stir to dissolve sugar. Bring to boil.

2. Combine semi-sweet and unsweetened chocolate in a bowl. Pour hot cream mixture over chocolate. Let stand 5 minutes. Whisk until smooth. Now you have espresso ganache.

3. Place foil cups on a baking sheet. Spoon two level tablespoons of ganache into each cup. Refrigerate 1 hour until firm. Top each cup with an espresso bean . Serve immediately or store in a tightly sealed plastic container in the refrigerator.

Yield: 2½ dozen espresso cups

~THE CORNER PANTRY~
~LIMEKILN, PENNSYLVANIA~
~KIM NEIN, OWNER~

EMMY GILBERTSON'S BRAZIL NUT TOFFEE

This is an easy recipe with candy store results. Surprise your friends with a tin under the Christmas tree, but do not be surprised if they expect one each year.

2½ sticks unsalted butter

1⅔ cups sugar

4 teaspoons corn syrup

¼ cup water

1¼ cups coarsely chopped Brazil nuts or almonds

1 (12-ounce) package semi-sweet chocolate morsels

¾ cup finely chopped Brazil nuts

1. Melt butter in a heavy saucepan. Add sugar, corn syrup, and water. Cook, stirring frequently, until candy thermometer reads 300 degrees or candy reaches the hard ball stage (a little dropped into cold water becomes hard and brittle). Immediately remove from heat.

2. Stir in nuts. Spread mixture into a buttered 15x10x1-inch jelly-roll pan. Sprinkle chocolate morsels over hot toffee. Gently mix until chocolate melts and is evenly spread. Do not press in, just gently spread morsels.

3. Sprinkle with finely chopped nuts. Refrigerate until cold. Break into pieces.

Yield: 1¾ pounds of candy

Tip: Other nuts may be substituted but the Brazil nuts are worth the trouble to find.

Desserts

From the Pantry

SAUCES

JAMS AND MARMALADES

CHUTNEYS AND RELISHES

MISCELLANEOUS

From the Pantry

STU'S RIBS BARBEQUE SAUCE

This recipe was originally given to me during a flight to the west coast by a state barbeque champion on his way to the national barbeque championship. He had a carry-on bag full of uncooked ribs on ice. I do not know how he did in the contest, but the sauce has been a winner whenever it is served. It can be used with equal success on chicken.

1 cup packed dark brown sugar

1½ teaspoons onion powder

½ teaspoon paprika

½ teaspoon salt, or to taste

½ teaspoon pepper

½ teaspoon barbeque seasoning

Dash of garlic salt

2 cups vinegar

1 cup bottled barbeque sauce

½ cup ketchup

2 tablespoons Worcestershire sauce

1 tablespoon Tabasco sauce

1. Combine brown sugar, onion powder, paprika, salt, pepper, barbeque seasoning, and garlic salt in a saucepan.

2. Whisk together vinegar, barbeque sauce, ketchup, Worcestershire sauce, and Tabasco in a bowl. Pour into dry ingredients and mix until well blended.

3. Cook over low heat, stirring frequently, until sugar dissolves. This thin sauce should be applied repeatedly to coat meat.

Yield: 3 cups

 Tip: For best results, cook ribs for at least 2 hours over low heat. Chicken will take less time. Apply sauce every 30 minutes at the start and every 10 to 15 minutes during last hour of cooking.

"Appetite, a universal wolf."

~WILLIAM SHAKESPEARE, *Troilus and Cressida*

BBQ SAUCE

From the Pantry

GORGONZOLA SAUCE

 Use this versatile sauce over grilled steaks or lamb chops. It can be folded into mashed potatoes or used as an elegant pasta sauce, as well.

4 cups heavy cream
3-4 ounces crumbled Gorgonzola cheese
3 tablespoons freshly grated Parmesan cheese

Salt and pepper, to taste
3 tablespoons minced parsley

1. Bring cream to boil in a saucepan over medium-high heat. Boil 45 to 55 minutes, stirring occasionally, until thickened like a white sauce.

2. Remove from heat. Whisk in Gorgonzola cheese, Parmesan cheese, salt, pepper, and parsley until cheese melts.

Yield: 3 cups

 Tip: To reheat sauce, warm over low heat until cheese melts. Whisk vigorously until sauce is blended.

"Music is the voice of all sorrow, all joy. It needs no translation."
~HELEN EXLEY

CHICKEN BARBEQUE SAUCE

 Barbequed chicken, prepared with this classic sauce from Cornell University, is a delicious and nutritious summertime favorite.

1 egg
1 cup vegetable oil
2 cups cider vinegar

2 tablespoons salt
1 tablespoon poultry seasoning
1 teaspoon pepper

1. Beat the egg, then add oil and beat again. Whisk in vinegar, salt, seasoning, and pepper until well blended.

Yield: 3 cups, enough for 6 chickens

Tip: While the recipe calls for raw egg, the acid in the vinegar will kill any bacteria that might be present. Cooking chicken to the well-done stage will also kill any salmonella present on the raw poultry or in the egg.

APPLE BUTTER

A Pennsylvania Dutch staple, apple butter was traditionally made in huge copper pots suspended over an open fire. It is served with biscuits, cottage cheese, or as an accompaniment to roasted chicken or meat. Today, the copper pots are sought-after treasures at antique shows and flea markets in the region.

8 cups apple cider
1 teaspoon salt
2½ teaspoons ground cinnamon
½ teaspoon ground cloves
½ teaspoon ground allspice
½ teaspoon grated nutmeg
½ teaspoon ground cardamom (optional)

Juice of two lemons
½ cup frozen orange juice concentrate, thawed
1-2 cups water
6 pounds Granny Smith apples, peeled, cored, and cut into cubes
3-4 cups sugar

1. Boil cider, stirring occasionally, in a 5-6-quart pan until reduced to ⅓ its original volume. Set aside. Combine salt, cinnamon, cloves, allspice, nutmeg, and cardamom. Set aside.

2. Mix lemon juice, orange juice with 1 cup water. Add apples. Add more water to keep apples from browning while cooking. Cook apples until tender. Force through a cone strainer. Do not use a food processor or blender as it ruins the homespun texture.

3. Measure apple pulp. Measure ½ to ⅔ cup sugar for each cup apple pulp, according to desired sweetness, and mix together.

4. Add apple mixture and spice mixture to cider syrup. Bring to boil, stirring constantly. Spoon off foam as it forms. When foam formation subsides, reduce heat to a gentle boil. Cook, uncovered, 20 to 25 minutes, stirring occasionally and removing any foam.

5. Set a small plate in the freezer to test apple butter. It is finished cooking when a ½ teaspoonful, chilled on a cold plate, forms a soft gel. Ladle hot liquid into sterilized jars. Clean away any sticky residue. Cap immediately and screw lids tight. Wipe jars clean and invert on a rack to cool.

Yield: 8-10 half-pint jars

"We know an age more vividly through music than through its historians."
~ANONYMOUS

From the Pantry

QUICK STRAWBERRY-ORANGE MARMALADE

Celebrate the start of strawberry season by making this quick and delicious spread. The fresh berry flavor is deepened by the cinnamon.

3 cups halved hulled strawberries
¼ cup sugar
1 cup premium orange marmalade
1 cinnamon stick, broken in half

1. Place strawberries in a heavy saucepan. Stir in sugar. Let stand 15 minutes, stirring occasionally, until juices release. Cook over high heat 3 minutes, stirring occasionally.

2. Add marmalade and cinnamon stick pieces. Bring to boil. Reduce heat and cook 15 minutes, stirring occasionally, until mixture is thick enough to coat the spoon.

3. Transfer to a bowl. Remove cinnamon stick pieces. Refrigerate until cold, then cover and keep refrigerated.

Yield: 2 cups

Tip: May be made 2 days in advance.

"There's sure no passion in the human soul, but finds its food in music."
~GEORGE LILLO

JAM

From the Pantry

226

NEW JERSEY PEACH MARMALADE

This recipe allows you to enjoy the delicious taste of summer peaches long after the season is over.

1 (6-ounce) can frozen orange juice concentrate, thawed

½ cup lemon juice

4-5 pounds fresh peaches, peeled and diced

Slivered peel of one orange, cut into ⅛-inch thick strips

6 cups sugar

1 teaspoon salt

1. Combine orange juice and lemon juice in a large bowl. Place diced peaches in juice mixture. Measure 8 cups peaches.

2. Mix peaches, citrus juices, peel, sugar, and salt in a 5-6-quart pan. Bring to boil, stirring constantly. Spoon off foam. When foam subsides, reduce heat to a gentle boil. Cook, uncovered, 20 to 25 minutes, stirring and removing foam.

3. Place a plate in the freezer. Jam is finished when a ½ teaspoonful forms a soft gel on the plate.

4. Ladle into sterilized jars, cleaning residue off seal. Cap immediately and screw lids on tight. Invert on a rack to cool.

Yield: 7 half-pint jars

"To write a symphony is, for me, to construct a world."
~GUSTAV MAHLER

 # RED-ONION MARMALADE

This is a wonderful condiment for filet mignon or roast pork, or spread on goat cheese topped bruschetta.

1 stick unsalted butter

2 pounds red onions, halved lengthwise, thinly sliced

½ cup red wine vinegar

4 tablespoons honey

¼ teaspoon salt

⅛ teaspoon pepper

Crostini toast

1. Melt butter in 3-quart saucepan. Sauté onions, uncovered, 8 minutes stirring occasionally, until softened.

2. Stir in vinegar, honey, salt, and pepper. Cook, covered, 1 hour, 15 minutes to 1 hour, 30 minutes, stirring occasionally, until tender. Serve at room temperature.

Yield: 2 cups

~MASON'S, EASTON, MARYLAND~

Tip: Marmalade can be frozen up to 1 month. Thaw and reheat to warm before serving.

From the Pantry

CUCUMBER JELLY

♫ *For a nice Christmas presentation, serve a dish of red cranberry sauce and dish of cucumber jelly with the holiday meal.*

12 cucumbers, peeled and seeds removed
7 cups sugar
1 cup vinegar

1 (6-ounce) bottle liquid fruit pectin
Green food coloring

1. Purée cucumbers in a food processor. Strain off 1½ cups juice. Use pulp for relish.

2. Combine cucumber juice, sugar, and vinegar in a saucepan. Bring to boil. Boil 2 minutes. Add fruit pectin and cook, stirring constantly, until thickened.

3. Add a few drops of food coloring. Ladle into hot sterilized jars and seal.

Yield: 6 half-pint jars

SUMMER HARVEST CHUTNEY

All of New England's late summer bounty is combined in this delicious relish which is sensational with pork or chicken and also stars as a delectable appetizer when served over cream cheese.

5-6 large ripe Bosc pears, peeled, cored and chopped

3 apples, peeled, cored and chopped

3 peaches, peeled, pitted and chopped

2 ripe tomatoes, peeled and chopped

2 lemons, seeded and chopped, including rind but not bitter white pith

1 lime, seeded and chopped, including rind but not bitter white pith

1½ cups golden raisins

2-3 tablespoons finely chopped red jalapeño pepper or 1 tablespoon crushed red pepper flakes

3 cups packed brown sugar

½ cup crystallized ginger, chopped

1 large garlic clove, minced

2 cups cider vinegar

1 teaspoon salt, or to taste

1½ teaspoons cinnamon

1 teaspoon ground cloves

¼ teaspoon ground nutmeg

¼ teaspoon ground allspice

1. Combine pears, apples, peaches, tomatoes, lemons, lime, raisins, jalapeño, brown sugar, ginger, garlic, vinegar, salt, cinnamon, cloves, nutmeg, and allspice in a large stockpot.

2. Simmer 2 hours, 30 minutes. Spoon into sterilized jars and seal.

Yield: 1½ quarts

 Tip: You can adjust the "heat" to taste by adding or reducing the quantity of jalapeño or pepper flakes.

BANANA CHUTNEY

The banana is an unusual ingredient in this tasty chutney. Try it with grilled chicken or pork chops or as a condiment to curry dishes.

3 cups sugar

2 cups vinegar

1 teaspoon salt

1½ teaspoons curry powder

2 (10-ounce) packages chopped dates

¼ cup candied ginger, finely chopped

1 cup candied mixed fruit

2 cups golden raisins, chopped

6 large firm bananas, sliced into 1-inch chunks

2½ cups coarsely chopped onions

1. Combine sugar, vinegar, salt, and curry powder in a saucepan. Bring to boil. Add dates, ginger, fruit, and raisins. Boil 10 minutes.

2. Add bananas and onions and boil an additional 6 minutes. Ladle into hot sterilized jars and seal.

Yield: 11 half-pint jars

From the Pantry

CRUNCHY PICKLE CHIPS

The Pennsylvania Dutch would take 8 days to make these delicious pickles. Here is a shortcut recipe that achieves the same results.

1 (2-quart) jar whole baby kosher dill pickles
1 teaspoon celery seeds
1 teaspoon mustard seeds

1 teaspoon salt
1 cup cider vinegar
4½ cups sugar

1. Rinse pickles and slice thinly. Wash jar. Place slices back into jar.

2. Combine celery seeds, mustard seeds, salt, vinegar, and sugar in a saucepan. Bring to boil. Pour over pickles in jar and refrigerate. Allow flavors to blend for 3 to 4 days. Keep refrigerated.

Yield: 2 quarts

"Dill Piccolino—
A wind instrument that plays only sour notes."

CRANBERRY, GINGER, AND LEMON CHUTNEY

Of the many versions of cranberry chutney that we have tasted, this one was the clear winner!

Zest of one lemon
1 medium lemon, remove white pith and discard
    Dice fruit into ¼-inch pieces
1 (12-ounce) package cranberries
2 cups sugar
½ cup diced crystallized ginger
⅓ cup finely chopped onion

1 garlic clove, minced
1 jalapeño pepper, seeded and minced
1 cinnamon stick
½ teaspoon dry mustard
½ teaspoon salt

1. Combine zest, lemon pieces, cranberries, sugar, ginger, onion, garlic, jalapeño, cinnamon stick, mustard, and salt in a nonreactive saucepan.

2. Bring to boil, stirring often, until sugar dissolves. Reduce heat and simmer 25 to 30 minutes until cranberries burst and sauce is thickened. Cool completely.

3. Remove cinnamon stick just before serving. Serve at room temperature.

Yield: 3 cups

From the Pantry

CANDIED CITRUS PEEL

 This is an old-fashioned recipe from Grandmother Patch who "wintered" in central Florida surrounded by citrus trees and happy memories.

2 large grapefruit	**2¼ cups sugar**
3 naval oranges	**1¼ cups water**
2 lemons	**¾ cup sugar**

1. Cut fruit and remove flesh for another use. Cut each half of rind into 4 quarters. Remove white pith and flesh away from peel. Slice peels into thin strips ⅓-inch wide.

2. Bring a few quarts of water to boil. Add peels and boil 5 minutes. Drain and rinse under cold water. Repeat the blanching two more times.

3. Combine 2¼ cups sugar with water in a saucepan. Cook over low heat until sugar dissolves. Add peels and bring to boil. Reduce heat and simmer, uncovered, 30 to 40 minutes until peels are translucent.

4. Remove peels with tongs, allowing syrup to drip into pan. Place peels on rack to cool completely. Roll in sugar. Store in airtight container for up to two months.

Yield: 2 pounds peels

Tip: For the best and juiciest citrus fruit, always pick fruit that has the smoothest skin. Select fruit that seems heavy for its size. This rule applies to all citrus: lemons, limes, oranges, and grapefruit. Additionally, when extracting juice, 15 to 20 seconds in the microwave will increase the yield as will rolling them back and forth on the counter using moderate pressure from the heel of your hand. A sprinkle of salt will dramatically sweeten a grapefruit.

"A harp is a naked piano."
~ANONYMOUS

From the Pantry

INDEX